THE VIEW
FROM COWLEY:

The Impact of Industrialization
upon Oxford, 1918–1939

R. C. WHITING

CLARENDON PRESS · OXFORD
1983

Oxford University Press, Walton Street, Oxford OX2 6DP
London Glasgow New York Toronto
Delhi Bombay Calcutta Madras Karachi
Kuala Lumpur Singapore Hong Kong Tokyo
Nairobi Dar es Salaam Cape Town
Melbourne Auckland
and associated companies in
Beirut Berlin Ibadan Mexico City Nicosia

Oxford is a trade mark of Oxford University Press

Published in the United States
by Oxford University Press, New York

British Library Cataloguing in Publication Data

Whiting, R. C.
 The view from Cowley.
 1. Industry—Social aspects—Oxford (Oxfordshire)
 I. Title
 303.4'83'0942574   HC256
 ISBN 0-19-821897-4

Typeset by Joshua Associates, Oxford
Printed in Great Britain
at the University Press, Oxford
by Eric Buckley
Printer to the University

ACKNOWLEDGEMENTS

I must thank the following for permission to consult and use material in their possession: Sir John Boyd (A.U.E.W.); Professor Elizabeth Brunner; Mr Harry Cole (Oxford City Labour Party); Mr T. J. Foden (Coventry and District Engineering Employers' Association); Mr Jack Jones (T. & G.W.U.); Mr H. K. Mitchell (Engineering Employers' Federation); Mr S. Murphy (T.U.C.). I am grateful to The Architectural Press for permission to reproduce two tables from T. Sharp, *Oxford Replanned* (1948).

Mr Norman Brown, Mr Henry Jones, and Mr Jack Thomas gave up much of their time to tell me about factory life and politics in Oxford; I owe them a great deal.

Mr Malcolm Graham and his staff at the Oxford City Library were unfailingly efficient and helpful over many years, as were Dr Richard Storey and his staff at the Modern Records Centre, University of Warwick. Mr David Horsfield, Librarian of Ruskin College, deserves particular thanks. He not only provided pleasant conditions in which to work but was also continuously watchful for new source material, in a way which far exceeded his immediate professional responsibilities. Mrs Deborah Baboolal typed successive drafts of the text with the highest degree of efficiency and care.

In the early stages of the research I received guidance and encourgement from Professor Peter Mathias and Mr P. J. Waller. I would like to acknowledge formally my gratitude to the Warden and Fellows of Nuffield College for electing me to a Research Studentship; my supervisor there, Mr John Goldthorpe, provided critical comment of the most useful kind. Mr Alan Fox and Professor Sidney Pollard made a similar contribution as examiners of the D.Phil. thesis on which this book is based. In the later stages Dr Steve Tolliday, Dr Jonathan Zeitlin, and Nina Fishman were particularly helpful. I cannot give an adequate account of my debt to Mr A. F. Thompson, of Wadham College, Oxford, except to say that he has been my supervisor for many years and has given invaluable advice and support.

University of Leeds   R. C. Whiting
September 1982

CONTENTS

MAPS

ABBREVIATIONS

In text:

A.E.U.	Amalgamated Engineering Union
A.S.E.	Amalgamated Society of Engineers
A.S.W.	Amalgamated Society of Woodworkers
A.S.L.E.F.	Associated Society of Locomotive Engineers and Firemen
B.U.F.	British Union of Fascists
E.T.U.	Electrical Trades Union
F.B.I.	Federation of British Industries
I.L.P.	Independent Labour Party
L.R.C.	Labour Representation Committee
N.U.D.A.W.	National Union of Distributive and Allied Workers
N.U.G. & M.W.	National Union of General and Municipal Workers
N.U.P.P.W.	National Union of Printing and Paper Workers
N.U.R.	National Union of Railwaymen
N.U.V.B.	National Union of Vehicle Builders
S.D.F.	Social-Democratic Federation
T.A.	Typographical Association
T. & G.W.U.	Transport and General Workers' Union
T.U.C.	Trades Union Congress
W.E.A.	Workers' Educational Association

In footnotes:

C.D.E.E.A.	Coventry and District Engineering Employers' Association
E.A.E.F.	Engineering and Allied Employers' Federation (now the Engineering Employers' Federation)
G.E.C.	General Executive Council of T. & G.W.U.
H.L.P.	Headington Labour Party
N.E.C.	National Executive Committee (of the Labour Party)
O.C.L.P.	Oxford City Labour Party
P.R.O.	Public Record Office
V.C.H.	*Victoria County History*

INTRODUCTION

Car workers have been deeply involved in the triumphs and crises of Britain's recent industrial performance. They have also changed the face of Oxford's economy. This book examines them in both these roles, at the meeting point between the national and the local, and during the transition in the inter-war years from the traditional to the modern economy. The aim here is not simply to write the history of an occupational group: the car workers have particular interest in the light of broader themes of depression and recovery, and labour relations and economic performance. Because they were not completely integrated into the national economy, in that attitudes and organizations bore the imprint of local as much as of strictly industrial factors, it is appropriate to look at car workers in a particular town, to assess their emergence within, and their effect on, a local society as well as their place within a national framework.

The assessment of the economic growth of the inter-war period, of which the Oxford car factories were a product, is not without its problems. Twenty years or so ago the picture would have been clearer than it is now: the motor industry, as one of Britain's 'new' industries, not only provides a sharp contrast to depression in the export sectors but was also part of a growing sector in the Midlands and South which initiated some measure of recovery in the 1930s and also supported more sustained growth after 1945.[1] Now that view has to be revised to take account of later research,[2] and the 'new' industries no longer appear so dynamic or important.[3] They

[1] See H. W. Richardson, 'The Basis of Economic Recovery in the 1930s; a Review and a New Interpretation', *Economic History Review*, 15 (1962), 344-63.

[2] The most recent summary is that of B. W. E. Alford, 'New Industries for Old? British Industry between the Wars', in R. C. Floud and D. McCloskey (eds.), *The Economic History of Britain since 1700. 2: 1860 to the 1970's* (Cambridge, 1981), pp. 308-31.

[3] Usually these are accepted to be vehicle manufacture, electrical engineering, rayon, non-ferrous metals, and paper, printing, and publishing. There is a considerable disagreement, however, about whether 'new' industries were also those which were expanding faster than others or showing unusually high gains in productivity.

had no monopoly of increasing productivity and had insufficient weight within the economy—in terms of investment, or employment, or of links between themselves—to act as a kind of 'development block' which might have provided an alternative basis for prosperity. They did little to meet problems of international competitiveness. By comparison with the motor industry in the United States, productivity in Britain was lower and firms still had a long way to go in standardization and penetration of the market. Perhaps even more telling (since the American producers had such advantages with size of their domestic market) was the failure to match the growth of European car producers.[4]

There was, of course, a very significant change in geography, in that certain types of industries, which in a national context were quite successful, had from the beginning of this century tended to be located in the Midlands and South, light engineering and motor-car production, for example. In the inter-war period these regions took an increasing share of net industrial output, which meant that the most prosperous towns were Coventry, Luton, Oxford, and Reading, whereas before 1914 these were to be found in the industrial centres in the North and on the Celtic fringe.[5] Continuity of economic performance and discontinuity of location can be yoked together around the central theme of labour. Both before 1914 and after 1945 British industry has been characterized by the development and resilience of shop-floor bargaining, problems of demarcation, and restrictive practice. This is true even though the location of industry and types of work involved have changed markedly through this century. If industrial relations are involved in the explanation for a secular decline in productivity then, as Dr Alford has suggested, 'the inter-war years are a period of particular

[4] Alford, 'New Industries for Old?', p. 320.
[5] The percentage of net industrial output was distributed as follows:

	1924	1935
North and Celtic fringe	49.6	37.6
Midland and South	28.7	37.0

Source: G. von Tunzelmann, 'Britain 1900–45: a Survey' in Floud and McCloskey (eds.), p. 247.

relevance in this process'.[6] Within this period the attempts of trade unions to recruit members from the expanding industries, the strategies of managements to meet this challenge, and the responses of the rank and file all merit discussion in order to 'place' the inter-war period within longer-run themes of labour history. Inevitably then, to look at Oxford from Cowley brings in a slice of national industrial history which requires some attention.

As a study of a section of the industrial working class between the wars, this book is conventional enough, but it might seem perverse to have chosen Oxford as a town on which to focus attention. The University population of dons, their wives, and servants must surely have distorted the more anonymous forces of class and politics which provide the main theme here. These characteristics are, however, very much to the point. One of the very obvious features of the 'new' industries in the inter-war period was that some were located in towns which had already experienced some industrial development, such as Coventry or Birmingham, while some expanded where manufacturing industry had been largely absent—Luton, Slough, and Oxford, for example. The comparison between labour organization in these two types of town will shed some light on the place of the inter-war period in labour history. Was there advantage in having some continuity with pre-1914 developments, or was there a very real hiatus or hiccup between 1914 and 1945 such that towns where workers had to be organized *de novo* were at no particular disadvantage?

The point is raised by contemporary assessment of the economic changes affecting Oxford between the wars. It was agreed that Oxford was going through industrial change which in its essential features (for example, the absorption of rural labour into manufacturing) had already been experienced elsewhere.[7] The economic history might therefore be written in terms of the integration of Oxford into the wider national economy, with parallel developments on the

---

[6] Alford, 'New Industries for Old?', p. 329.
[7] Barnett House, *A Survey of Social Services in the Oxford District*, ed. A. F. C. Bourdillon, 2 vols. (Oxford, 1938–40), 1, *Economics and Government of a Changing Area*, p. 155.

labour side—workers joining trade unions and supporting the Labour Party. As regards the local economy there is much to be said for this point of view, but it is not necessarily possible to extend the characterization to industrial relations and politics. If the wider industrial society was changing in such a way—principally in the weakening of labour organization—so as to converge with the 'late developers' like Oxford, then 'integration' is a misleading label to apply such a process.

This is also a study of a town, and not only of the two car firms located there. In addition to examining the impact on industry and politics of a working class of unprecedented 'mass' on the south-eastern periphery, the particular fascination of Oxford among English towns has to be recognized. This is the peculiar strength of Oxford for this kind of study. Because many who lived there saw their political lives in both national and local aspects, the relationships between classes have a special interest which is an asset rather than a liability. Such an interest, of course, has been pursued selectively, perhaps ruthlessly so. The main link between town and University is through politics, but to a large extent such questions as the strength of the Left within the University, or the role of University members in local government, have been neglected, except where 'the Labour Movement' was a common theme.

This way of viewing Oxford accounts for the book's arrangement. After an introductory chapter sketching in the outlines of Edwardian Oxford, the subsequent section deals with the motor industry in Cowley up to 1939, with comparative reference where necessary to what was going on elsewhere. Then the effects of the development of Cowley on politics and industry in Oxford are assessed. This does violence to chronology but it prevents needless interruption of perspective. The concluding chapter outlines the effects of the Second World War and the characteristics of the post-war period, by which time the particular conditions which justify a local study such as this cease to apply.

1

POLITICS AND INDUSTRY BEFORE 1914

There was very little sign before 1914 of the industrialization which was to affect Oxford in the inter-war years, and
in the Edwardian period it was still a pre-industrial town.
The nature of the working class, the divisions within it,
and its relations with the intellectual and professional middle
classes in the town all reflect this. It was numerically small,
split between a group of skilled workers and a pool of casual
labourers from whom the former wished to keep their
distance. Both, none the less, received charitable help from
the men and especially the women in the University who felt
this was a society to which they owed some responsibility,
as well as being one which they could comprehend and
penetrate. In the industrial world, trade unions had sup-
planted friendly societies as the most important agencies for
working-class welfare; in Oxford, this displacement had not
occurred before 1914. This introversion and 'backwardness'
throws into relief the changes of the inter-war period and
requires delineation, since some of its features persisted after
1918. Oxford's was not, of course, a common condition of
the 'new' industry towns before 1914—Coventry provides a
useful case for comparison here.

By 1914 the work-force in Coventry's 'new' industry was
established in a way that was clearly not the case in Oxford;
the Cowley car factories to the south-east of Oxford grew more
rapidly in the inter-war period. A comparison of occupational
structure in 1911 brings out the way in which Oxford not only
was hardly affected by the growth of cycle and motor manufacture, but also had a high proportion of its population employed
in domestic service and the professions, which indicates the
effect of the University. The size of the industrially-employed
population was inevitably a much smaller percentage of the
total working population than in Coventry: 16.5 per cent in
the former and 73.7 per cent in the latter.

Table 1. Oxford and Coventry in 1911
(percentage of occupied population over 10 years of age)

	Oxford n = 25,272	Coventry n = 50,382
1. Professions, local govt., defence (I–III)	10.9	4.3
2. Domestic service (IV)	26.9	5.7
3. Commerce (V)	3.9	6.2
4. Railways (VI, 1)	2.1	0.9
5. Metals (X, 1-9)	2.0	18.3
6. Vehicles (X, 10)	0.8	23.3
7 Craft occupations: carpenters; joiners; bricklayers; masons; leather; printers; bookmakers; tailors; boot and shoe. (XII, 1; XVI, 1-2; XVII, XIX)	11.1	6.4

Source: Census of England and Wales for 1911, vol. 10 (Cd. 7019), part 2, table 13.

Before 1914 the Midlands region as a whole showed strong demand for labour within the location there of the metal trades and coal-mining, as well as the newer industries of cycle, electrical, and motor-car engineering. Expansion in these trades absorbed a great deal of agricultural labour, as well as workers from elsewhere; growth in the metal trades accounted for twice the numbers leaving agriculture.[1]

Coventry was very much in the van of this growth. It led the field in cycle production and did the same with cars before 1914. While this was the stage of early specialized production which depended heavily on the skills of the mechanic rather than the semi-skilled assembly-line worker, some of the Coventry firms were sizeable—Daimler employed 5,000 in 1913, Wolseley 4,000, and Humber and Sunbeam

[1] E. H. Hunt, *Regional Wage Variations in Britain, 1850–1914* (Oxford, 1973), p. 117.

between 2,500 and 3,000.[2] Not only did this growth entail
absorption from rural labour from Warwickshire, but it
had also drawn workers from Staffordshire, London,
Leicestershire, Northamptonshire, and Worcestershire.[3] In the
initial period, of course, this meant a somewhat heterogeneous
labour force in the cycle trades and motor manufacture, the
ploughman or watchmaker working in the same firm as the
skilled mechanic, or even displacing him.[4] But such heterogeneity was less marked by the inter-war period in Coventry
than it was in Oxford, where the expansion of motor manufacture occurred later. It is very difficult to get precise
information on the previous occupations of car workers or
engineers in the two towns; a very rough guide to the milieux
from which workers were drawn can be gained from marriage
certificates, which give the occupation of the bridegroom's
father—an indirect, but not unhelpful, insight into the
origins of early car workers.

The qualifications to be added to Table 2 are several and
weighty. There are a relatively small number of cases; the registers came from Church of England, Methodist, and United
Reformed churches, because of the lack of access to civil
registers; most of all, it gives only the crudest of pictures of the
historical background of workers. This table bears out the
point suggested by the different timing of industrial development in Oxford and Coventry. Whereas both towns went
through similar stages in the recruitment of labour, with firms
drawing on a variety of sources, including the nearby rural
areas, Oxford experienced this later than Coventry and so the
heterogeneous background of labour was probably more
marked in the former than in the latter by the inter-war period.

Before 1914 the Oxfordshire countryside had not been
seriously affected by the wage levels in Oxford itself; it was
simply regarded as a rather expensive place in which to live.[5]

[2] S. B. Saul, 'The Motor Industry in Britain to 1914', *Business History*, 1
(1962), 25.
[3] Census Report, 1911, birthplace details, vol. 9 (Cd. 7017), table 2.
[4] R. Hyman, 'The Workers' Union' (Oxford Univ. D. Phil. thesis, 1968),
pp. 30-1, later published as *The Workers' Union* (Oxford, 1971).
[5] Flora Thompson was told that a man might earn 25s. a week in Oxford,
'But as he would have to pay "pretty near half" of it in house rent, he'd be a
fool to go there' (*Lark Rise to Candelford*, Oxford, 1945, p. 20).

Table 2. Occupations of fathers of car workers in Coventry and Oxford
1910–1937
(percentage)

	Rural or non-industrial	Engineering	Other industries	Craft	Non-manual work
Coventry n = 299	9.0	58.7	10.5	15.0	6.5
Oxford n = 120	35.8	9.1	23.3*	17.5	14.1

Source: Marriage registers. From Coventry: Alderman's Green, Foleshill, Broad Street, Lockhust Lane (Wesleyan Methodist, in Coventry City R.O.), Wyken and Stoke (C. of E., in Warwickshire R.O., DR 266). From Oxford: Cowley, Garsington, Wheatley, Headington, St. Ebbe's (C. of E., Bodl. Lib., MSS D.D.Par), Temple Cowley (United Reformed, registers in chapel).
Note: *Half of these were coal miners, very probably from South Wales.

By 1939 the position had changed quite markedly: not only had farm labourers left the land to work in the car factories and elsewhere, but the occupation distribution shows how far the motor industry had displaced the University (in numerical terms) as an employer. Car production also involved larger concentrations of workers.

Table 3. Occupations in 1939
(percentage)

1. Motor vehicles	30.25
2. Distributive trades	17.8
3. Building	11.93
4. Public services and professional	8.39
5. Other metal and engineering	5.1
6. Printing	4.72
7. Transport	3.17
8. Food and drink	1.59

Source: T. Sharp, *Oxford Re-Planned* (London, 1948), p. 57.

Coventry continued to expand, at a faster rate than Oxford: its occupied population practically doubled during the inter-war period, whereas in Oxford the increase was only 41.8 per cent. Although the change in distribution of employment was inevitably more dramatic in Oxford than in

Table 4. Employment in Oxford firms in 1939

Pressed Steel	5,250
Morris Motors	4,670
Morris Motors Radiators	1,190
University Press	840
*Lucy's (engineering)	500
*John Allen (engineering)	270

Source: Sharp, p. 57.
Note: *Established before 1914.

Coventry because of its later start, the pattern of employment still carried the idiosyncrasies of a university town:
a professional sector of 12.1 per cent in 1931 (compared
with 1.8 per cent for Coventry and 1.9 per cent for Luton)
and 19.2 per cent engaged in domestic service (compared
with 6.1 per cent in Coventry and 5.9 per cent in Luton).
Oxford's distributive sector was more akin in size to a
country town in an agricultural region than an industrial
centre.

The new labour force made the same impact residentially;
it did not swamp the centre of Oxford but settled to the
south-east, in Headington and Cowley, and many lived
beyond the city. The number of those working in the motor
industry who lived outside the city increased in the 1930s, as
Table 5 shows.

While the smallness of Oxford tended to encourage a
concentration of workers near the factory, it also required

Table 5. Residence of workers in Oxford car factories

	1931	Percentage share	1936	Percentage share
Oxford*	4,278	69.8	6,148	60.3
Suburbs	473	7.7	1,627	15.9
Villages				
6–7 miles	392	6.4	893	8.75
7–15 miles	594	9.7	784	7.7
Towns				
20–40 miles	252	4.1	415	4.6

Source: Derived from Barnett House, *Survey*, vol. 1, appendix IV.
Note: *Includes Cowley, Summertown, Botley, and Hinksey.

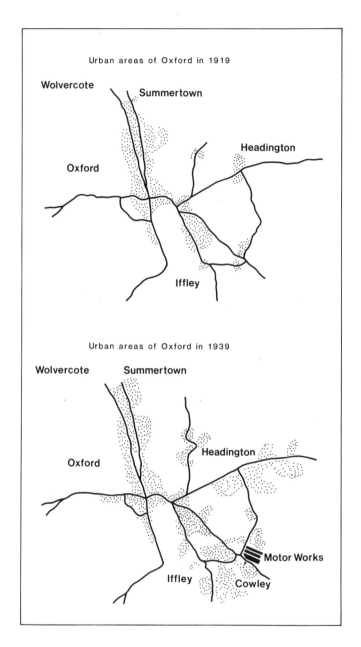

Map 1. Urban areas of Oxford in 1919 and 1939

the dispersal of a section further away than was typical in larger industrial centres.[6] The tendency for these numbers to increase when workers were coming to Oxford from some distance, suggests that the newcomers may well have had to live some distance from the factories. Certainly the high cost and shortage of lodgings (30s. a week compared to £1 in Birmingham) was a frequent complaint of those migrating to Oxford from the depressed areas.[7] The connections between factory and neighbourhood were therefore more tenuous than might be supposed at first glance. The 'one-industry' suburbs near the factories showed few signs of the social solidarities which such a label usually connotes, while a significant proportion of the labour force was dispersed at the end of the day beyond the easy reach of union organizers. While the changes in population and occupation were distinctive enough[8] they did not in any sense displace the University, and the extent to which semi-industrialism was going to affect politics and industrial relations was not going to be decided by sheer weight of numbers.[9] Before these larger questions are tackled however, it is necessary to discuss further the nature of the Oxford working class, such as it was, before 1914.

Employment in Oxford in the main reflected the fluctuating demands of the University.[10] Printing, the largest skilled trade in the city, became quiet during the long vacation, especially in the smaller firms doing specialized work for the colleges; though this resulted in short time rather than unemployment.[11] The problem was not too severe for the

[6] K. Liepmann, *The Journey to Work* (London, 1944), p. 154.

[7] *Oxford Times*, 28 Sept. 1928.

[8] The city's population increased from 62,000 in 1911 to 97,000 in 1939; whereas in 1911-21 the population increase was mainly natural, in 1921-31 two-thirds of it was caused by immigration and in 1931-7, five-sixths. See Barnett House, *Survey*, vol. 1, p. 26.

[9] Unlike the position in Slough, where the newcomers engulfed the older inhabitants and so dominated local government. M. E. Attlee, *Mobility and Labour* (London, 1944), p. 36.

[10] 'The recurrence three times a year of the eight weeks' term is still the important factor in employment, when the normal population of 53,000 is reinforced by some 5,000 undergraduates and tutors, full of "effective demands" for goods from the shops and for services from their scouts and the unseen army dependent on their desires.' C. V. Butler, *Social Conditions in Oxford* (London, 1912), p. 81.   [11] Ibid., p. 82.

college servants, for those not on a quarterly salary went into hotel work during vacations.[12] The building trade suffered the fitful requirements of the University in reverse, since masons, painters, and decorators were required out of term and were therefore busy in the summer. The problems of season and term were linked by the question of overtime and the colleges' use of it. During the building workers' dispute in June and July 1914, regulation of overtime was demanded in Oxford to ease local unemployment, and the University was asked to provide work in the winter months for the same purpose.[13]

Most of the skilled workers in the town—the printers, the tailors, those in the food trades, the college servants, and the small numbers in the cycle and engineering works—earned 30s. a week or more, that is, a ' "good average" adult male urban workers' wage'.[14] The skilled building workers were not consistently within this range. Although their rates of pay were nominally the same as those earned in the local engineering trade, namely 8d.-10d. an hour, these were declared to fall by at least 1d. an hour when the effects of irregular employment were taken into account. Only during the busy summer weeks would the wage of a skilled building worker rise significantly above 30s. a week.[15] The main group outside the influence of the University were the railway workers, who lived to the west of the city around Osney.[16] They were not very well paid: only drivers, firemen, goods guards, and mechanics could hope to earn more than 30s. a week.[17]

As could be expected, trade union organization was stronger amongst the skilled workers than the labourers, but it was far from uniform. The coverage of the Typographical Association was almost complete: in 1910 it had 400

[12] Ibid.

[13] *Oxford Chronicle*, 22 May 1914; Trades Council minutes, 26 Oct. 1910.

[14] H. A. Clegg, A. Fox, and A. F. Thompson, *A History of British Trade Unions* (Oxford, 1964), vol. 1, pp. 480-1. In 1906 the average wage nationally for engineering workers was 32s. 6d. per week, and for hand compositors 32s. 8d. if they were on piece-work; for tailoring it was 30s. 2d. A.E.U. District Committee Minute Book, 29 Aug. 1919.

[15] *Oxford Chronicle*, 19 June 1914.

[16] *V.C.H. Oxfordshire*, vol. 4, *Oxford City* (London, 1979), p. 215.

[17] Clegg, Fox, and Thompson, p. 489.

members, roughly the same as the number of hand compositors who made up the majority of the union's membership.[18] The engineers were far less well organized. They were
employed at two engineering works (Lucy's and John Allen's)
and one motor garage; but of 320 possible members only
twenty-five were in the A.S.E. Of the building workers the
masons were probably the best organized, though the bricklayers had a membership of 160 in 1914 having recovered
from a fall in membership during a downturn in local house-
building in 1909-10.[19] It is unlikely that wages were seriously
affected by these variations in union organization.[20] Organization amongst the railwaymen was distributed between
A.S.L.E.F. and the Railway Servants.

The major exceptions to union organization amongst the
better-paid trades were, of course, the college servants.
College work was highly regarded within the local population
and it was felt that their unionization would, in setting a
minimum rate for the servants themselves, also have an uplift-
ing effect on the earnings of other local workers.[21] Not only
because of their particular status within the town, but also
as a result of the internal division between and within the
colleges, they proved impossible to recruit into trade unions.

The way in which trade unionism underwrote rather than
eroded differences flowing from labour market conditions
was still true in Oxford up to 1914, even though it had
become less so elsewhere.[22] The skilled workers were in the
main sharply distinguished from the unskilled groups by
standards of living and degrees of organization. Casual labour
gathered around the building trades, although even in the
summer they could not all be absorbed. In the winter it was
a question of going to the gas company, the corporation, or
the coal merchants to ask for work.[23] For a carter or a

[18] Butler, p. 40; A. E. Musson, *The Typographical Association* (Oxford,
1954), p. 103.
[19] Butler, p. 50; Operative Bricklayers' Accounts, 78/OB/2/2/26, Modern
Records Centre, University of Warwick.
[20] 'Most of the masters pay at union rates and are on very friendly terms
with their employees', Butler, p. 50.
[21] Ibid., p. 21; *Oxford Chronicle*, 9 Jan. 1920.
[22] See Hunt, *Regional Variations*, p. 331.
[23] Of 550 men who applied for municipal relief in 1910, a large proportion
were unskilled builders' labourers. Butler, pp. 84-5.

painter's labourer, earning about 25s. a week when in employment, the margin left over at the end of the week after rent, food, and lighting had been deducted was small, usually only one or two shillings.

In the working-class district of St. Ebbe's 'a man can drop into any one of fifteen public houses, within five minutes' walk of his house', and it was found that 'the labourers have, as a whole, responded less than the better paid men to the temperance ideal'.[24] To make ends meet, many of the women of St. Ebbe's were casually employed during the term taking in washing and charing.[25] Here, more than with the skilled workers, was the 'low wage' aspect of Oxford. Whereas building workers in the big cities such as Birmingham and Leeds earned almost 30s. a week, those in Oxford were often earning as little as 22s. 6d.[26] In this respect Oxford wages were characteristic of those of the Home Counties and the South-East in the later nineteenth century, in being lower than elsewhere, with sizeable numbers employed in domestic service.

Attempts to organize these less skilled workers came to nothing. In 1912 the local branch of the I.L.P. wrote to the Trades Council expressing 'a real desire on their part to assist in organising the unorganised workers of Oxford'. In response to this, the Trades Council tried to get a branch of the Workers' Union established, but 'the difficulty of organising the unskilled workers of Oxford was in evidence at the meeting called by the organisers of the above named union [the Workers' Union] at their meeting on January 24, a very small attendance being present. No branch of the Union was formed.'[27]

Even when some measure of organization was achieved it was difficult to exploit this when bargaining with employers. The local tramway workers were a case in point. In 1913 they had formed a branch of the Amalgamated Society of Tramway and Vehicle Workers, which included fifty out of the fifty-six regular shifts.[28] When they went on strike over

[24] Butler, pp. 220, 226.
[25] *Oxford Diocesan Social Service Committee*, Report (1908), p. 33.
[26] Ibid., p. 36.
[27] Trades Council minutes, 18 Dec. 1912, 29 Jan. 1913.
[28] *Oxford Times*, 29 Mar. 1913.

increased Sunday working, without the support of their union, they found that their places were taken by other men, the whole thing fizzled out, and the Trades Council was left with the burden of supporting those strikers who had lost their jobs until they were able to find alternative work.

Inevitably, then, the local working class was internally divided by levels of earnings, degree of unionization, and relations with its employers. But how far did these occupational differences determine relations within the local working class and affect its general political identity? To look at relations between the various groups, those from the better-paid trades enjoying stable employment were all represented in the key offices of the Trades Council, with the printers predominant. A printer was president of the Council for eight of the years between 1900 and 1914, and secretary for thirteen.[29] Only one representative of the unskilled, Broadhurst of the Building Labourers, held office, that of treasurer in 1899. In the main Trades Council was concerned with the interests of the skilled workers, even in the case of the building trade where unskilled casual labour constituted one of the more serious social problems in the city.[30]

The wish of the skilled workers to keep themselves apart from the labourers was expressed more explicitly in the arguments over the provision of working-class housing in the city. Oxford had two housing problems. First, there was inadequate housing in the poorer districts of St. Ebbe's and St. Clements, either in small courts or rows of badly-built cottages which were damp, poorly ventilated, and had no private sanitation. They were usually rented at between 2s 9d. and 4s. a week.[31] The second problem was a shortage of the better, three-bedroomed houses in the West ward of the city, for the railway workers who wished to live near the station, and the printers at the University Press who congregated in Jericho. It was the high rents resulting from this shortage which concerned the officers of the local A.S.L.E.F. branch when they made representations to the

<hr/>

[29] A member of the Shop Assistants' Union filled the post three times and a postman twice.

[30] See Trades Council minutes, 29 Jan. 1908.

[31] Butler, p. 99.

city council.[32] More generally the Trades Council opposed municipal housing purely for the benefit of the labourers; what it wanted was houses at varying rents to meet the needs of the better-paid artisan.[33]

Although the working class in Oxford was very small by comparison with such groups in other more obviously indust-rial towns, it did not live in isolation from other classes. In particular it received some attention from the University, and from Ruskin College,[34] though the reasons for the connection were somewhat varied, being in part political and in part social. Over the period as a whole the balance between these sources of connection did alter. By the 1930s the Oxford working class had grown in size, achieved some economic independence, and acquired the elements of industrial organization. It became of political interest to those involved in a national framework, and the relationship was not biased heavily in favour of the University. Before 1914 when the working class was small, and showed an essentially nineteenth-century division between skilled artisans and a pool of casual unskilled labour, it attracted attention mainly as a social problem, through a sense of obligation on the part of Uni-versity members. The inter-war years will be dealt with later: here the focus is on the 'reforming élite' who tried to understand and improve social conditions before 1914. According to Dr Harrison, it was a 'quartet of don's wives (Mrs H. A. L. Fisher, Mrs A. L. Smith, Mrs H. A. Prichard, and Mrs J. Wells) who at that time presided over Oxford's world of social work'; and they had continued the endeavours of Mrs Toynbee, Mrs T. H. Green, and Mrs Arthur Johnson.[35] These activities were encouraged by several factors. 'Emanci-pated by domestic servants from routine duties, and often discouraged by social convention from seeking a career, the younger women of Edwardian Oxford naturally moved into philanthropy.'[36] A tradition of service to the wider community

[32] *Oxford Chronicle*, 29 Apr. 1910.
[33] AGM of Trades Council, 1901, in *Oxford Chronicle*, 12 Apr.
[34] Founded in 1899 (as Ruskin Hall) by two Americans, to provide education for the working class, and not formally part of the University.
[35] B. Harrison, 'Miss Butler's Oxford Survey', in A. H. Halsey (ed.), *Traditions of Social Policy* (Oxford, 1976), p. 69.
[36] Ibid., p. 64.

was given a new force in the later nineteenth century by T. H. Green's philosophy, and, in addition, there was an interest in economic and social studies. Violet Butler, who was active in the local Charity Organization Society (C.O.S.) as well as the author of *Social Conditions in Oxford* (1912) read for an economics diploma following her First in History.[37] The impulses of the 'reforming élite' were expressed most concisely in the first issue (in 1891) of the *Economic Review*, the journal of the Oxford branch of the Christian Social Union:

On the one hand there has been a quickened sense of responsibility for the conditions under which the poorer members of the community live; and on the other, a new departure in Economic Thought has relaxed the dread of interfering with natural laws felt both by professed economic teachers and by the world at large.[38]

Social work did not demand a particularly tightly defined political framework, although in retrospect Miss Butler claimed that 'we were partly socialist without knowing what we were . . . it was a mixture of attempts to be good Christians and of common sense, with a tinge of unconscious Marxism thrown in'.[39] Only a tinge of course, for social work could be done by Conservatives; but it did require some view of what the working class needed and the condition to which it ought to aspire, and here there was scope for disagreement.

Those in the C.O.S. wanted to encourage the casual labourers 'to help themselves by thrift and foresight' in much the same way as the skilled workers were able to provide for misfortune by prudential saving.[40] The chief cause of local unemployment was seen to be the 'want of character in the men who were unemployed', who 'spent many weeks of each year loafing at street corners',[41] and who had failed to respond to the temperance ideal as positively as the artisan. In a sense this analysis was not borne out by Miss Butler's

[37] Harrison, 'Miss Butler', p. 47.

[38] For the opposition which this expressed to the views of Marshall and Cambridge economists on the public role of economists, see A. Kadish 'Oxford Economists and the Young Extension Movement', in T. Rowley (ed.), *The Oxford Region* (Oxford, 1980), p. 252.

[39] Harrison, 'Miss Butler', p. 61.   [40] C.O.S. Report 1909, p. 3.

[41] Ibid.

social survey of 1912, which showed that even in employment labourers did not earn an adequate wage and could not obtain decent housing. None the less, the C.O.S. directed most of its funds to those reduced by some misfortune from better circumstances, in particular widows with large families. Those who received the weekly pension were those who 'have seen better days, have led honourable lives; they have saved money, but have lost it by unfortunate investment or have seen it dwindle away during years of sickness'.[42] For those fit to work such relief was seen simply as misguided charity, a point which ignored the discovery of the inadequacy of labourers' earnings by Edwardian social investigation.

Others in the University were critical of the C.O.S., placing greater stress on the economic dependence of labour, and recommending its political representation. Four men should be mentioned here, all of whom were members of the University Fabian Society: Sidney Ball, fellow of St. John's since 1882, founder and supporter of the Fabian Society, and the recognized head of University socialism; A. J. Carlyle, of University College, Lecturer in Economics and Political Science; T. W. Chaundy, Student of Christ Church; and H. B. Lees-Smith of Ruskin, who later sat on the Oxford Committee to consider the extension of tutorial classes to working men.[43] Of these, Carlyle probably had the closest links with the local labour leadership, Miss Butler relying upon him for introductions to trade unionists.[44] His interest in economic and social questions was first aroused (as for many others) by Toynbee and Ruskin,[45] and this had practical effect not only in articles on housing and 'sweating' in the *Economic Review*, but also in representing working-class interests. He participated in the West Ward Housing Association and with another Christian Socialist, John Carter of Pusey House, he drew up lists of 'fair' employers in the city.[46] Carlyle had no wish to bring the working class to a

[42] C.O.S. Report 1903, p. 5.

[43] A. Mansbridge, *University Tutorial Classes* (London, 1913), p. 28.

[44] Harrison, 'Miss Butler', p. 43.

[45] According to notes made by his wife, in Carlyle MSS, MS Eng. Lett. c. 482, fos. 1–3, in Bodleian Library, Oxford.

[46] Trades Council minutes, 5 Jan. 1899.

state of independence through thrift. 'There is nothing to be more desired by anybody who is a real lover of human nature, than that the working classes should desire unnecessary things.'[47] He expressed a radical biblicism, claiming that 'Freedom, justice, brotherhood, equality, these are the mooter principles of the revolt of the Proletariat, and surely they are also the principles, the first and rudimentary principles, of the doctrine of Christ.'[48] These values were contrasted with 'the blind collision of immoral forces' in existing society. But while Carlyle was ready to criticize existing inequalities in Edwardian society—of which the strikes of 1911-12 were seen as the inevitable consequences[49] —the remedy did not lie in any changes in the control of industry or in the redistribution of wealth. Labour relations were potentially harmonious: employers had to pay high wages to secure efficient workers, while the latter had an interest in limiting wages to secure future investment.[50] Legislation for minimum wages was likely to be more effective than trade unions. Carlyle believed in class co-operation for the common good, rather than in class conflict as the means of overcoming an inegalitarian class system.

Ball took the same view: 'Socialism is not simply a working man's, or an unemployed, or even a poor man's question', he argued, in *Moral Aspects of Socialism.*[51] Like Carlyle he had little sympathy for the C.O.S.'s view of the working man's position, which, he argued, focused on a misdirected benevolence and lack of thrift as causes, rather than on the economic dependence of labour.[52] When this group (Ball, Carlyle, Chaundy, and Lees-Smith) encouraged the idea of labour representation, there was no idea of underwriting working-class sectionalism. When Carlyle presided over the inauguration of a Muncipal Labour Representation Committee in 1902, he suggested 'The City ought to be governed by no class but by the whole for the good of the whole.'[53] A few of the University members, therefore, had a sense of purpose

[47] In *Wages* (London, 1912), p. 46.
[48] In 'Social Liberalism', an essay in *Anglican Liberalism by Twelve Churchmen* (London, 1908), p. 208.
[49] In *Wages*, p. 101.   [50] Ibid., p. 81.   [51] In the 1908 edn., p. 80.
[52] Ibid., p. 82.   [53] *Oxford Chronicle*, 7 June 1902.

and engaged in sustained thought about the working class, and in a way which cast them in a responsible role. However mild a view of labour representation this produced, it was rather more 'progressive' than the Liberalism of the town. Although Ball was a member of the Oxford City Liberal Association, other Liberals were less keen on an independent working-class representation, one claiming that it 'would only create friction'.[54] This did not mean a neglect of material concerns, such as efforts to help the unemployed, to provide special cars for workmen on trams, or to appoint more Poor Law Guardians for the populous working-class parishes.[55] They also claimed that working-class Liberal candidates could be elected, but in this they were wrong. They put forward only two 'working-class' candidates, the president of the Trade and Benefit Society and a compositor: neither was elected. Liberal candidates in general were similar by occupation to Conservative candidates, solicitors, builders, and shopkeepers being mixed in similar proportions.

However, before about 1906 there was no great demand on the Labour side for independent representation. Carlyle and Lees-Smith had been instrumental in setting up the Municipal Labour Representation Association in June 1902, following a meeting at Ruskin,[56] but by the following year they were asking the Trades Council to take it over because it was not representative of organized labour. However, there was little support for this,[57] and it was only in 1906 that the response was more enthusiastic, with a motion in favour of achieving labour representation on all public bodies.[58] Up until then there had been little to disturb a low-key Lib-Labism. The local Labour Movement was more keen on free trade than on the ownership of production,[59] and, like the Methodist minister who attended their annual meetings, did not wish trade unions to be 'antagonistic', but 'to unite with employers to make it possible to work amicably under conditions which they found at present in the country'.[60] There was, too, some degree of nonconformist allegiance in

[54] E. P. Thornton in *Oxford Chronicle*, 7 June 1902.
[55] *Oxford Chronicle*, 12 Apr. 1901; Trades Council minutes, 1 Jan. 1900.
[56] Trades Council minutes, 28 Jan. 1902.　　　　　[57] Ibid., 27 July 1903.
[58] Ibid., 29 Aug. 1906.　　　　　[59] Ibid., 3 Nov. 1903.
[60] *Oxford Chronicle*, 12 Jan. 1906.

working-class Liberalism, although the evidence is somewhat ambiguous. The chapels certainly drew on artisan support, and the Trades Council sent a resolution against the proposed 1902 Education Act to the city's Conservative MP, Viscount Valentia.[61] But any electoral advantage is hard to discern: while the Liberals put particular emphasis on their opposition to the Act during the 1902 municipal election, they lost one of their seats in so doing, and one of their few working-class candidates did worst of the three Liberals. In 1906 the Trades Council was 'entirely satisfied'[62] with the views of the (unsuccessful) Liberal candidate, but after the formation of a Labour Representation Committee in 1906 attitudes changed. Before the 1909 municipal elections it was announced that 'There will never again be any combination of Labour and Liberal forces at municipal elections' because 'there is no essential difference between Liberal and Tory'.[63] This development was probably engineered not by the more left-wing members in the University, but by Frederick Ludlow, a printer and a newcomer to working-class politics who put a more forthright Labour view.

Some trade unionists continued to be doubtful of labour representation which implied any sort of socialism, and there were the college servants and brewery workers who were likely Conservative voters anyway. By 1914, however, working-class candidates had been regularly contesting municipal elections (always unsuccessfully), and ward committees had been set up to provide more continuous organization.[64] Modest though these developments may have been, they were in line with what was happening elsewhere.[65] But in terms of local politics Labour had made little impression on Conservative dominance of parliamentary and municipal

[61] Trades Council minutes, 20 Sept. 1901. The eventual Act abolished the local school boards and also provided voluntary—mainly Church of England—schools with assistance from the rates.

[62] *Oxford Leader*, June 1909 (journal of Oxford I.L.P., edited by Chaundy).

[63] *Oxford Chronicle*, 12 Jan. 1906.

[64] Trades Council minutes, 4 June 1913.

[65] In Coventry a L.R.C. had been set up in 1902, in Luton (to be another 'new' industry town) in 1907. Labour Party Archives, LPGC 22, letter of 3 Dec. 1907. For the wider trend of an increasing number of Labour candidates see M. Sheppard and J. L. Halstead, 'Labour's Municipal Election Performance in Provincial England and Wales 1901-13', *Society for the Study of Labour History Bulletin*, 39 (1979), 39-63.

elections. No Labour candidate was put forward at parliamentary elections, and of the eighteen who ran in municipal contests, only two finished higher than bottom of the poll. Whereas in other towns, such as nearby Reading, it was possible to get perhaps one or two candidates elected, this was never achieved in Oxford. The very limited franchise did not help[66] but, even more, Oxford's working class did not have the weight within the local social structure for it to achieve any importance. Unlike Reading, which had become a 'biscuitopolis', it had not experienced any shift towards large-scale industry before 1914.

The scope for action by the University Left in politics was therefore limited; it was as a social problem that the working class was most interesting. The same was true on the more strictly industrial side, as G. D. H. Cole discovered when dealing with the unsuccessful tram strike of 1913. Because of the weakness of organized labour he found his newly developing Guild Socialist ideas diluted into a modest labourism in their local application. Cole had come up to Oxford in 1908, and by 1912 had become critical of the Fabians for neglecting the possibility of social transformation at the point of production rather than of distribution.[67] Cole became increasingly interested in trade unions rather than political parties as agents of change, particularly in delivering the Guild Society and releasing the active human will of the working class. While for Carlyle the labour unrest of 1911–14 indicated a degree of inequality which required legislative correction, for Cole 'the pre 1914 unrest was presented as evidence of the vitality of the aspiration to control'.[68] While Carlyle saw the need for management and labour to recognize mutual interest, Cole did not. In *The Tram Strike— A Letter to the City and University*, written with G. N. Clark in 1913, he argued that wages should not be dependent on the level of profit but on the needs of labour. Because of the

[66] In the elections of 1911 in Oxford only 18.9 per cent of the total population could vote, the same as in Wolverhampton. G. W. Jones, *Borough Politics* (London, 1969), p. 31. By the inter-war period the figure was nearer 40 per cent, being 42.9 per cent in Cowley in 1930.

[67] See A. W. Wright, *G. D. H. Cole and Socialist Democracy* (Oxford, 1979), pp. 21 ff.

[68] Ibid., p. 89.

weak position of the tramway workers, Cole's interest in unions as agents of social change had to take second place to the more modest aim of encouraging union growth and supporting the strike; and this applied to the country areas around Oxford too, from which replacement labour could be drawn.[69] Ultimate ambitions for trade unions, which appeared not too distant in the wider world, were a long way off in Oxford and had to be replaced by more immediate objectives. Cole's activities were reminiscent of L. T. Hobhouse's in the 1880s. Like Cole, Hobhouse had shown interest in trade unions, taking 'a leading part in the campaign to unionize the local agricultural labourers'.[70] But by the 1890s Hobhouse's interest had waned, with the weakening of the unions.[71] Those who saw the working class as a political grouping capable of achieving some broader transformation of society inevitably had to look beyond Oxford. This was the case even at quite a modest level. Leonard Cotton organized Sunday meetings in Oxford for the S.D.F. in the 1890s and became a target for undergraduate humour; but he went on to a seat on the S.D.F. Executive and in 1910 was a founder member, and later secretary, of the Socialist Party.[72] For those of a primarily political concern, of a left-wing nature, the local context was uninspiring. This was true not only for the town but also in the University. As Ball put it in 1909, when explaining in essentially political terms his failure to get the presidency of St. John's, 'one of the permanent conditions under which Liberal and progressive people stand in Oxford is that they must never have official predominance'.[73]

The relations between the town and the University reinforced the way in which Edwardian Oxford was essentially

[69] For the activities of University members of the strike see Kingsley Martin, *Harold Laski* (London, 1953), p. 20, and for those at Ruskin, see H. Sanderson Furniss, *Memories of Sixty Years* (London, 1931), p. 132.

[70] S. Collini, *Liberalism and Sociology: L. T. Hobhouse and Political Argument in England 1880–1914* (Cambridge, 1979), p. 54.

[71] Ibid., p. 72.

[72] See H. E. Clayton, *Spiritual Needs of the City and Rural Deanery of Oxford* (Oxford, 1898), and W. Kendall, *The Revolutionary Movement in Britain* (London, 1969), p. 325 n.

[73] Oona Ball, *Sidney Ball: Memories and Impressions of 'an Ideal Don'* (Oxford, 1923), p. 99.

a continuation of late-Victorian developments; this seems clear whether the focus is on Toynbee and the tradition of social work, or Cole following the example of Hobhouse. This complemented the way in which the structure of working-class society had remained largely unchanged in the early twentieth century from what it had been in the later nineteenth. The only development which does not fit easily into this, the emergence of a Labour interest rejecting Liberalism, came from within the Labour Movement and was not engineered from without by the University Left.

Coventry, of course, was a much more important town before 1914, and labour there was in a markedly different position from that of Oxford. Its standard of living was higher, because wages in most trades, including building and engineering, were better, and rents and prices were lower.[74] In part this reflected economic factors, in the general buoyancy of demand for labour and the greater opportunities for female employment (in watchmaking, for example) which gave higher and more regular earnings than were to be had in Oxford.[75] But in part also the position of the labourer and the semi-skilled engineering worker reflected their successful unionization and their ability to turn this to good account in strikes at three engineering firms in May 1913. The advance in pay conceded by employers of roughly 1½d. per hour meant that an engineering labourer earned 27s. a week, something approaching a reasonable wage, and some semi-skilled drillers and lathe operators about 35s. a week.[76] The Workers' Union had been able to exploit the developments of semi-skilled machine work in the motor industry to good effect. Whereas it had been unable to make lasting gains in the cycle trade, by 1912–13 the union had made real headway within engineering and motor-vehicle production with a membership of about 2,100. It was from this position that the increases in rates in 1913 were achieved.

[74] Miss Butler agreed that the cost of living for the working class in Oxford was about the same as in Reading; Reading was worse off, in wages, rents, and prices than Coventry. Board of Trade, *Enquiry into Working Class Rents, Housing, Retail Prices and Wages* (Cd. 3864, cvii, 319, 1908), pp. 159–64, 386–90.

[75] In watchmaking a woman could earn 16s. a week, as opposed to the 8s.–11s. in term-time Oxford for laundering or cleaning.

[76] J. Hinton, *The First Shop Stewards' Movement* (London, 1973), p. 219.

The success of the Workers' Union did show for this period the way in which developments in machinery were making life more difficult for the skilled man. While the skilled unions wanted to ban semi-skilled workers from operating certain machines, the Workers' Union was anxious for any such promotion which might have benefited its members.[77] The skilled unions were well established; of those grades in the engineering and motor-vehicle trades from which the A.S.E. could reasonably have hoped to draw members, 23 per cent were in the Society. In the coach-building section their position was stronger: in 1913 roughly three-quarters of the coachmakers were in one union or another.[78] Both the A.S.E. and the coachmakers had their own social clubs, and in this way reinforced their occupational identity. The density of Workers' Union membership was roughly half that of the Engineers, being around 10 per cent. None the less, from the beginning of the century there were complaints from A.S.E. members about unskilled labour being used on machining work, and some machinists operating lathes.[79] Like the engineers, the coach-builders were also being troubled by the use of non-union or semi-skilled labour.[80] While the Workers' Union was far weaker than the craft societies, it had still made some members in the trim shops, and received some backing from the N.U.V.B. in its strike of May 1913.[81]

Even where some recruitment had been achieved, the rough calculations indicate that in the broad industrial categories a majority of workers in Coventry did not belong to a union. There were of course some industries where unionization had failed completely. The Courtaulds silk factory, set up in Foleshill in 1905, because of the abundant

[77] According to James Hinton's calculations, 45 per cent of the labour force in Coventry's engineering factories was semi-skilled, compared to 16 per cent in an older-established centre like Sheffield. Hinton, *Shop Stewards*, p. 218.

[78] The categories used from the 1911 census for the potential A.S.E. membership were: erectors, fitters and turners, metal machinists and toolmakers, cycle and motor mechanics. This sort of exercise only ever provides a rough guide since 'none of the occupational groups is co-terminous with the trade union group with which it is compared'. Clegg, Fox, and Thompson, p. 467. In the case of the coachmakers, the estimate comes from N.U.V.B. Minute Book for Coventry, 2 June 1913.

[79] A.S.E. Journal, Coventry Division, May 1899, June 1899.

[80] N.U.V.B. Minute Book, 30 Sept. 1913, 6 Oct. 1913.

[81] N.U.V.B. Minute Book, 7 May 1913.

supplies of female labour, saw two rather violent strikes in November and December 1911 which brought no lasting membership.[82] Labour in the cycle trade was less well organized than in the motor industry, not least because it contained a higher proportion of women.

Politically, a Labour interest had emerged rather earlier in Coventry than in Oxford (1902 instead of 1906), but there are aspects of similarity between the two towns, in the participation of middle-class individuals and in the politically fragmented loyalties of trade unionists. The Labour interest was split between the Labour Representation Committee set up in 1902 at a meeting organized by the Trades Council and two more explicitly socialist organizations, the S.D.F. and the I.L.P.[83] The I.L.P. drew in several members from outside the working class, including the first Labour councillor, S. O. Poole. He had no affiliations with the trade union movement, but was the founder of a local Clarion cycling club.[84] Also of middle-class background was Arthur Bannington of the S.D.F., who won the All Saints ward in 1913. There was some success for those from within the Trades Council, H. Wale, its president, winning Hillfields in 1913. From 1907 the Liberals had tried to contain the growth of Labour, which held at that time two council seats and places on the Boards of Guardians. Even though they moved towards a more 'progressive' programme they still met Labour opposition. The agitation over the National Insurance Act (in which the local Labour Movement was against the element of contribution) showed the gulf between them.[85]

The main concerns of Labour locally were with municipal ownership of the tramways, more municipal housing, and free school places for working-class children. Despite the clear stand for Labour representation,[86] the L.R.C. did not

[82] D. C. Coleman, *History of Courtaulds* (Oxford, 1969), vol. 2, pp. 162-3.

[83] K. Richardson, *Twentieth Century Coventry* (London, 1972), p. 192.

[84] J. Yates, *Pioneers to Power* (Coventry, 1950), p. 28.

[85] They faced Labour candidates on eight occasions between 1904 and 1913; Labour won only twice. R. A. Wright, 'Liberal Party Organisation and Politics in Birmingham, Coventry and Wolverhampton, 1886-1914, with particular reference to the development of independent Labour representation' (Birmingham Univ. Ph.D. thesis, 1978), p. 303.

[86] For the views of the Coventry L.R.C. see Labour Party General Correspondence files, LPGC 5/99, letter of 26 June 1906.

receive the whole-hearted backing of local trade unionists. The secretary of the L.R.C. complained about lack of enthusiasm amongst them, and in 1909 four trade union branches left the Trades Council because of its involvement in politics.[87] In the main the trade union contribution— whether assessed by those who sat on ward committees, sent delegates to the L.R.C., or tried to organize support for Labour candidates—came from the skilled workers, particularly the engineers and coach-builders.[88]

As with most studies of labour which take organizations as their focus, it is important not to overemphasize the numbers which fell into their orbit. It has already been shown, by some admittedly rough calculations, that there were far more non-trade unionists than members in the engineering section in Coventry. In other industries very few if any were in a union. In addition, the political organization of these men and women was still very limited, not least because of the technical factor of a limited franchise. But looked at in another way, what had been achieved was quite impressive. The disturbing effects of technological change on labour organization had been coped with in one way by the growth of the Workers' Union, and the skilled unions were fairly strongly placed. It was also true that the new industrial growth and the housing estates which went with it developed in areas where some sort of manufacturing activity had already been established. Harnall, where Labour achieved its first success in 1905, had been the home of ribbon workers from the later nineteenth century, and an ordnance works and two housing estates had been built there before 1906. This meant that new growth did not take place in raw and unformed surroundings, and the sense of discontinuity from the past was not as strong as it was to be when Oxford experienced industrialism during the inter-war period. And so while many of the changes in economic life which tended to increase the heterogeneity of labour—the modifications of work practice, the entry of those from nearby rural

[87] Wright, 'Liberal Party Organisation', thesis cit., p. 302; F. Carr, 'Engineering Workers and the Rise of Labour in Coventry' (Warwick Univ. Ph.D. thesis, 1978), p. 44.

[88] N.U.V.B. Minute Book, 19 Mar. 1909, 2 Dec. 1911; Carr, 'Engineering Workers', thesis cit., p. 47.

regions, or example—had clearly been at work in Coventry before 1914, they had not frustrated totally the efforts of the Labour Movement.

Even by 1914 Oxford was still a non-industrial university city, carrying an essentially nineteenth-century division between the skilled man and the casual labourer in its working class. Relations between classes had yet to be disturbed by the institutions and organizations of the wider industrial society, and the contrast with Coventry where new industrial growth was already in evidence before 1914 and where the adaptation to change had already shown visible results, was quite striking. However, as later chapters will show, this contrast did not persist so forcefully into the inter-war period, when similarities became as obvious as differences.

2

MORRIS MOTORS IN THE 1920s

Oxford's industrialization began in the 1920s with the emergence of William Morris as a major producer of motor cars. The location of the Pressed Steel company at Cowley in 1926 was a direct result of this growth and it was this latter firm which was the source of the political and industrial changes which affected Oxford in the 1930s. Although the expansion of Morris Motors in the 1920s had marked effects upon the city and the surrounding countryside, industrial relations at the factory (and also at the radiator plant in north Oxford) followed rather than deviated from the attitudes of labour in the past; in the 1920s workers there were not noticeably more aggressive or militant than unskilled workers in other occupations in Oxford.

Morris's use of the old military college at Cowley for producing cars indicated the lack of constraint on industrial location and meant that the social impact of his factory was spread between town and country. Cowley had been a largely agricultural village up to the mid-nineteenth century, and this was not fundamentally altered by the subsequent location there of the Oxford Steam Plough company and the Church Army Press.[1] Although Morris went through a characteristic progression from bicycles through motor cycles to cars he did so in an area with no accompanying industrial development. The key question as far as labour organization went was the extent to which the influence this had on industrial relations perpetuated the contrast existing before 1914 with other towns which had made an earlier start with the 'new' industries, such as Coventry. As this chapter will show, even though some differences remained up to 1930, the degree of convergence of their experience was even stronger.

Morris's experience in the cycle and motor trade had begun before 1914 with his activities as a bicycle repairer

[1] *V.C.H. Oxfordshire, vol. 5, Bullingdon Hundred* (London, 1957), p. 89.

(from 1893), motor-cycle producer (from 1902), and a garage owner (from 1907). The business was a fairly small-scale enterprise with most investment funds being generated within it. On the eve of the war, however, he was employing only 80–100 men,[2] and the most rapid growth came in the inter-war period. The First World War helped a great deal by providing an opportunity, at government expense, to try out methods of production and to build up the labour force by producing munitions. The ideas behind such experimentation came from his visit to America in 1914 where he saw for himself techniques of high output based on interchangeable parts, subdivision of labour, and standardization of product.[3] Organizing the assembly at Cowley of parts made elsewhere demanded a close supervisory relationship with contractors which was important not only in moving to high output of cars after the war but also in avoiding the weight of high overheads of more integrated plants like those of Daimler and Austin. At this stage Morris was still dependent on the Midlands engineering industry for the supply of components.

Once the major technical problems of making cars had been solved, the production engineer rather than the mechanic became increasingly important in the economics of the car firm. The emphasis on the organization of production in order to cut costs was important for Morris since his products lay in the medium range of cars (10–15 hp), rather than in the luxury bracket, where profit margins could be more generous.

Before the First World War the main factory was a three-storey building in which machining and drilling were done on the ground floor, chassis assembly on the first, and the mounting of bodies on the second. The chassis was stationary on each of these floors. After the war a production line was organized with the chassis being pushed from one group of workers to the next. It was at this point that improving the organization of work by subdividing operations, by using single-purpose machines to drill the chassis frame, and by

---

[2] *Oxford Chronicle*, 3 July 1914. The factory employed 1,650 in 1923; by 1927 it had reached roughly 5,000 where it remained for the rest of the inter-war years.

[3] R. J. Overy, *William Morris, Viscount Nuffield* (London, 1976), p. 18.

synchronizing the work of various assembly lines, began to have serious effect. By 1926 each worker was engaged in a task of about 2½ minutes' duration, and the factory was producing about 1,300 cars per week; before the war it had been turning out the same number in a year.[4] Interchangeability of parts still had some way to go, judging by the prevalence of hand tools in the final assembly, but Morris was still quicker to adopt these techniques than his other competitors, including Austin.[5]

The other major change in methods of output came in 1934 with the installation of a mechanically-driven assembly line which gave much tighter control over labour, and permitted much closer synchronization of the supply of sub-assemblies with the final production line. Such mechanization gave greater flexibility, in that output could be increased within the working day.[6] With the introduction of the mechanical assembly line, production increased to 300–400 chassis per day, or at 2,000 per week, roughly double the 1926 level. This increase in output had been achieved without anything like a commensurate increase in the size of the labour force, which stayed at about 5,000 from 1924 to 1934, showing an impressive use of labour. The same was true elsewhere in the Morris enterprise: according to a report by the Board of Trade, the organization of production at the engine plant in Coventry was second to nothing in America and it appeared to have reached what were then considered to be the limits of economies of scale.[7]

Work at Morris's was representative of trends in the more advanced car factories, in that the typical attributes of skilled or craft labour were nowhere to be seen. No broad knowledge of engineering procedures was required, nor was there discretion over how a job was to be done. In particular the time in which tasks were carried out by workers was entirely at the control of the employers. A frequent theme of papers

---

[4] *Automobile Engineer*, Sept. 1926.   [5] See Overy, p. 90.
[6] Only the enamelling department had a night shift in order to keep up with the main assembly line. *Automobile Engineer*, Sept. 1934. See also F. Woollard, *Principles of Mass and Flow Production* (London, 1954), p. 85.
[7] 'There is in engine making little if anything to be gained by increasing outputs beyond 200 per day, the actual level of output at the Coventry factory.' Treasury papers, P.R.O. T 171/249. See also Overy, pp. 84–5.

on factory organization was the importance of controlling time in the factory, so that sub-assembly and assembly lines could work in unison and no time be wasted. The close timing of job cycles, in addition to the subdivision of work, were fundamental aspects of semi-skilled work. This was true not only for chassis construction but also on the body-building side. Morris was able to achieve lower costs in the Cowley body shops than in the Coventry firms where traditional craft methods were used.[8] The increasing use of standardized parts and their progression through successive stages of assembly meant savings of time and money. Workers in these conditions became mere assemblers, their confinement to a specific, closely-timed operation being worlds apart from the specialized coachmaker's shop, where the work overlapped between departments and where there was 'a needless hurrying to and fro, instead of a steady progression of effort'.[9]

In terms of the motor industry as a whole, Morris's rise had been dramatic, for by 1925 he was the country's largest producer of cars, and remained so up to 1938, even though his share of the market declined in the 1930s from the high point reached at the end of the 1920s. In 1920 Morris had been producing only 5 per cent of cars built, but by 1925 his share was up to 41 per cent; by 1929 he was, with Austin, taking 60 per cent of total car production. By the later 1930s, with the switch of demand towards smaller cars (that is, below 10 hp) as well as severe competition from Ford and Vauxhall, his ascendancy was challenged, but he still produced 23 per cent of Britain's cars.[10]

Morris had managed to exploit a confused and insecure period of the motor industry in the post-war years. Many firms geared to low output and high profit margins found themselves in difficulties once the boom broke in 1920-1.[11] Although Morris increased his prices between 1918 and 1920 during the post-war inflation, he managed to cut prices

[8] P. W. S. Andrews with E. Brunner, *The Life of Lord Nuffield* (Oxford, 1954), pp. 92, 103.

[9] H. Butler, *Motor Bodywork* (London, 1924), p. xxii.

[10] Andrews and Brunner, pp. 112, 189; G. Maxcy and Z. A. Silberston, *The Motor Industry* (London, 1959), p. 107.

[11] See Overy, p. 16.

thereafter and still increase profits.[12] Once Morris had established such a lead, he had a major advantage over the competitors: Rover and Clyno, his nearest rivals, were in great difficulties by the end of the 1920s. Whereas Rover's sales had been the same as Morris's in 1922, they were only 7 per cent of his by 1928, and by the end of the 1920s Morris held a virtual monopoly of production in the 12–15 hp range.

The only cloud on the horizon as far as Morris was concerned was the threat of foreign competition if import duties on cars were removed. The McKenna duties of 1915 imposed a duty of 33½ *ad valorem* on motor cars and parts in order to save shipping space for military materials. They were removed by the Labour government in July 1924 and restored by the Conservatives in July 1925. In a widely-regarded speech in Liverpool in May 1924, Churchill attacked Labour for the 'rough and harsh' decision to repeal the duties.[13] In the Commons the Labour Chancellor, Snowden, rested his case on the diminution of welfare and of aggregate demand by the protection of any one industry.[14] However, while Baldwin met this head-on by claiming that Britain would be swamped by imports from America, and that 'mass production under free trade in a competitive world is an impossibility', Churchill denied that it was protection versus free trade. He simply affirmed the virtue of obtaining revenue by taxing a luxury item.[15]

Morris took a rather gloomy view of the removal of the duties which was not regarded seriously in every quarter.[16] Imports of foreign cars would mean lower output and less employment, 'It did not take much brain power to work that out.'[17] He saw the alternative equally clearly: 'If Baldwin is returned to power I will guarantee to employ during 1924 another 1,000 employees.'[18] When he announced a price reduction in September 1924 he was quick to point out that

[12] The Morris Cowley cost £290 in 1918, £465 in 1920, and £299 in October 1921. Profit per unit of output increased from £36 in 1920 to £50 in 1921. Overy pp. 20–1.

[13] M. Gilbert, *Winston S. Churchill, V. 1922–29, A Companion* (London, 1979), pp. 152 ff.

[14] *Hansard*, fifth series, clxxiii, 13 May, cols. 1193–4, 1213.

[15] *Hansard*, 28 Apr. 1925, cols. 69–70.

[16] See W. Wedgwood Benn in *Hansard*, fifth series, clxxxvii, 7 May, col. 1218.

[17] *Oxford Times*, 30 Nov. 1923.   [18] Ibid.

had the duties remained the fall in price would have been greater.[19]

Free trade opinion was quite categoric about the desirability of removing the tariff on motor cars. *The Economist* not only believed that Churchill's interest in the duties as a revenue-producing instrument was spurious, but more interestingly, argued that the prosperity of the motor industry without the duties demonstrated 'the mitigating effects of competition'.[20] The same point could be made more specifically about Morris Motors: taking sales and profits for the 1923–5 period, there is no sign of the firm being hard hit by the repeal of the duties in 1924.[21] The Unemployment Committee Minute Book for Oxford also shows no increase in unemployment during the time the duties were off.[22] It is quite possible to reconcile this evidence with the fact that repeal did bring a significant increase in the number of foreign cars imported into Britain; imports in the early months of 1925 were always at least double those of the previous year, and they fell off as soon as the tariff was reimposed.[23] However, *The Economist* pointed out that home producers more than maintained their share of the market, which suggests that there was no straightforward substitution of foreign for home-produced cars, since they were of different design, and in many cases of larger engine size than most of the British cars. It has been argued, however, that this imperfect substitution of imported for home-produced cars did none the less allow for some net gain as a result of protection, the loss as a result of higher import prices being more than outweighed by the gains of lower prices through economies of scale allowed in a protected market.[24] What does emerge from the history of the industry is that

[19] *Oxford Times*, 5 Sept. 1924.
[20] *The Economist*, 2 May 1925, pp. 845–6. The £3 million that Churchill expected to derive from the duties during a full year was put against the £35 million in tax relief awarded in the same budget.
[21] Andrews and Brunner, pp. 112, 139.
[22] Oxford City Council Unemployment Committee Minute Book, May 1923–September 1924.
[23] J. S. Foreman-Peck, 'Tariff Protection and Economies of Scale, the British Motor Industry before 1939', *Oxford Economic Papers*, N.S. 31 (1979), 253.
[24] Of the cars showing a marked reduction in price, only the Citroen 7.5 hp was in the small-car category. Of the American cars, many were in the 20–30 hp class. Foreman-Peck, pp. 237, 255. *The Economist*, 26 Apr. 1924, pp. 863–4.

under protection it developed in much the same way as the free traders claimed it would without the duties, with the elimination of many inefficient producers unable to take advantage of scale.[25] It has been suggested that had the duties remained off, the effect at its most negligible would have been to reduce production by just under one-third in each year.[26]

However alarmist Morris might have appeared over the repeal of the McKenna duties, given the negligible impact on his own factory in the very short time when there were no duties, he was probably right about the long-term benefits of retaining them. In any event, Morris's political interests were tied to protection,[27] and the debate over the McKenna duties throws light both on his position in the wider political world, and on his relations with the workers at Cowley.

During the agitation to prevent the repeal of the duties in 1923 Morris quite overshadowed the Conservative candidate in Oxford at that time, R. C. Bourne. Morris had turned down the offer of the Conservative candidacy in 1923, and it is not difficult to see why. Apart from any view he might have had about the intrinsic attractions of being an MP, it is clear that his political interests as an industrialist did not necessarily require him taking such action. A place in Parliament was not so important as making the case locally or with those in government, and his eminence as a manufacturer ensured that his point of view was known in ministerial circles.[28] This role was established more formally in 1930 when Morris set up the National League of Industry which sought co-operation between employers and employed and required protection as the safeguard of industrial prosperity,[29] the firmly protectionist line of the League in fact forcing the F.B.I. to follow suit.[30]

[25] The number of firms halved during 1924–38. Overy, p. 136.

[26] Foreman-Peck, p. 255.

[27] Apart, that is, from his contribution of £50,000 to Mosley's New Party in 1932.

[28] Morris's views were mentioned in discussions between Amery and Birkenhead, P.R.O. T 171/249. In 1924 Churchill wished to discuss with Birkenhead 'two points of considerable difficulty: the McKenna duties and the Irish boundary situation'. Gilbert, *Winston S. Churchill*, pp. 152 ff.

[29] Andrews and Brunner, p. 25; *Oxford Times*, 22 July 1932.

[30] R. F. Holland, 'The Federation of British Industries and the International Economy', *Economic History Review*, 34 (1981), 289.

This indicates quite clearly where Morris's political priorities lay. As long as local politics were in Conservative hands there was little point in deep involvement. Although he was president of the Cowley Conservative Club, he was rarely seen there,[31] and Morris did not face the same problems as the Coventry engineering employers who in the early 1930s became somewhat alarmed at Labour success in local elections and wanted to get some of their own men elected.[32] Apart from a belief in free enterprise and his penchant for the efficient dictator, his main concerns were clearly with any state action which might affect the size of the market for cars. Given the opportunity for important businessmen to catch the minsterial ear, local political office-holding was irrelevant for Morris's political purposes.

The McKenna duties were not defended only in national politics; the argument had a specific local context which was bound up with Morris's relations with his workers. During the campaigns to defend the duties in 1924 and 1930 there were demonstrations of support from the work-force. In 1924 'a big mass meeting was held at Cowley to express indignation at the removal of the McKenna duties', and in 1930 a similar meeting decided to send Snowden, the Chancellor, the resolution that 'The employees of Morris Motors Ltd. pray that Her Majesty's Government may not repeal the McKenna duties.'[33]

It was always likely that these meetings were orchestrated by management but this was denied by the Morris workers, and there were no indications of a contrary view.[34] An Oxford branch of the League of Industry was set up in June 1931. At the inaugural meeting 'the majority of those present were employed at the motor works in Cowley', and workers from both factories sat on the Oxford council and gave exhibition tug-of-war matches at fêtes organized by the League.[35] In the sense that this activity was directed against Labour governments by generally Conservative employers

---

[31] One of his directors, S. G. K. Smallbone, was a vice-president, *Oxford Times*, 27 Feb. 1931.

[32] Coventry and District Engineering Employers' Association minutes, 21 July 1930.

[33] *Oxford Chronicle*, 9 May 1924; *Oxford Mail*, 5 Mar. 1930.

[34] *Oxford Chronicle*, 30 Nov. 1923.   [35] *Oxford Times*, 30 June 1931.

it appeared to give an anti-Labour ring to the whole debate. In Cowley the appeal to the workers to support protection was being made in the context of a strongly anti-trade union policy of both Morris Motors and Pressed Steel. Did agreement over protection among the workers imply sure acceptance of employers' hostility to the Labour Movement?

Clearly in Oxford it gave the appearance of doing so, particularly since there was little commitment to trade unions by labour. However, in Coventry, with a Labour MP and a recent history of successful union organization, trade unionists also joined the employers in opposing repeal.[36] Purcell's position as the Labour MP was obviously rather awkward, but in Coventry the protection debate had a rather different aspect from that in Oxford precisely because of trade union organization in the motor industry. In Coventry the trade unionists supported protection because they believed it would ease the threat of unemployment and strengthen their position with the employers. They were still having to follow the employers' lead; and repeal of the duties threatened to bring a more aggressive stance towards labour by the employers in Coventry.[37] Support of protection could therefore be quite consistent with basic trade union attitudes, in a way that was not apparent in Cowley.

Looked at more broadly, Morris's attitude to labour was quite straightforward: 'I have no particular reverence for tradition—especially for industrial tradition. I never allow trade unions to interfere with me.'[38] Morris believed that paying a reasonable wage was the key to getting commitment and loyalty from his workers, rather than elaborate 'welfare' arrangements: 'Much has been said and written about welfare schemes for workers. I do not believe in over-doing it. You cannot intermingle work and pleasure. Pay a good day's wage

---

[36] C.D.E.E.A. minutes, 25 Apr. 5 May 1924.

[37] 'Many of them who are friends of mine and who have been concerned with negotiations, tell me that immediately this matter got going then relationships with the employers were cut off, that there was very little chance of bargaining with safety, and that there have been adjournments and suspensions of negotiations again and again. If, for no other purpose than to establish them in a stronger position and enable them to bargain more effectively with their employers, I should be in favour of the maintenance of these duties.' A. Purcell, *Hansard*, clxxiii, 13 May 1924, col. 1243.

[38] *Oxford Times*, 1 July 1927.

for an honest day's work and he will soon find out how to enjoy himself properly.'[39]

Despite this attitude there were various social activities for the workers which were sponsored by the firm. Morris himself took an active, or at least a visible, part in all this: he gave out the trophies at football matches, presided at annual dinners, and attended sports meetings.[40] Of more material benefit was a life insurance scheme, set up in January 1926 and paid for by the firm, which provided coverage up to £100.[41]

In the 1920s there was little difficulty in attracting labour. Because the Cowley plant was mainly concerned with the assembly of parts, most of the work required little skill, tasks could be learnt quite quickly, and the demand for skilled labour was slight.[42] An A.E.U. member who arrived at Morris's in 1921 (and asked unsuccessfully for the district rate for a skilled engineer) found that 'the firm seemed to prefer semi-skilled labour and had subdivided operations in the assembly shops so that men who were quite unskilled could learn their portion in a day or two.'[43]

Morris's factory inevitably attracted workers from the rural regions around Oxford, and for this as well as other reasons the relationship between the city and the countryside was no longer the same as it had been before 1914. At that time the rural population had had very little to do with the city, which was simply an expensive place in which to live. After 1920 the interpenetration of urban and rural was far more marked. It would be wrong, of course, to place Cowley within the city in the discussion of urban and rural relations.[44] There were certain ways in which Oxford as a town within a largely rural area was bound to have some attraction as a centre for social activities once rural transport improved. In this way there were general changes which brought the

[39] Oxford Times, 28 Jan. 1927.

[40] According to H. W. Gray, one of the firm's directors, 'Sport had proved an important adjunct to the business side of the firm. They were in a better position today than most other car manufacturers.' Oxford Chronicle, 17 June 1921; and see also Oxford Chronicle, 6 May 1927, for Morris's participation.

[41] Oxford Chronicle, 2 Apr. 1926.

[42] Particularly after 1930 when the machine shop and foundry were closed.

[43] A.E.U. District Committee Minute Book, 10 Mar. 1921.

[44] It only became part of the city for purposes of local government in 1928.

rural and urban worlds closer together; the impact of the Cowley works, located within what was still an outlying village, was more specifically economic.

Motor transport brought the town in general and Oxford in particular into much closer reach of the rural inhabitants, though Saturday night dancing in Oxford and Sunday travel were 'the devil' as far as rural churchmen were concerned.[45] In addition to a more wide-ranging social life there was the attraction of higher wages and shorter hours in non-agricultural work, and the numbers employed in agriculture in Oxfordshire fell more quickly than for the country as a whole.[46] Whereas the number of agricultural workers in England and Wales fell by 17 per cent between 1921 and 1931, the number in Oxfordshire over the same period fell by 32 per cent, and over the period 1911 to 1931 it declined by roughly one-half.[47] These workers went into the aluminium factory at Banbury, which opened in 1931, cement production at Shipton, aerodrome construction, and the Witney blanket mills.[48] Morris's also pulled in many ex-farm workers, many rural vicars reporting a drift from farm work to the Cowley factory.[49] It is difficult to give a precise figure, but in 1936, 1,332 workers who had first taken out employment books in the rural areas of Oxfordshire from the Bicester, Chipping Norton, Thame, and Witney branch districts exchanged them in Oxford.[50] Many of them travelled into Cowley every day from villages nearby, and in 1936 the 'satellite' villages around Oxford sent 1,677 workers into the two car factories.[51] This gives a very rough estimate of around 3,000 ex-agricultural workers in the Cowley motor industry by 1936.

[45] Oxford Diocesan Visitation 1928, fos. 146-8; reports from Horspath and Weston-on-the-Green, in MSS Oxford Dioc. c. 388, Bodleian Library.
[46] A Ministry of Agriculture inspector, commenting on the position in Oxfordshire, wrote: 'The farm worker certainly has become more alive to the possibility of earning a higher wage in shorter hours for the reason that he only has to look to see it around him.' In 'The Economic Position in Agriculture', P.R.O. MAF 47/3.
[47] Barnet House, *Survey*, vol. 1, p. 139.   [48] P.R.O. MAF 47/3.
[49] Oxford Diocesan Visitation 1928, fos. 140-2, 146-8, 154-6, 408-10.
[50] Barnett House, *Survey*, vol. 1, p. 290.
[51] Ibid. See also R. Samuel, ' "Quarry Roughs": Life and Labour in Headington Quarry 1860-1920', in Samuel (ed.), *Village Life and Labour* (London, 1975), p. 243.

There were obvious incentives for such men to switch jobs, particularly since many of them still lived in the villages and so avoided paying high rents.[52] Wages in the rural industries for the woodmen and basket makers around Oxford were regarded as very low.[53] For the agricultural labourers the problem was more pressing, since during the depression of the 1920s farmers were keen to dispense with labour.[54] Even for those remaining in work the differences in pay were quite striking: for most of the 1920s the minimum wage of labourers on the Oxfordshire farms was 30s. a week for forty-eight hours in winter and fifty in summer; by 1932 it had fallen to 28s.; it then recovered by the mid-1930s to between 32s. and 36s. a week.[55] At the car works earnings were irregular but averaged out between 70s. and 80s. a week for between forty-four and forty-seven hours.[56] The interpenetration of rural and industrial employment brought home these differences, often in rather painful ways: 'The parish is being increasingly overrun by Morris workers—who offer three times the previous rent—and are even desirous to purchase. The clash with the agricultural workers is great—especially the jealousy owing to the contrast in wages.'[57]

Agricultural workers have often been thought of as deferential and submissive towards their employers—a result either of their 'free will' or of the difficulties of organizing people dispersed over many farms in any particular region. This assumption cannot be easily made in the case of Oxfordshire. At the end of the First World War quite impressive gains had been made by the Workers' Union, not least because of the establishment of the Agricultural Wages Board. In 1919 the Oxford Trades Council received affiliation fees from branches at Kidlington, Stanton Harcourt,

[52] 'The Economic Position in Agriculture', P.R.O. MAF 47/3.

[53] 'Rural industries may still be a refuge for inefficiency and a source of danger to rural standards of work and life.' K. S. Woods, *The Rural Industries Round Oxford* (Oxford, 1921), pp. 44, 120–1.

[54] E. H. Whetham, *Agrarian History of England and Wales, 1914–39* (Cambridge, 1978), p. 156.

[55] Oxfordshire Agricultural Wages Committee, P.R.O. MAF 64/57–9.

[56] Barnett House, *Survey*, vol. 1, p. 59. The car workers' earnings fluctuated, of course, with seasonal unemployment: this figure is an estimate which attempts to allow for this. At busy spells, earnings could reach £6 a week.

[57] Oxford Diocesan Visitation 1928, fos. 154–6.

Weston-on-the-Green, and Wootton; membership was still increasing in 1921 and new branches were springing up everywhere.[58] Trade unionists in the city were somewhat envious of this recruitment of agricultural workers and found that 'they were a long way in front of the town workers in trade union ideals'.[59]

While the trade union penetrated Oxfordshire rural life quite successfully, bringing with it various social activities, and affecting too those in rural industries,[60] it was not an enduring feature. The Workers' Union had done well when conditions were favourable, but it was not capable of providing much protection when decontrol of wages coincided with a sharp drop in agricultural prices. The income of the Workers' Union branch in Oxfordshire suffered severely, its income dropping by 82 per cent between 1921 and 1924.[61] Trade unionism was never completely wiped out in Oxfordshire, and when the Wages Committee was re-established, the officials of both the National Union of Agricultural Workers and the Transport and General Workers' Union were able to use that machinery to moderate the demands of farmers for reductions in wages.[62] But there is little doubt that the optimism of the early post-war years was not sustained. In the 1930s the T. & G.W.U. officials found the organization of agricultural workers a difficult, expensive, and unrewarding task, and there is no reason to suspect that it was any different in Oxfordshire from other regions.[63]

Trade unions, then, had a doubtful and erratic status in the rural regions from where many of Morris's workers were drawn. The same applied among those who had

[58] Oxford Trades Council minutes, 30 Apr. 1919; *Oxford Chronicle*, 9 Sept. 1921.
[59] *Oxford Chronicle*, 8 July 1921.   [60] Ibid., 9 Jan. 1920.
[61] Hyman, 'The Workers' Union', thesis cit., p. 307.
[62] Oxford Agricultural Wages Committee, 16 Jan 1932, P.R.O. MAF 64/58.
[63] See Bevin's quarterly reports to G.E.C. for May 1933, December 1935, November 1939. On the last occasion, Bevin complained of the lack of commitment to the union, even when it was beginning to show some results. 'Wages are being increased for agricultural workers all over the country, but the membership shows very little sign of improvement. It is, in fact, the one section for whom the union is always working where the men just take it as manna from heaven, without paying for it.'

left shop jobs in Oxford itself for the higher earnings in Cowley.[64] These groups were unlikely to have had any experience in their original milieux to encourage them to challenge Morris's hostility to trade unions. There was little reason for them to change their minds once they started work at Cowley. There was no one union well placed to recruit amongst the semi-skilled car workers; rather, the Trades Council had to rely on the efforts of several trade unions concentrating on particular groups in the labour force. In 1925 the Trades Council tried to bring in the National Union of Foundry Workers and the Electrical Trades Union, although, as it discovered, 'no union exists with either the foundry workers or the E.T.U. locally, and we consider the foundry workers the key to the situation'.[65] A branch of the N.U.F.W. had existed at Reading but had been transferred to Slough. The union itself was going through a difficult time in the 1920s. In 1920 the membership stood at 54,617; by 1930 it had fallen to 33,196.[66] By 1926 no representative of either union had visited Oxford[67] and organization from within the departments in question was difficult for fears of unemployment or victimization.[68]

This left the A.E.U. and the N.U.V.B. For the A.E.U. members the position was pretty hopeless; although the union had opened an industrial section in 1926, this did not affect recruitment until much later. In the meantime the few members who were employed at Morris Motors were left to hold out for the district rate, and when this meant they lost their jobs they not unnaturally 'felt it had to subsist on the Donation Benefit of 15 shillings a week while by the aid of overtime and Sunday working these unskilled men were drawing from £6.10.0 to £7 a week'.[69] The local committee recognized that in the end it was powerless to do anything until the firm had been 'brought into line', but in the 1920s

[64] Interview with Miss C. V. Butler.
[65] Letter from Oxford Trades Council to T.U.C., 9 Dec. 1925, in T.U.C. TC 79.
[66] H. J. Fyrth and H. Collins, *The Foundry Workers* (Manchester, 1959), p. 138.
[67] Letter from Elvin to Tewson of T.U.C., 3 June 1926, in T.U.C. TC 79.
[68] Letter from Oxford Trades Council to Tewson, 9 Dec. 1925, in T.U.C. TC 79.
[69] A.E.U. District Committee Minute Book, 10 Mar. 1921.

this never happened. Local membership of the union (which included other firms besides Morris's) declined up until 1927, the year that the Pressed Steel factory began operation. A fairly meagre eighty-one members in 1922 had dwindled to thirty-four in 1927.

The N.U.V.B. had potentially far greater scope for recruitment in the body-making section of Morris's; there were 659 mounters and finishers on the assembly line and 400 workers in the paint shop. However, there was a similar problem here to that of the engineers, for the N.U.V.B. had been concerned with representing the craftsman coach-builder, and an industrial section was not opened until 1931. And yet, as a member discovered, 'all kinds of tradesmen and unskilled men were working there assembling car bodies'.[70] Despite the fact that some members of the union had transferred to Oxford from Coventry, Wolverton, and Swindon (where they had been working as railway coach-builders) the local branch of the union made little headway.[71] Local officials had very great difficulty kindling any interest in the branch; it lapsed in 1921, and was reconstituted only on the initiative of the head office.[72] In 1925 another visit was requested to revive interest in the branch, but during yet another poorly attended meeting in 1927 'it was agreed that the secretary write to Head Office to point out the futility of any attempt at organisation in this district'.[73]

Little more was happening on the shop-floor: although shop stewards were appointed, there is no sign that they took up any grievances on behalf of members, and they appear to have been primarily concerned with the collection of union dues. When a member proposed in 1925 that a shop committee be set up the scheme fell through for lack of support,[74] and, not surprisingly, the labour force remained at work during the General Strike.[75] Morris was able to be fairly ruthless with anyone who tried to push the firm towards accepting unions; and when the N.U.V.B. membership decided to affiliate to the Trades Council the decision was

---

[70] N.U.V.B. Journal, Jan. 1929, London District Organizer's Report.
[71] N.U.V.B. Minute Book, 7 Aug. 1927.
[72] Ibid., 21 Aug., 6 and 21 Oct. 1921.   [73] Ibid., 7 Sept. 1927.
[74] Ibid., 25 Nov. 1925.   [75] Ibid., 6–10 May 1926.

quickly reversed, 'the reason given being that many members had had to leave town. Delegates said that several who were in favour of affiliation had been got rid of by Morris Motors.'[76] In such an atmosphere most of the men were diffident about doing anything which might offend their employer. In 1927 a group of workers who had been temporarily laid off in the summer had not asked for their insurance cards, with which they might have claimed unemployment benefit, because 'they were afraid it would prejudice their re-starting when the works re-opened again'.[77]

There were several factors which confirmed the unions in their marginal role, beyond those associated with jurisdiction or lack of geographical coverage. The fact that many workers lived outside Cowley, and the way in which they were confined to their particular departments because of the tight time-cycle around which the works was organized, meant that it was very difficult for outsiders to publicize the union case amongst the labour force. Their heterogeneity of background, in which any experience of trade unions was quite unusual, meant that any general commitment to organization was rare.[78] A more fundamental problem which arose was the way in which trade unions were seen to have very little effect upon workers' standards of living. The 'high wage' effect was a key point of Morris's strategy. As he put it: 'A low wage is the most expensive method of producing. A moderately high wage gives a man an interest in life. Men are only going to work if they are going to earn more comforts, hobbies and amusements.'[79] There were two elements in this: the first was the comparisons wage-earners made with other workers in order to evaluate their earnings, and the second concerned the relationship of these earnings to trade union rates of pay.

The first factor can be simply demonstrated. The sharp contrast in wages between agricultural work and employment in the car factories has already been commented on, and union organizers found this to be an obstacle: 'A comparison of their standards with rural workers outside their district

[76] Oxford Trades Council minutes, 21 Apr. 1926.
[77] N.U.V.B. Minute Book, 7 Aug. 1927   [78] Ibid.
[79] In *System*, Feb. 1924. 'Policies that Have Built the Morris Business'.

created a sense of satisfaction which reflected itself in the attitude of disregard for trade union organisation.'[80] The N.U.V.B. also found that one of the main difficulties in recruiting new members lay with the low basic rates paid in other local industries.[81] This does indicate the extent to which, as far as labour was concerned, the motor industry was in its infancy. Wage comparisons were still made across occupations, usually with the industry from which particular groups of workers had moved. There is little evidence to suggest that comparisons of earnings were drawn between car firms, as they were after the Second World War, most probably because of the absence of union organization in the industry.

On the question of the second component of the 'high wage' effect, the comparisons with trade union rates, the point was simply that Morris paid above these. If recognition was granted to unions, there was always the threat that wages would be lowered to their rates. The difference was in some cases considerable. The foundry workers at Morris's, for example, were paid 1s. 8d. an hour in the 1920s, 30 per cent above the basic union rate,[82] for a forty-hour week, which was three hours less than the norm. Similarly, the local N.U.V.B. members were opposed to any moves (however unlikely these might have been) to make the factory a 'union shop', owing to Morris's paying over and above the union rates.[83]

Much of the evidence, then, suggests that workers in the Morris factories in Oxford were not much interested in unions; and in this they hardly differed from unskilled labour locally before 1914. But even for those who did feel antagonism or resentment towards Morris as an employer, there was little to be done collectively; the practical constraints were too great, the advantages, in terms of pay, doubtful. Unless there were a number who felt that, in general, workers ought to be in trade unions, there was little to trouble Morris's desire to keep them out of his factories. Although Morris had located his factory at Cowley simply because he was a local

---

[80] A.E.U. Journal, May, 1931.   [81] N.U.V.B. Journal, 11 Nov. 1925.
[82] A. Smith of Morris Motors to N. Brookes of N.U.F.W., 12 May 1924, in T.U.C. TC 79.
[83] N.U.V.B. Minute Book, 19 Nov. 1924.

man, he was able to exploit the possibilities of setting up shop in a largely non-industrial area. It was not a question of using low-paid labour, but rather of being free from any jarring influences of less compliant workers. The advantages were commented upon by business writers: 'Workers in country centres, or in small towns and villages have less of what one might call an industrial sense. They are less obsessed by socially inherited prejudices and more inclined to give full effort and full co-operation. The wages offered will be much beyond what they have previously earned, and thus act as an incentive to output and effort.'[84]

The establishment of the car firms had clearly affected the region quite markedly in the 1920s, not because they had brought trade unions with them, but through the juxtaposition of very high earnings for unskilled manual labour with the low pay in traditional local occupations, whether in the rural areas or in the town. Although this produced no signs of labour shortage, it did encourage the declining independence of village life which had been apparent before 1914. In the main this meant closer links with the city and industrial employment, but not always both together. By 1930 there was still no definite urban milieu for the workers employed in jobs near Oxford. Viewed from the common standpoint that the large units of production and assembly-line technology of motor-car factories have provided the basis for quite intense industrial conflict since 1950, the acquiescence of labour in the two Morris factories might seem surprising. Placed within the context of the 1920s, both national and local, it is less so. As *The Economist* commented in 1926: 'The explanation probably lies in the fact that motor car production is a young industry, able to start with a clear sheet, free from the innate prejudices of a chequered past.'[85]

The Economist was probably right to be fairly cool in its assessment of industrial relations at Cowley; after all, most of the relevant factors were operating in Morris's favour. It is interesting therefore to look at how the employers in the Coventry motor industry fared, who had to operate in a far

---

[84] C. Northcott, O. Sheldon, L. Wardropper, and L. Urwick, *Factory Organisation* (London, 1928), p. 4.

[85] *The Economist*, 10 July 1926, ciii, p. 55.

more strictly industrial town, where no single manufacturer could dominate employment, and where the elasticity of labour supply was less marked, particularly as regarded skilled labour.[86] There were some similarities: Coventry, like Oxford, acted as a magnet for labour from the surrounding countryside, and by a rough estimate 12,000 workers were making the journey into Coventry each day.[87] This was nothing new in the case of Warwickshire and Coventry, but it did perpetuate to some degree the heterogeneity of labour, with continued input of those from non-industrial backgrounds, which had already been noticeable before 1914.

However, within Coventry there was a more stable, self-recruiting industrial working class, and one which had experience of trade union organization. The skilled unions had been strongly established prior to 1914, and the semi-skilled had also used their organization to good effect. However, in the 1920s the contrasts with Cowley gave way to similarities. Although the inheritances from the pre-1914 period were clear enough in Coventry, labour was on the defensive, and no new gains were made in the 1920s. Thus Morris, who had purchased supply firms in Coventry,[88] had as little trouble there as in Cowley. When the Oxford Trades Council was searching for a way of bringing pressure to bear on Morris Motors of Cowley, it turned to the Coventry Council with a proposal for joint action, but the response was negative:

I have to inform you that a similar position obtains in Coventry to that of Oxford. Wages are certainly higher, in some areas it is reported that men earn exceedingly big money. The A.E.U. is fairly well organized in the toolroom, but only a smattering so far as other departments are concerned. The Workers' Union also have a few members there I believe . . . At the moment however it will be impossible to do anything.[89]

There were a number of trade union members at the

---

[86] When Morris moved his foundry from Cowley to Coventry to enlarge it, it was harder to find suitable labour there. *Automobile Engineer*, Jan. 1930.

[87] C.D.E.E.A. minutes, 30 May 1927; see also J. Saville, *Rural Depopulation in England and Wales, 1851–1951* (London, 1957), p. 84.

[88] Including the Hotchkiss works which had been the scene of labour troubles in the First World War. See Hinton, *Shop Stewards*, pp. 215–16.

[89] T. Baird, Secretary of Coventry Trades Council to Organization Committee of T.U.C., 3 July 1926.

Morris factory in Coventry, but they were no more powerful than those at Cowley. They were not recognized by management, and they stayed at work during the General Strike, even though they had been classified as transport workers and called out.[90] A broadly similar position held good for the engineering industry as a whole in Coventry up to the 1930s. The T.U.C. survey on union organization in the 'new' industries noted that craftsmen and skilled workers were still quite well organized, but not the less skilled.[91] Labour as a problem for employers concerned the skilled workers, of whom there had been very few in Oxford. In Coventry in the 1920s the main strategy of the engineering employers was to try and dilute certain skilled work, especially that of the coach-builders. By the end of the 1920s they had achieved some measure of success, and had yet to face any obstructive organization by the semi-skilled. So while in certain respects the position in Coventry in the 1920s reflected its early start industrially, the particular conditions of that decade were eroding the gains that labour had made.

To deal first with those in engineering (as opposed to coach-building), Coventry had been affected by the industrial militancy of the First World War, though not in the same way as the older-established industrial centres. As Dr Hinton has argued, the weakness of traditional craftsmen in Coventry's industrial structure before 1914 meant that dilution was a less novel threat, and one which did not inspire a search for quasi-revolutionary political solutions. The wartime militancy in Coventry did not leave the engineers in a stronger position at the end of the war. A fully-fledged workshop organization had failed to develop, and the efforts of the skilled men to maintain their position as a reserved occupation and their job mobility led to conflicts with the semi-skilled and split the Coventry Engineering Joint Committee.[92]

Unable to establish an effective platform, the engineering shop stewards were vulnerable to the slump of 1920–1 which saw many Coventry firms go out of business, and by 1921

[90] Documents on General Strike in Coventry, at Modern Records Centre, University of Warwick.
[91] Trade Union Survey, in records of Organization Department, T.U.C. D30.
[92] Hinton, *Shop Stewards*, p. 221.

they had 'to all intents and purposes been eliminated.'[93]
Within the Coventry and District Engineering Employers'
Association only five firms out of forty-six were working full-
time; of the remaining forty-one more were operating only
two or three days a week with a nucleus of men.[94] The
Workers' Union was hit hardest of all by the heavy unemployment of the immediate post-war period, and its decline in the
Midlands, previously its main area of strength, was particularly
marked. The Amalgamated Engineering Union was in trouble,
unable to get its own members to stand firm against wage
reductions, and it came to grief during the 1922 lock-out.[95]
The A.E.U. failed to make any headway in the national
dispute with the engineering employers over their right to
introduce changes in working practice, and the lock-out
hit the local branches hard. In Coventry their membership
roughly halved from 11,000 to just over 5,000.[96] Shop
steward organization of any real significance ceased to exist,
and in many of the motor firms only a nucleus of membership remained. The unions had very little involvement in the
negotiation of piece-work prices.[97] By 1927 the A.E.U.
membership had halved again to 2,000, and efforts to win
the engineers back into the union met with a poor response.[98]

It is doubtful, however, whether the earnings of the
engineers were critically affected by the failure of their union
to retain their membership. Even after the depression of
1920–1, some of the firms were paying as much as 75 per
cent above the basic rate on piece-work earnings, with similar
bonuses for time-rated toolroom workers, and there was no
noticeable decline in such earnings by the mid-1920s.[99]
Certain strategies of the union had been defeated. It had
failed, for example, to impose limits on piece-work earnings

[93] C. G. Reynolds, *Joint Consultation over Thirty Years* (London, 1950), p. 54.
[94] C.D.E.E.A. minutes, 6 Dec. 1920.
[95] See disputes at Triumph and Rover discussed with Midland organizers, report for February, March, and April in A.E.U. Journal, and C.D.E.E.A. minutes, 21 Feb. 1921.
[96] Carr, 'Engineering Workers', thesis cit., pp. 198–227.
[97] C.D.E.E.A. minutes, 26 Mar. 1925.
[98] A.E.U. Monthly Report, June figures; A.E.U. Journal, August, 1923, December 1928.
[99] See the rates at Humber and White & Poppe; C.D.E.E.A. minutes, 1 Feb. 1922, 27 Feb. 1922, 26 Apr. 1926.

in particular departments. Some reductions in earnings from
wartime levels had been pushed through in 1921 and 1924,
and the employers had kept clear of granting any increases
to basic pay in order to protect unit costs, but none of these
problems appear to have generated any significant hostility
from engineering labour.[100] In the main their earnings were
well above the district rates, and in 1926 at the time of
the General Strike, they felt themselves to be in a much
better position because of piece-work earnings than those
dependent on day rates in the heavier sectors such as
shipbuilding.

For those on the vehicle building side the position was
rather different: here the status of the skilled worker was
more clearly dependent on union strength because dilution
was still a live issue. Whereas the scope for dilution in the
machine shops and toolrooms had been diminished, as the
distinction between the highly skilled non-production worker
and the semi-skilled machinist became more firmly established,
the question was very much alive on the body building side.
In the early 1920s the Coventry employers were facing a
shortage of coach-builders, and this lead to competition
between firms for such labour and to distortions of earnings,
the Daimler company in particular paying above district
rates in order to attract skilled men.[101] In 1924 the employers
considered 'the desirability of dilution by introduction of
second grade labour' and it was agreed to use 'every endeavour'
to pursue such dilution.[102]

It was not merely a question of labour shortage, but the
change in nature of the occupation itself. As the output of
cars increased, the specialist body builder catering for a small
number of customers faced a declining market. In 1924 it
was reported that 'Low prices and ever vanishing profits are,
of course, the great evil. Quantity production has done much
to put them down to absurdly low levels and the body
builder who caters for the individual customer has been
drawn into the vortex of low priced competition.'[103]

[100] C.D.E.E.A. minutes, 28 July 1924.
[101] C.D.E.E.A. minutes, 19 Feb. 1924; 23 Apr., 7 May 1923.
[102] C.D.E.E.A. minutes, 18 Feb. 1924.
[103] Editorial in *Motor Body Building and Vehicle Construction*, March 1924.
The most powerful indication of the market pressures on this side of the industry

By 1928 the N.U.V.B. branch in Coventry was feeling the effects of dilution and changes in the industry. Having reported in 1925 that organization was good, by 1928 their Midlands organizer confessed that 'our members in Coventry are fighting rearguard actions', and that they had failed to contain the spread of semi-skilled labour to painting work.[104] The use of car bodies made up in metal sections with a timber frame, instead of those made entirely with wood, reduced many of the requirements for skilled woodworking and hit the N.U.V.B. membership hard. Although the numbers in that union did not decline significantly until the 1930s, the anxieties of its officials, and the frequency of strikes in Coventry over reductions in earnings or the use of unskilled labour (sometimes female) indicate clearly enough the pressures members were under.[105] Even the sheet metal workers, regarded as being a peculiarly strong local union, could not resist the use of boy labour in certain operations.[106]

By the 1920s the sources of organization in Coventry were drying up. Skilled workers previously well organized were becoming less so; the heterogeneous group of less skilled workers were hardly touched by trade unions. The breaking of connections with the past was therefore as evident in a town like Coventry, where industry and labour organization had been established before 1914, as in Oxford, where they had been almost entirely non-industrial. Measured simply in terms of pay, of course, most of these workers were well off, and their standard of living had not suffered much by the absence or weakness of unions.

However, from the point of view of 'the Movement',

was the decision of the Daimler Company to close down its body building shop and contract out the work to volume producers. N.U.V.B. Journal, Jan. 1930.

[104] N.U.V.B. Journal, Sept. 1928.

[105] Of the fourteen recorded strikes (recorded, that is, in the Ministry of Labour dispute books), twelve were in vehicle building departments as opposed to the engineering side. P.R.O. LAB 34/36–43. For female labour issues, see the strikes at Rover, 8–9 Feb. 1926, and the Motor Body and Sheet Metal Co., 23–8 Sept. 1925. Before 1914, the number of women employed in the motor industry had been negligible; by 1930, women constituted about one-sixth of the labour force.

[106] C.D.E.E.A. minutes, 18 Nov. 1929. For the acknowledgement of their power as a craft society, see J. Hilton (ed.), *Are Trade Unions Obstructive?* (London, 1935), p. 141.

union organizations were of importance, especially in the 1920s. The old labour strongholds were being weakened by heavy unemployment and the defeat of the miners in 1926. As the weight within the union movement came to be with the major general unions, the need for these to recruit in areas of industrial expansion, such as Oxford and Coventry, was pressing, hence the T.U.C. survey of the unions' position in such towns. The sources for such growth thus acquire much interest and significance since the industrial expansion of the 1920s occurred where the links with historically well-organized labour were either weakening or non-existent. That is, a town like Coventry by the early 1930s appeared to be no easier a proposition for the organizer of semi-skilled labour than Oxford, even though conditions in the latter seemed at least historically so much less promising. It is necessary now to turn to the other Oxford car factory, Pressed Steel, to see precisely how and why industrial relations there developed a markedly different way from the patterns that have been outlined in this chapter, and did provide a source for organization in the 1930s.

3

THE EMERGENCE OF CONFLICT AT PRESSED STEEL

The growth of Morris Motors at Cowley in the 1920s had had very little effect on the strength of local industrial organization: the apathy, acquiescence, or powerlessness of those outside the skilled trades which had been apparent before 1914 had been confirmed rather than challenged by the behaviour of the Morris workers. The major change brought about by industrial growth was the interpenetration of rural and urban areas for which there had been no real basis before 1914. This had provoked an often quite painful juxtaposition of depression and affluence which had served to underline the attractiveness of work in the car factory. In the wider context of the difficulties of trade unions nationally the absence of any straightforward connection between factory employment and trade union organization was hardly surprising.

What had been quite striking was the extent to which the same was true in Coventry in the 1920s. Even though skilled and semi-skilled workers had been effectively organized there before 1914, and had been able to win some ground against employers, their position in the 1920s became significantly weaker. Skilled engineers and vehicle builders were less well organized and were unable to restrict changes in work practice; organization amongst the semi-skilled had virtually disappeared. Shop steward influence was negligible. Therefore Morris was as untroubled in Coventry as in Cowley by labour organization. Improvements in productivity had come not from the need to counter trade union pressure on wage rates but from the incentives to cost-cutting in the market conditions of the 1920s. The main impact of his factories in both towns had been to underline quite simple propositions about the benefits of paying high wages, assessed either in rural or industrial terms.

By the mid-1930s the position in Oxford had altered

significantly. Pressed Steel, located at Cowley to produce car bodies for Morris, had been unable to maintain a pacific labour force. Sporadic unrest had served as a preface to a major strike in 1934 which led in turn to trade union recognition and growth. These developments affected industrial relations and politics in the city in a quite fundamental way: the Labour Party and the trade unions were much stronger by the end of the 1930s than either had been in the 1920s. For the University the local working class had become more interesting, though less docile than it had been either in the 1920s or before 1914. The main purpose of this chapter is to show as precisely as possible why labour at Pressed Steel turned out to be both more restive and more powerful than workers in other local occupations; subsequent chapters will pursue the consequences and significance of this.

The Pressed Steel factory owed its existence to Morris.[1] The company of the same name had been formed as an Anglo-American enterprise with J. Henry Schroeder, Budd's of Philadelphia, and Morris as the chief architects, and began production in 1926. Its formation followed on quite logically from Morris's purchase of the Coventry engine-building firm of Hotchkiss, in the sense that it showed his appreciation of the need to control supply of parts in order to achieve the lowest possible cost. Whereas in the early years he had wished to take advantage of Coventry engineering skills without incurring the responsibility of ownership, this became unavoidable as his demands grew. By the late 1920s there was more scope for innovation on the body building than on the engineering side of the industry. In chassis and engine production the gains in reducing cost had been achieved by applying the principles of subdivision of task and the use of single-purpose machinery. Particularly in the process of assembly, with which the Cowley plant was chiefly concerned, the advances had involved the organization of production, rather than developments in components or design. When it came to body-making the position was different. While Pressed Steel was at one with the radiator and engine factories in being closely tied to Morris's high level of output, it departed from

[1] The relations with Pressed Steel are dealt with in Andrews and Brunner, pp. 131–4, and Overy, pp. 30, 86.

their example in so far as it was also committed to a novel method of producing car bodies. Following a visit to America in 1925, Morris was keen to exploit progress made there in the production of the car body using sheet-metal pressings instead of a timber frame and metal panels. Up to this time the production of car bodies had lain at the heart of the contradiction of the motor car as a consumer good: something which had to be turned out in large numbers and yet was susceptible to variations in fashion and taste. Whereas the chassis and engine could be turned out in large numbers because they could be common to several models, it was the car's body which had to respond to the whims of the customer. Hence the equipment for producing particular bodies often had to cover its cost in a shorter period of time than was the case with engine or chassis production.[2]

As far as Morris was concerned, the Pressed Steel project was not a success. The first factory of its type, it had great difficulty in producing bodies of reasonable quality.[3] Morris was the firm's only customer up to 1929, but in 1930 he severed his connection with it, having been unable to gain complete control. Thereafter he relied less on Pressed Steel than many other car producers, and this insulated him from any commercial damage which might have been caused by Pressed Steel's rather turbulent industrial relations in the 1930s.[4]

Mention of the early difficulties of Pressed Steel should not hide the record of rising profits in the 1930s, and it is appropriate to discuss these here. Despite the technical problems associated with the all-steel body, profits increased steadily, except for 1932, and after that year the firm's

[2] 'To follow the vagaries of fashion largely imposed by a hundred and one small bodymakers means amortising the cost of equipment in a very short time, and the provision of big and expensive facilities for the production of the necessary dies.' 'Report and Memorandum on U.K. Car Industry', in P.R.O., Board of Trade Papers, BT 56/22.

[3] See M. Thomas, *Out on a Wing* (London, 1964), pp. 152–3: 'The actual delay in the production of bodies from Pressed Steel was nothing like so troublesome as the appallingly low standard of quality when the first output began to come off the line.'

[4] During the 1934 strike at Pressed Steel, which closed down that factory for a while, production at Morris's was hardly affected since it merely supplied some steel panels which were attached to a timber body-frame made elsewhere.

consumption of sheet metal grew consistently. Comparing Pressed Steel's performance with that of Morris's and those of seven leading vehicle manufacturers shows the strength of Pressed Steel's position and the slow recovery from the slump by Morris's.

Table 6. Index of trading profits
1930 = 100

	Morris	Pressed Steel	Leading firms
1928	102	62	n.a.
1929	n.a.	93	89
1930	100	100	100
1931	56	102	81
1932	64	78	70
1933	29	233	89
1934	46	308	120
1935	102	425	144

Sources: For Morris Motors, see Andrews and Brunner, p. 185; for Pressed Steel, see accounts in Company's House; for Austin, Humber, Morris, Standard, Vauxhall, A.E.C., Leyland, see G. Maxcy and Z. A. Silberston, *The Motor Industry* (1959), p. 153.

When trading profits are considered in relation to fixed assets, these again reveal a sharply rising rate of return after the early years, to levels comparable with Morris's. A decline after 1936 probably reflected an increase in fixed costs through extension of the factory in 1937, and a decline in demand which began to show itself later in that year. These factors continued to operate in the following year when further extension was fully accounted for. The development of the integral body and chassis unit and facilities for producing aircraft parts demonstrated the vitality of the company. Not surprisingly, labour matters did not intrude prominently into the published reports, and while higher wage costs were used to explain in part the slight decline in net profits in 1937, this did not prevent the introduction of holidays with pay, or the building of a works hospital the following year.[5] The main problem on the supply side was

[5] Information on the firm comes from company reports in *The Times*, 21 May 1938, 20 May 1939.

not labour but steel. Motor manufacturers criticized the high cost of the domestic product compared to the American, and at Pressed Steel the quality was poor for much of the period.[6] However, by the end of the 1930s quality had been improved and costs reduced somewhat.

Working at Pressed Steel was undoubtedly more unpleasant and materially less rewarding than at Morris's. In the first place, it was more dangerous: the major risk lay not in the assembly of the parts into Pressed Steel bodies but in the pressing out of sheet steel prior to its assembly. In 1930 the Factory Inspectorate successfully prosecuted the firm for neglecting to fence a power press, which was classed as dangerous machinery, and out of sixty-three presses in operation, seventeen had no guard at all.[7] In addition, the grease which covered the steel panels and the metal dust produced by the grinding of parts made the work much more dirty than at Morris's; whereas those at Morris's could go to work 'respectably' in jacket and tie, the Pressed Steel men were quickly recognizable by their greasy overalls.[8]

Pay was also less good at the Pressed Steel factory. At Morris's wages were paid as a flat rate on which a 'bonus' was earned once output exceeded a certain level. At Pressed Steel the system was one of straight piece-work, with no guaranteed minimum. With interruptions or short-time working this meant that wages could fall to very low levels.[9] The management at Pressed Steel had tried to follow some of the elements of Morris's strategy by paying high wages but refusing to recognize unions,[10] but the poor performance of the firm in its early years and difficulties in producing satisfactory bodies perhaps led them to try and economize on wage costs,

[6] The problem of steel supply is discussed in R. A. Church, *Herbert Austin: The British Motor Car Industry to 1941* (London, 1979), pp. 122 ff.

[7] *Oxford Times*, 13 Feb. 1930.

[8] Interview with J. B. Clarke, former Pressed Steel worker.

[9] The organizer for the N.U.V.B., which had a small membership at Pressed Steel, reported in 1931, 'The prices were impossible for members to earn a bare living. It would be safe to say that this firm would compare favourably with Woolworth's—nothing over 6*d*.' N.U.V.B. Journal, Jan. 1931.

[10] The A.E.U. District Committee was told that the firm was 'not opposed to paying out more money, but was very decidedly opposed to any appearance of falling in line with trade union practices in any way.' A.E.U. District Committee Minute Book, 31 May 1928.

even though the firm operated at a profit during this time. Whatever the reason, reductions in wages in particular departments led to strikes in 1929, 1930, and 1931. These were small-scale affairs, only one of them lasting longer than a day and none involving more than 100 workers. They did not match the scale of strikes occurring at other factories in the same period, one at Austin's in 1929 lasting ten days and involving 7,000 workers, and two at Dagenham which saw 8,000 workers striking for fifteen days.

Small and isolated though these strikes were, they did show that the managers at Pressed Steel had failed to succeed where Morris had done so in the blending of paternalism with authority. Although the firm had claimed that it was in the forefront as regarded the provision of social, athletic, and welfare institutions, and its managing director dutifully attended various social functions,[11] alongside Morris's benevolence to the wider community the managers were bound to appear as faceless men. In addition, of course, they had to operate in far more difficult conditions than Morris. Whereas the latter had been able to exploit economies in the organization of production, at Pressed Steel they were facing technical problems as well as uncertainties over demand for their product. There were, in short, obvious material conditions which overrode the attractiveness of welfare provision and social entertainment, and produced a less than docile labour force.

But there was more to it than this. It has been suggested earlier that the success of authoritarianism and generosity at Morris Motors was rooted in the social character of labour supply, which was heterogeneous in terms of previous occupation, and in general without a background of trade union membership. Labour recruited to Pressed Steel differed in two respects from that which went to Morris's. First, there was a larger proportion of skilled workers, and second, some of the semi-skilled workers came from outside the immediate area, and amongst these were some from districts where trade unions were firmly embedded in certain industries.

The skilled men were mainly in the non-production departments away from the assembly lines, working as machinists,

---

[11] *Oxford Times*, 9 May 1930.

toolfitters, and patternmakers, 298 in all, and many of these had to be brought in from outside the district. Such labour was not always easy to 'manage' because of its stronger position in the labour market, and the greater density of trade union membership within particular skilled occupations. However, the main impression they leave of their role in the early years of Pressed Steel is one of sectionalism and weakness. A strike by engineers to remove a ban on smoking failed because of 'a very decided lack of cohesion',[12] while an attempt to operate a ban on overtime until the conditions of the national engineering agreement were observed had to be abandoned because of the refusal of members of the United Patternmakers' Association to join such an embargo.[13] Even if many of the incoming skilled workers had been members of unions elsewhere, they showed no signs of joining branches in Oxford. The A.E.U. could not keep track of new workers coming into the district, and the fact that branch meetings were held in St. Ebbe's, an old working-class district some way from Cowley, was another discouragement against joining.[14] The N.U.V.B. also failed to make any headway, its membership actually declining from sixty-five in 1927 to forty-seven in 1932.[15] It is quite clear then that in the early years of Pressed Steel's operation the skilled workers did not pose any particular threat to management and were not the source of any significant accretion of trade union strength. Yet it was precisely this group, the skilled men, who held out most hope for trade union organizers in the very difficult conditions of the 1930s.[16]

The effect of technology on skill did not support this view, however. In the motor industry 'where the super-skilled press tool designer and toolmaker, and the quick adaptable machinist are most in demand',[17] dilution and concentration of skill had gone hand in hand at the expense of the traditional

[12] *Oxford Times*, 5 Aug. 1930.

[13] A.E.U. District Committee Minute Book, 22 Aug. 1929.

[14] The A.E.U. membership in Oxford only increased from forty-four to sixty-eight between 1928 and 1933, far short of the number of engineers coming to the district.

[15] Figures from N.U.V.B. Journal for July of each year.

[16] Conference of 10 January 1937 on organization at Dagenham, in T.U.C. T 604 57.4(D).

[17] 'Notes on Mass Production', in A.E.U. Journal, Mar. 1939.

craftsman. The gulf between the toolmaker and the pattern-makers on the one hand, and the semi-skilled assemblers on the other, was too wide for any real sense of identity to develop. In the main characteristics of their work, discretion and control, they were worlds apart—toolmakers and pattern-makers were never subject to the discipline and interference of piece-work payment systems. The presence of skilled workers at Pressed Steel, forming at first sight a link between earlier industrialization and the 'new' industries, did not, however, have any serious consequence for industrial relations.

As well as having to bring in skilled labour, Pressed Steel also had to go further afield for semi-skilled workers. Some, at least, had already turned up in Oxford in 1927 from the depressed regions, the local employment committee reporting that 'quite considerable numbers of miners and other workers from South Wales had come to Oxford' because of the development of the motor industry,[18] and to meet their needs Pressed Steel took them on.[19] Their demands coincided with the period in the late 1920s when anxieties were growing that unemployment in the mining industry would prove to be long term and not merely cyclical. Before the Special Areas policy was launched in 1934, the main response to the problem had been to encourage miners to leave the coalfields and find work elsewhere. As official policy this took the form of the Industrial Transference Board set up in 1928 to provide financial help to those moving some distance in search of work, and Baldwin also appealed to employers to play their part by taking on such labour.[20] Many of the unemployed had begun to reach similar conclusions about their fate and had begun to migrate in search of work. But whether they travelled with government help or not, there were some anxieties about their impact on the regions receiving them, the Ministry of Labour noting 'some apprehension

[18] *Oxford Times*, 18 Mar. 1927.
[19] The London organizer of the N.U.V.B. reported in 1929 that 'at Press(ed) Steel Co. we found a large number of men from the Welsh coalfields'. N.U.V.B. Journal, Jan. 1929. In addition to the Welsh, the motor industry absorbed more 'outsiders' than any other. Barnett House, *Survey*, vol. 1, p. 53.
[20] The Oxford Employment Committee reported that 'The Pressed Steel Co., through Mr. Campbell, had been very helpful, taking young men chiefly from Wales.' *Oxford Times*, 18 Sept. 1928.

that these workers will impart into areas to which they may be transferred elements of unrest and disturbance'.[21]

However, before 1934 these migrants made very little impact upon industrial relations at Pressed Steel, since it was only after 1933 that their position became at all settled. The mobility of labour from the depressed areas was dependent on the level of prosperity in the towns to which they went, and so it is not surprising to find that transfers from coal-mining to other occupations were substantially reduced in 1932 as unemployment hit even the more prosperous industries.[22] Although Oxford escaped the worst of the Depression, it still had 3,614 unemployed in September 1932.[23] It is therefore unlikely that the 259 men from the depressed areas who were in Oxford in 1928 had been joined by many others before 1933; certainly the movement from South Wales, the region nearest to Oxford, was negligible before 1933 and only picked up thereafter.[24]

Those who did move to Oxford before 1933 were likely to have been the most mobile of their population, the young, single men, who were also able to move away again in the face of unemployment or poor working conditions. Sometimes this involved return to Wales because it was cheaper to live there as an unemployed man than in Oxford; sometimes it meant moving to a job elsewhere, perhaps to Vauxhall's at Luton.[25] Local societies catering for the Welsh in Oxford suffered from this mobility: at the annual dinner of the Pressed Steel Rugby Club, at which a Welsh choir provided the music, the secretary complained of a large number of

[21] Ministry of Labour, *Industrial Transference Board Report*, Cmd. 3156 (1928), p. 10. It is relevant to point out here that of the regions of Great Britain between 1911 and 1947 South Wales was the most strike-prone, as was mining of all the industries. K. G. J. C. Knowles, *Strikes: a Study in Industrial Conflict* (Oxford, 1952), pp. 197, 210.

[22] Ministry of Labour *Gazette*, Nov. 1932, pp. 408-9.

[23] *Oxford Times*, 23 Sept. 1932.

[24] According to Daniel, 'prospects of employment in other districts during the depression were so poor that very little immigration took place', whereas 'in 1933-5 there was a marked improvement in the prospects of employment in Oxford, and large numbers of men migrated from Wales'. G. H. Daniel, 'Some Factors Affecting the Movement of Labour', *Oxford Economic Papers*, 3 (1940), 156.

[25] Ibid., p.. 174; and an interview with E. Williams, Pressed Steel worker 1927-9; and from 1930.

men leaving the district in comparison with the previous year.[26] The Welsh glee singers were similarly affected, the secretary reporting in 1931 that 'at present they were badly affected by the trade depression, a number of members having had to leave Oxford'.[27] The consequences of uncertain employment were remarked upon by a union organizer who visited Pressed Steel in 1930: 'I found that our would-be helper had been discharged along with a number of others who were possibly also interested, and had departed for his native woods and hills, not to say colliery refuse heaps of South Wales.'[28]

Without any effective leadership within the factory, which the migrants might have provided, the strikes over piece-work remained small scale, ineffectual, and unrelated to any more general pressure for the recognition of trade unions by management. But before 1933 there was little encouragement for this from outside Oxford, since the union most likely to recruit car workers, the Transport and General Workers' Union, showed little interest in expanding its membership there. Bevin recognized that amalgamation with the Workers' Union in 1929 meant that they inherited responsibility for semi-skilled workers in engineering, and in the event it was his union which recruited most heavily at Pressed Steel after the strike there in the summer of 1934.[29] However, the main involvement by the union in the Oxford region before 1934 was purely negative, involving the dismissal of Hembury, an officer of the Workers' Union who had been taken on with the amalgamation.[30] The view of Transport House was that 'at the present time there was only a nucleus of organisa-tion in the district', and Bevin, faced with the need to eco-nomize on staff because funds were depleted by the Depres-sion, refused to be swayed by talk about 'potential member-ship which has not fructified in the majority of cases'.[31]

---

[26] *Oxford Times*, 4 May 1929.   [27] *Oxford Times*, 20 Mar. 1931.
[28] N.U.V.B. Journal, Jan. 1930.
[29] Report of the National Joint Committee between A.E.U. and T. & G.W.U., 7 Aug. 1931, in minutes of G.E.C.
[30] T. & G.W.U. Finance and General Purposes Committee, May 1933, minute 536.
[31] T. & G.W.U., G.E.C. minute 67, 10 Feb. 1930; Bevin's report to the Biennial Delegate Conference. 7 July 1927.

Financial worries were only half the story. While in 1928 Bevin had been willing to launch an expensive campaign to organize the provincial bus industry, it was always unlikely that the motor industry would receive similar treatment because at that time it did not have a settled place within the union's structure. In February 1931 the formation of a trade group for the metal, engineering, and chemical industries was still posing problems which were not fully sorted out until November 1933.[32] In conjunction with the fluid conditions of employment, the outlook of the T. & G.W.U. meant that the problems at Pressed Steel caused few upsets in Cowley and had no repercussions beyond. Certainly what happened there showed that the successful strategy pursued at Morris's could not easily be copied, but the failure to do so had, up to 1933, no serious consequences for either industrial relations or politics in Oxford.

By 1934 this had changed: a strike at Pressed Steel in July led to the recognition there of trade unions, forcing a change of front by management, and bringing with it a substantial number of new members to the T. & G.W.U. If one event marked the point when economic and social change began to affect politics and industrial relations in Oxford, then it was this strike. The consequences of the strike, and the activities of those involved in it, reached through to most aspects of industrial and political behaviour in subsequent years. The growth of the Labour Party in the south-east of Oxford, the formation of local housing associations to combat high rents, the unusually active Communist Party are all difficult to explain except in terms of that strike. It now deserves explanation and description.

The strike began on Monday, 16 July, as a dispute involving 180 workers in the press shop, the immediate cause being low piece-work earnings on a new body intended for the Motor Show in October.[33] Unlike previous strikes at the firm it did not end after a few days with no clear result, but spread to other departments so that within three days the factory was closed. The strike was not resolved until ten

---

[32] Bevin's report to G.E.C., 17 Feb., 17 Nov. 1931; 16 Nov. 1933.
[33] N.U.V.B. Journal, Oct. 1934. According to the London organizer, 'the rates paid to semi-skilled workers were a disgrace'.

days later when trade union recognition—which had become the major issue—was conceded. While the management had originally stood firm and rejected the demands of the strike committee for the abolition of the piece-work system, it eventually ended the strike by agreeing to join the Engineering and Allied Employers' Federation which required them to recognize trade unions. But why did the strike, which had promised to be no more than a minor piece-work dispute, become much more broadly based and have such a fundamental effect on the relations between management and workers?

Conditions in the wider industrial world were certainly more favourable than they had been since the company began operations. While the firm was enjoying healthy profits, it was still dependent on the demand of car producers for the all-steel car body. Pressed Steel's position as a supplier to the industry made it vulnerable to strikes during busy periods, as July was with preparation for the Motor Show. When the strike was a week old and the factory had been closed down, the larger car firms were demanding the return of their jigs so that the work could be done elsewhere;[34] and when the strike was over the secretary of the Engineering Employers' organization reported some relief in the Midlands that the strike had been settled. The strike was eventually brought to an end by the intervention of Andrew Dalgleish, the national officer of the trade group of the T. & G.W.U. which covered the motor industry. This reflected the way in which, by 1934, the union had become far more interested in building up membership in towns like Oxford than it had been in earlier years. First reports of attempts to organize at the Cowley works, in the face of the anti-unionism of the management, appeared in October 1933, and by the spring of 1934 some recruits had been made at Pressed Steel. The union officials were quick to act once the strike had broken out, enrolling 600 new members within a short time.[35]

But while the result of the strike—the recruitment of a large number of semi-skilled workers into the T. & G.W.U. —was in part the reflection of a new emphasis in the policy

[34] *Oxford Mail*, 24 July 1934.
[35] Finance and General Purposes Committee, 10 August 1934, minute 669.

of that union, this was not the whole story. In fact, in the early stages of the strike it was clear that the T. & G.W.U.'s propaganda campaign, which had begun some nine months before, had not produced immediate benefit, for the strike committee was anxious to exclude trade union officials from the organization of the strike.[36] Even when the question of the enrolment of workers in a union did arise, the T. & G.W.U. was not the immediate beneficiary, for the original intention was to put the strikers into the A.E.U., to give one union a monopoly of membership. However, this wish was frustrated because the local members of the A.E.U., mainly in the toolroom, were unenthusiastic about opening their ranks to semi-skilled production workers.[37]

Responsibility for organizing the strike lay initially with the strike committee drawn from various sections in the factory, rather than with any outside group; and what is surprising about the strike committee is the extent to which it was composed of those who had moved to Oxford from the older-established industrial regions of the North and West. Precise information on the committee is unavailable, and estimates of its size have varied. Goronwy Daniel, investigating the Welsh in Oxford in the 1930s, reported sixteen of them among the twenty-three members of the committee, and a later estimate gave much the same proportion.[38] The rest came from either Scotland or the North of England. Three key individuals may be identified. The secretary, Rowland Garrett, was a toolmaker (and a notable exception to the aloofness of skilled men from the strike) and in Darlington had been chairman of the ward committee of the Labour Party. Harris, a crane operator in the press shop

[36] An official of the N.U.V.B. reported that he and the secretary of the Pattern-makers' Association had 'offered to accompany the strike committee on a deputation to the firm, but were turned down by the strike committee. They were asking for trade union rates and conditions but were not prepared themselves to recognise trade union officials.' N.U.V.B. Journal, Oct. 1934. According to an A.E.U. member, the strike committee decided that no trade union official was to be allowed to interfere in the dispute, A.E.U. District Committee Minute Book, 23 July 1934.

[37] Interviews with Donovan Brown (Ruskin College) and Henry Jones, two of those involved in the organization of the strike.

[38] Daniel, 'The Movement of Labour', p. 157 n.; interview with Rowland Garrett, secretary of the committee.

where the strike originated, had been active in trade unions for several years before he came to Oxford in 1934, and had been a member of the South Wales Miners' Federation; the same was true of Huish. These two were to emerge as leaders of the Pressed Steel work-force, Harris becoming secretary of the Pressed Steel branch of the T. & G.W.U. as well as chief shop steward, and Huish its chairman.

The contribution of the migrants from the depressed areas was out of all proportion to their numbers in the factory. In 1936, 1,266 workers from Wales, the North, and Scotland were employed in the local motor industry,[39] and even if they had all gone to Pressed Steel, they would have made up only half the work-force; their domination of the strike committee is therefore evidence of the rather special contribution they had made. While they were reluctant to involve trade union officials they did need some outside help, and one of the committee, probably Huish, approached the local Communist Party.[40] Like the T. & G.W.U., the local Communist Party's interest in Cowley was not long-standing. Up to a year before the strike, the party had been mainly confined to students, and had operated through the October Club.[41] But by 1933 greater emphasis was placed on the importance of winning members through industrial action on the shop-floor. Instead of trying to set up independent trade union organization, greater emphasis was to be placed on work within the established trade union movement, and on the day-to-day struggles of the working class. Whereas the earlier efforts of the Minority Movement to set up independent organization had tended to concentrate on workers already strongly organized and evidently militant, the change in outlook after 1933 encouraged interest in unorganized workers, particularly those in the 'new' industries, as a way of winning support for the Communist Party.

The Oxford Communist Party was rather unusual (and was regarded by King Street as such) in having good facilities

---

[39] Barnett House, *Survey*, vol. 1, p. 55, table 8.

[40] Interview with Henry Jones.

[41] For a typical meeting, with Harry Pollitt as visiting speaker, see *Oxford Mail*, 5 May 1933.

for producing leaflets and factory newspapers, and in being able to use students at Ruskin and in the University for the creation and distribution of this material. In these respects it was far more active than the average local party.[42] In 1933 an attempt was made to penetrate the Pressed Steel factory, and some twenty members joined the T. & G.W.U.; yet like that union the party was unaware of what was going on in the early stages of the strike, which was hardly surprising since none of the strikers was a member of the party.[43] To gain control of such a large strike involving inexperienced workers was also quite beyond the capabilities of the local party.[44]

To provide some support, the party's head office sent an organizer, Abe Lazarus, to Oxford. Previously he had helped to organize a strike at the Firestone Tyre factory in north London. Although he operated outside the official Labour Movement, Lazarus was to play an important part in working-class and left-wing movements in the city over the following years. He was an outstanding speaker,[45] and his ability to capture the attention of workers at meetings in various parts of the city during the strike was invaluable. In addition pickets had to be organized to thwart the efforts of management to weaken the strike by reopening the factory. Because of the enormous problems in organizing a strike in Oxford in 1934, Lazarus's presence was of major importance. Although the strike committee had done a great deal to bring together the grievances of the various departments, not one of them at this stage could assume the role of a public figure in the way that Lazarus did and so command, by force of personality, the attention of the whole labour force and other working-class groups.

Lazarus took up a different position from that of the strike committee towards trade union officials, arguing that their help was vital. However much support the committee

---

[42] Interview with Donovan Brown.

[43] *Communist Review*, Sept. 1934, 146 ff.

[44] As one member has recalled, 'The Party just couldn't cope with it, and we didn't know what to do next. They all came out on strike, they were all very "green", none of them—or very few of them—were in a union, it was a wonderful July, blazing hot, and discipline was falling to pieces.' Interview with Donovan Brown.

[45] Interviews with Donovan Brown and Henry Jones; the comments of Christopher Hill at the time of Lazarus's funeral in 1969, on file in the Abe Lazarus Library; and F. Pakenham, *Born to Believe* (London, 1951), p. 88.

had from the shop-floor it still required the backing of a major union if its bargaining strength was to have any durability. The ability of the T. & G.W.U. officials to secure wage increases for new members at Pressed Steel was demonstrated soon after the strike, when Dalgleish won increases on basic rates and piece-work allowances which meant an increase of about 18 per cent for most assembly-line workers.[46]

It has been useful to trace the development of this strike in some detail to show the sources of protest and their forms of organization. What had been very clear about the 1920s had been the way in which the motor industry at Cowley had developed with so few connections with the wider industrial economy, particularly on the labour side. The attempts to recruit workers into unions also showed formidable problems of structure and geography which underwrote that isolation. Inevitably, the success of the 1934 strike depended to a great extent on the way in which conditions outside Cowley had become more favourable: the pressures on Pressed Steel as a supplier undoubtedly provided some incentive to end the dispute; and the haphazard way (if at all) in which trade unions had operated in the motor industry in the 1920s had been replaced by the more systematic efforts of a major union. But quite clearly it was not because of organizations alone that Pressed Steel ceased to be confined within its particular Oxford context and became part of a more nationally based system of industrial relations. In the first instance the links with the industrial economy and the sources of continuity with the Labour Movement as it had developed in the past lay not with the energies of a national union but with changes in the supply of labour. And even here there is a distinction to be made. It was not the skilled workers who had provided such links, even though their position in the labour market was stronger than that of the less skilled, and had to a degree been inherited from the past rather than created anew by the motor industry itself: they had pursued sectional ambitions and concerns with little reference to the semi-skilled. Rather, if there was any group responsible for

---

[46] Dalgleish, report to Metal Engineering and Chemical Trade Group, December 1934. The union also gained support through paying out strike benefit, even though at the time the strike had not been official.

bringing the desire to organize within the factory to Cowley, it was the migrants from the depressed areas, always fewer in number than those who had come from regions nearer to Oxford but still significant in the role they had played.

It is worth emphasizing the comparative 'newness' of working-class society in Cowley in the early 1930s. The organizations of the Labour Movement had yet to establish themselves locally; while the T. & G.W.U. at national level was becoming increasingly interested in towns like Oxford, its presence in Cowley was still intermittent. The nearest district official of any standing was based in Birmingham; there was no local district secretary until 1937. Full-time union organizers were therefore seen only rarely, perhaps at one of the trade union weeks which never appear to have achieved very much.[47] The Labour Movement might not have existed to any worker whose only experience of the world came from Cowley.

The local social context, too, was rather barren. While the new housing estates in Cowley and Headington were very much the products of the local motor industry, the residential concentration of the working class which this produced did not imply any obvious social solidarity. The workers who lived on the estates had been attracted to Oxford from various backgrounds and were settled in an area which did little to break down the barriers of regional difference. In 1936 the Oxford Council of Social Service established a community centre in Cowley because 'There are many families residing in close proximity who are unknown to each other and have nothing in common, and it is the purpose of these community centres to provide an avenue of approach. We must assist these communities to get together and know each other.'[48]

The newly arrived migrants also very largely made up the strike committee and were not only able to transform an isolated piece-work dispute into a more broadly based

[47] According to one union organizer, 'The trade union campaign on the day of my visit was literally and physically a wash-out. Up to the time of my visit the efforts of the Oxford Trades Council closely resembled the game of 'Carting Coal to Newcastle'', the meeting audiences, so I was informed, consisting of trade union organizers and officials.' N.U.V.B. Journal, Jan. 1930.

[48] *Oxford Mail*, 23 Oct. 1936.

movement, in a social context which was far from supportive, but also ended the isolation of Cowley by travelling to the Midlands and to Dagenham to ensure that work normally done at Pressed Steel was not carried out elsewhere.[49] Although these efforts could never have been sustained for any length of time without the support of a major union, the shop-floor organization was never absorbed completely into the T. & G.W.U. and its outlook was never shared completely by that union. In view of the importance of these migrant groups in making, as it were, some connection between the established (though depressed) industrial sector and the 'new' industries, it is worth considering briefly the relationship between their social and cultural life in Oxford and their industrial activities.[50]

Of those moving to Oxford from the older industrial regions, the most numerous and 'visible' were the Welsh.[51] The process of migration and settlement tended to underwrite cultural differences, not only because migrants clung on to friends and activities which were familiar but also because of their contrast in type and character from the Oxford 'natives'. Although the government provided financial help and information about jobs to those wishing to leave the depressed areas, many made the journey on their own account. Most travelled on excursion or football trains; some 'jumped' lorries. Travelling from South Wales, across the South West and into Oxford without government assistance

[49] *Oxford Mail*, 25 July, 1934.

[50] Because of the absence of birthplace details in the 1931 census, it is particularly fortunate that the Institute of Statistics at Oxford conducted investigations into migration of labour, and that one member, G. H. Daniel, devoted particular attention to the largest group, those from South Wales. See H. W. Robinson, 'The Response of Labour to Economic Incentives', in P. W. S. Andrews and T. Wilson (eds.), *Oxford Studies in the Price Mechanism* (Oxford, 1951); the chapter by J. Marschak, Director of the Institute, in Barnett House, *Survey*, vol. 1, on industrial immigration; Daniel, 'The Movement of Labour'; and G. H. Daniel, 'A Sample Analysis of Labour Migration into the Oxford District' (Oxford Univ. D. Phil. thesis, 1939).

[51] When the Barnett House *Survey* was published in 1938 there was some surprise that only 10.8 per cent of those coming to Oxford from outside the town were from Wales; casual observation had suggested that east Oxford was dominated by Welsh people. It should also be pointed out that by far the greatest number of those from outside Oxford came from the South-West region (4,058 or 36.7 per cent of the total), and of these 3,480 came from towns within fifty miles of Oxford. Barnett House, *Survey*, vol. 1, p. 290.

Table 7. Migrants from depressed regions living
in Oxford in July 1936, by region of origin

Wales	1,195
North East	639
North West	518
Scotland	158

Source: Barnett House, *Survey*, vol. 1, p. 55,
table 8.

meant reliance on family and friends to help with housing
and jobs, and this in turn meant that particular villages in
Wales tended to supply a high proportion of migrants to any
one town.[52]
Once in Oxford the fundamentals of life might strike the
migrant in various ways. For the younger men in the motor
industry the work was probably fairly light compared to
mining and the pay was good: one reported that 'they had
never had so many material possessions before. Working
overtime he frequently earned £6 to £7 per week. . . .'[53]
On the other hand, for the older men the pressures of keep-
ing up with the assembly line could be hard to bear[54] and
rents were very high during periods of temporary unemployment.[55]
Making friends with other Welsh people, or knowing some-
one from one's own village, obviously helped make social
life bearable; the 'natives' were regarded as more restrained,
and less sociable than the Welsh were used to.[56] There was a

[52] One-sixth of all migrants to Oxford from Wales came from a small mining
village, Pontcymmer, Barnett House, *Survey*, vol. 1, p. 59; and 72 per cent of
those moving from all the depressed areas to town in England did so on their
own account, Industrial Transfer Scheme, General Review', in P.R.O. LAB
8/218.
[53] Daniel, 'The Movement of Labour', p. 174.
[54] One ex-miner reported that 'It was the man against the machine, and the
machine always wins; the faster the machine, the faster we had to work.' He had
to leave the car works and take a job as a builder's labourer. Ibid., p. 175.
[55] 'In Wales it would be possible to live far more cheaply on the "dole" than
in Oxford. Their main worry during such times was to find 20s. a week for
the rent.' Ibid.
[56] 'People are so independent here [in Oxford]. At home they wouldn't ask,
but come in and help if the children were ill; if things were bad they would
bring a loaf with them. In Oxford we could all be dead and no one would know
until the rent collector came round at the end of the week.' Ibid.

political slant to this, one of those whom Daniel interviewed
finding it 'hard to understand their Conservative politics
and apathetic attitudes towards trade unions'; and, more
generally, Cowley was not seen as a particularly working-
class place: there were no dances to go to, and those in
Oxford were expensive and snobbish.[57]

Many of the migrants coped with the difficulties of adjust-
ment to Oxford life by mixing mainly with Welsh people.
Because of the limited size of the Cowley suburbs this was
not too difficult. Those who moved from Wales to less well-
defined areas had a harder time of it. On the new estates in
Hayes and Southall, Middlesex, the Welsh were scattered and
isolated; in Oxford, as in communities already well defined,
such as Smethwick in Birmingham, it was easier to build
local connections.[58] Religion too played a part: the Congregational Church at Temple Cowley was having to meet growing
numbers by 1928, linked very closely with the growth of
Morris Motors and Pressed Steel. Although it did not serve
a solely working-class population, the church fostered links
with Wales—visits of Welsh churchmen, concerts by glee
singers, for example—and its vicar was active on behalf
of hard-pressed tenants on the Cowley estates.[59] As well as
its religious purpose, the church fulfilled certain social
functions of specific help for the incoming Welsh.

However, the commitment to maintaining a specifically
Welsh form of social life was not universal. While some
regretted the absence of other Welsh speakers, and joined
Welsh choirs and went to chapel as the only alternative to
returning home, the younger single men often travelled
to London to watch football matches, or visited the cinema,
the only Welsh aspect of their social life being the friends
they mixed with.[60] The variations in the intensity of attachment to a Welsh social and cultural life were not related
directly to the industrial and political activities of these
newcomers: involvement in labour organization was not

[57] Daniel, 'The Movement of Labour', pp. 177, 179. Interviews with F. Nicholls,
M. Williams, and R. Williams, who stressed the importance of the union in the
social life of the mining village.
[58] 'Religious Bodies and Transfer', in P.R.O. LAB 23/102.
[59] Log-Books of Temple Cowley United Reformed Church; interview with
M. Williams.   [60] Daniel, 'The Movement of Labour', pp. 173-9.

allied with any particular cultural pattern. The social supports of migration and existence in 'such lifeless and non-descript areas as the environs of Oxford'[61] were not in any necessary way linked with political or industrial activism, and if anything, the reverse was true. It was probably those who more fully embraced the more anonymous social life of English towns and showed no wish to return to Wales who became involved in the trade union or political party.[62] This is very much in line with the findings of the *Commission of Enquiry into Industrial Unrest in South Wales*, which considered the militancy there during the First World War. Political radicalism and industrial militancy were very much linked with the younger generation for whom the particular quality of Welsh chapel life, for example, was not attractive. And so, while the Welsh were a particularly distinctive group amongst the migrants by virtue of accent and culture, their specific industrial and political importance was not necessarily linked with this. Some tradition of collective action and a sense of class were what mattered, and in these aspects the Welsh were no different from others making the journey from the depressed areas. As a general category they had their impact upon local employers, it being reported in 1937 that 'A very definite preference exists amongst contractors and others for local workers off farms rather than for "travellers" from a distance.'[63] The Welsh, though, were sometimes singled out, since Pressed Steel tried to restrict the intake of Welsh after the 1934 strike.[64] The way these traditions affected Pressed Steel for the rest of the 1930s, the extent to which they could be communicated to others, and the typicality of industrial relations at that factory must now be assessed.

[61] The phrase comes from M.P. Fogarty, *Prospects of the Industrial Areas of Great Britain* (London, 1945), p. 458.

[62] See the member of the strike committee interviewed by Daniel, 'The Movement of Labour', pp. 177–8.

[63] 'Economic Position in Agriculture: Labour Aspect', in P.R.O. MAF/47/3.

[64] Daniel, 'The Movement of Labour', p. 157 n.

4

OXFORD AND THE NATIONAL EXPERIENCE,
1934–1939

The 1934 strike at Pressed Steel was an obvious break from
past experience at Cowley; it is therefore important to assess
its consequences for the Oxford car factories, and this will
require some discussion of what was going on elsewhere in
the industry. Conditions after 1934 certainly favoured labour
more than at any other time since the end of the post-war
boom. The upswing in the business cycle, which affected the
motor industry even though its output had not fallen drastic-
ally during the slump, inevitably gave workers greater
confidence about staking a claim.[1] The unions too were in
a better position with the motor industry than they had been
in the 1920s. Partly this was because some of the confusions
and uncertainties of structure were beginning to be resolved,
in that skilled unions were less tied to the defence of craft
practices and their sections catering for semi-skilled workers
were becoming operational; the general unions were also
showing willingness to expand.[2] But the level of prosperity
had a part to play as well; in a pre-Keynesian world union
leaders were bound to see their activities as closely dependent
on fluctuations in trade, and with an upswing were likely
to be less defensive than they had been during the Depression.
But while there was much promise, little of substance was
achieved. In this sense the very vivid contrast in industrial
relations between the firms at Cowley—Morris Motors
practically strike free, and Pressed Steel probably the most

[1] The Ministry of Labour reported in 1936 that 'The usual desire of work-
people to obtain higher wages as soon as there is an upturn in industrial conditions
furnishes an opportunity for irresponsible elements to encourage unconstitutional
action.' *Annual Report*, Cmd. 5431, p. 67.

[2] The Midlands' district officer of the T. & G.W.U. reported in June 1934 on
a 'considerable amount of work' in Derby, Nottingham, West Bromwich,
Coventry, and Oxford. Dalgleish's report to Metal, Engineering, and Chemical
Trade Group of T. & G.W.U., June 1934.

strike-prone plant in Britain between the wars—hid some basic similarities which were typical of the industry as a whole.

I. *Pressed Steel*

Industrial relations at Pressed Steel revolved, not surprisingly, around a tripartite division between management, unions, and shop stewards, the main issue being the power of the third against the other two. The suspicious attitude of the strike committee towards the trade unions, which had been apparent during the early days of the 1934 strike, continued after the settlement had been reached. The *Conveyor*, a factory newspaper produced by local Communists, was critical of the way in which the strike had been ended without consulting the labour force. 'It [the 1934 strike] was an opportunity of getting trade unionism into Pressed Steel; we knew the need for unity and accepted the T. and G.W.U., but we did not give them power to act as they did, and we must take care that they do not act without consulting us in the future.'[3] The paper went on to suggest that 'union members must appoint shop stewards and collectors which they can control', since 'we must be as wheels within wheels and grind out our own salvation'. Such courses of action appeared possible because the strike leaders of 1934 subsequently emerged as representatives of the work-force, as shop stewards and branch officials of the T. & G.W.U. Harris and Huish both became shop stewards, as did Martin Cone and Harry Hamilton. Harris, because of his position as secretary of the branch, acquired the informal status among the men of chief shop steward. Another connection was made through political affiliation. None of the members of the strike committee in 1934 had been members of the Communist Party, but its involvement in the strike left its mark on the shop steward group, and Huish and Harris were both closely associated with it.[4] A Communist Party member from Pressed Steel served on the Oxford Trades Council until February 1936.[5]

[3] The *Conveyor*, no. 7.
[4] Interview with Norman Brown, Pressed Steel shop steward, 1934–9, member of the Communist Party. Since both stood as Labour Party candidates in municipal elections it is unlikely that they were party members.
[5] Henry Jones, Trades Council minutes, 27 Feb. 1936.

The main issue between the union officials and the rank and file was not directly over union democracy but over the scope of shop stewards' actions and the use of the disputes procedure to which the union was committed. The essence of the disputes procedure in the engineering industry lay in the removal of discussions from the work place by successive conferences involving increasingly senior and more distant officials from both sides. Two conditions were attached to this procedure which tended to make it irksome for workers with an immediate or particular sense of grievance. In the first place, no strikes could be officially sanctioned until this somewhat lengthy procedure had been exhausted, and in the second, management could make changes in working conditions, which the labour force would have to accept until any grievances which might arise had gone through procedure.

Union officials tended to be firmly committed to such procedures since they had been written into agreements which they felt they had to stand by in the interests of orderly industrial relations.[6] If nothing else, such agreements preserved their negotiating status, which was bound to be valuable when their own position was essentially weak, as it was for most of the inter-war period.

The formal rights of shop stewards under the disputes procedure were very limited. They could deal with problems arising in the department in which they worked before the full-time officials of the union were brought in. In every other respect the stewards were subject to the same restrictions as other workers. They could not leave their department to make contact with other workers or stewards, unless they had the permission of their foreman. They had no right of access to higher management. An active role could not be played on such a limited base, and an important feature of the activities of shop stewards at Pressed Steel after 1934

[6] As a divisional organizer of the T. & G.W.U. put it during a conference with officials of the E.A.E.F.: 'I will agree with you that if you have an agreement, no matter whether that agreement is good or bad, that agreement should be carried out, and it is unfortunate that these difficulties [unofficial strikes] should arise in the way they do.' S. W. Clark, minutes of local conference between E.A.E.F. and T. & G.W.U., 8 Nov. 1938 (held at the Engineering Employers' Federation head-quarters, Tothill Street, London), p. 10.

was the development of their activities beyond these limited formal rights, particularly with regard to negotiations with management.

The Pressed Steel shop stewards did not regard themselves as officials of the T. & G.W.U. but as representatives of the men, and therefore as not committed to the formal agreements which the full-time officials felt bound by. After one unofficial strike in 1936 the management asked the shop steward involved, Huish, 'why, as a union official, he had not kept the men at work'. He replied 'that he was not a union official, inasmuch as he was not paid. He stated further that whatever the men wanted him to do, he had to act for them. He also stated that his position was very different from that of Geobey [regional officer of the T. & G.W.U.] as he was working for the men and not the union.'[7] The poor relations between management and workers which had been apparent before 1934 made it unlikely that the factory would be free from labour troubles in subsequent years, so raising more fundamental questions about the relationships between management, unions, and workers.

Two main bones of contention arose over the piece-work payment system. One was over the way in which the system underlined the lack of control workers had over the pace of work and the fixing of piece-rates; the other was over the adjustments which management made in the number of men working on assembly lines. To increase the number of workers was usually to increase output, but this often brought a decrease in the earnings of individuals. A dispute arose in November 1938 on an assembly line where 'strong objection was taken to the suggestion of intimidation, and the method adopted in the time study and fixing of rates',[8] and another in June 1936 over manning levels on an assembly line producing car bodies for the Standard Motor Company.[9] These and the other strikes which took place after 1934 were unofficial, and this was the main complaint of the union officials with the membership in the factory. During the strike of 1936 on the Standard assembly line, Dalgleish

[7] Report on disputes at Pressed Steel, 18 June 1936, by Birmingham E.A.E.F., held at E.E.F. headquarters.
[8] *Oxford Mail*, 18–19 Nov. 1938.   [9] *Oxford Mail*, 26 June 1936.

complained that 'There was constitutional machinery which the union had to observe, and those men who came out on strike without observing the machinery were strangling any efforts which the union could make on their behalf', and when he adressed a meeting of strikers he was heckled and criticized for betraying the rank and file.[10]

These points of difference between management, unions, and labour force came to a head in the autumn of 1938, when industrial relations had been strained by the downturn in the economy in that year which produced high unemployment at both Morris Motors and Pressed Steel.[11] Inside Pressed Steel piece-work rates were reduced and boy labour introduced. The shop stewards' committee was able to arrange some work sharing, but unofficial disputes over wages became more frequent. According to representatives of the Engineering Employers' Federation, 'in one period of 14 weeks there had been 13 strikes, all of them unofficial'.[12] The position had become so serious that the assistant secretary of the Employers' Federation felt it necessary to visit Cowley. The main point at issue was the ability of the union to control the shop stewards.

The two chief shop stewards had managed to acquire direct access to top levels of management from April 1937, which meant that the official disputes procedure, which was time consuming and clumsy, could be laid on one side. But when this failed to produce any diminution in unofficial disputes in 1938 the management decided to reimpose the formal agreement whereby a shop steward could deal only with matters arising in his own department. One of the branch secretaries of the union, Harris, who was also one of the chief shop stewards, refused to be bound by this and was sacked. A strike followed to reinstate him, and while at the subsequent negotiations the union put the workers' point of view, that 'If the discharge of Harris is allowed to go unchallenged, some of the other men feel they may be dealt with by the management similarly at a later date', there was a

[10] *Oxford Mail*, 30 June 1936.
[11] 3,300, according to Dalgleish in his report to the Trade Group, June 1938.
[12] Minutes of the Central Conference between E.A.E.F. and T. & G.W.U., 8–9 Dec. 1938, p. 7.

tendency for both sides to commiserate with one another over the snake-pit at Cowley. While Pressed Steel's managing director, Otto Mueller, complained that 'we are sick and tired of breaches of discipline on the part of members of unions', a union representative confessed that 'I know the Pressed Steel people; I have met those people in the early days. I had a few damn good dressings down. I knew what it was to try to handle this crowd. I have had as many dressings down as the employers, and probably more.'[13] The contention of the employers was that the T. & G.W.U. officials could not control the shop stewards, put rather graphically by Appleyard of the Federation:

You yourself took the matter in hand and told them, if I may put it colloquially, exactly where they got off, and instructed them that they must keep within the arrangement of the agreement.
    I could repeat to you comments of Mr. Harris which perhaps you may say were gossip but which refer quite clearly to his intentions in these works not only with regard to these works but with regard to the Executive of the Union, and the sum total of Mr. Harris's attitude was that nobody was going to tell him what he could or could not do.[14]

In the end the efforts to reinstate Harris were fruitless, as was a further strike which, in addition to opposing cuts in piece-work prices also demanded that the chief shop stewards be admitted to negotiations with the management.[15] As well as these attempts ending in failure, two of the shop stewards were refused re-employment, and when they tried to find work outside Oxford they 'were discharged as soon as it became known they had come from Pressed Steel'.[16]

    This was not the end of the matter, for in the early months of 1939 efforts were made to transfer some of the assembly-line workers from the T. & G.W.U. into the A.E.U. There were two probable reasons for this: the officials of the T. & G.W.U. were appointed by the General Executive Council whereas those of the A.E.U. were elected by the membership. Given the disgruntled attitudes towards the T. & G.W.U. officials and the obvious limitations on the power of shop stewards, this difference between the two unions had obvious

[13] Minutes of Local Conference, 8 Nov. 1938, pp. 16, 21.
[14] Minutes of Central Conference, p. 8.   [15] *Oxford Mail*, 26 Nov. 1938.
[16] Trades Council minutes, 1 Jan. 1939.

attractions. Secondly, the political views of the A.E.U. were somewhat to the left of the T. & G.W.U. under Bevin, and its members were less suspicious of the Communist Party; again, this aligned the A.E.U. more closely with the political affiliations of some of the leading shop stewards at Pressed Steel.[17] However, this strategy also failed, the A.E.U. agreeing with the T. & G.W.U.'s request to block the transfer of members, and after the removal of Harris as branch secretary and an inquiry by the union into the workings of the branch, it was described as 'functioning in a constitutional manner' by August 1939.[18]

The summer of 1939 therefore marks the end of a turbulent period at Pressed Steel which requires assessment. The level of union membership was impressive, since for semi-skilled groups in the motor industry to be organized at all was unusual. Probably about half the labour force were union members, the 800 recruited in 1937 being added to the 1,200 reported in 1935. The increase in wages after the 1934 strike was not a once and for all episode, levelling up earnings to national guidelines, but the prelude to the marginal wage increases which followed the unofficial disputes, and led to an agreement in 1936 'which cannot be equalled in any engineering shop in the country', because of piece-work allowances of $33\frac{1}{3}$ per cent instead of 25 per cent.[19] However, earnings probably suffered in 1938 when there was some pressure to lower labour costs through using boy labour and reducing piece-work prices on particular models. It was still the case too that car factories were relatively isolated from one another. Although Pressed Steel had become more prominent nationally, being cited by enthusiasts for the United Front as a good example of collaboration between the 'official' Labour Movement and the Communist Party,[20] there was little evidence of comparisons of earnings between different car factories.

[17] See editorial in A.E.U. Journal, Oct. 1936, asking for a 'stronger and more worthy opposition to the Bevin–Citrine Combination', which was hostile to the Communist Party.

[18] T. & G.W.U., G.E.C., 2 Mar. 1928, minute 307; and G.E.C., 18 Aug. 1939, minute 857.

[19] Dalgleish report to Trade Group, 17 July 1936.

[20] T.U.C. Conference Report, 1934, p. 349.

Inevitably then, membership was far from complete at Pressed Steel and earnings still followed the influence of cyclical fluctuations in the economy. Similar limitations were also evident in the more ambitious aims of the leadership within the factory, namely those of establishing 'closed shops' in certain departments, having direct access to management, and participating in the negotiation of piece-work prices. The first was never achieved, while the other two had been curtailed by the management by 1938. These aspirations towards some control or influence over management were therefore of the most basic and elemental kind, namely to establish some security of earnings. Concern by shop stewards over manning levels on piece-work prices had little to do with tendencies towards workers' control which were evident during the First World War and its aftermath. Extending or defending discretion over work itself was clearly ruled out by the subdivision of tasks and the lack of distinctive skills attached to them; in fact the tendency was for union negotiators to press for labour mobility within the factory so that those away from the production line would not invariably be denied the possibility of high piece-work earnings.[21] Goodrich's prediction of 1920 that 'control' in the newer industries would have very little connection with the protection of craft skills relevant for older-established industries was clearly fulfilled by the motor industry in the 1930s.[22]

The evidence of the internal solidarity of the work-force, derived mainly from the strikes which took place, is ambiguous. On the one hand, many of the disputes, arising in a particular department over piece-work rates, tended to emphasize sectional loyalties. On assembly lines, where earnings were pooled, workers had to be quite combative towards others in order to protect their pay. Those producing the Standard car body at Pressed Steel went on strike in 1936 because the assembly line was overmanned and earnings were suffering. 'With less men employed in the department, each man would receive more if the same number of bodies were turned out, and

---

[21] Dalgleish report to Trade Group for June 1937.
[22] C. Goodrich, *The Frontier of Control* (London, 1975 edn.), p. 264.

the strikers claim that a "closed shop" would solve this problem.'[23]

When a strike by one department affected others who did not share the grievance, pressure was sometimes put on the former to return to work and so protect the earnings of the latter. But such divisions inevitably reflected conflicts of interest around particular issues, themselves affected by the organization of the factory. Where trade union matters were at stake, such as the efforts to increase membership in April 1937, or to defend a shop steward from the sack in November 1938, then a sense of common purpose was evident. In April 1937 the issue of non-unionism arose in the trucking department, responsible for moving material around the factory. Other departments came out in sympathy, and pressed the cause of union membership in their own cases.[24] As a consequence, many, including some girls in separate sections of the factory—in the canteen, and in a department making refrigerators—joined the T. & G.W.U. But in both the 1937 and 1938 strikes barriers of skill remained intact, those in the machine shop staying at work in both instances even though other members of the A.E.U. had become involved.

However, while the position of certain skilled men in the machine shop and in the patternmaking departments was very different from that of those on the assembly lines, in that they were still paid by time and had some control and discretion over their work, this was not true of all those falling under the wing of the A.E.U. Like the shop stewards of the T. & G.W.U., the A.E.U. officials were concerned with manning levels on the assembly lines, and their main effort (which was unsuccessful) was to try to get some control over these.[25] In addition they faced the continuing problem of unskilled, often trainee, workers being put on jobs thought to be the preserve of skilled men; but even here the aim was to defend the wage rather than the status of the work, the union deciding that any worker was acceptable as long as the skilled rate was paid.[26] While it was appropriate to think of craft skills in certain departments, the strategies of skilled

[23] *Oxford Mail*, 1 July 1936.   [24] *Oxford Mail*, 21–3 Apr. 1937.
[25] A.E.U. District Committee Minute Book, 26 Mar. 1936.
[26] Ibid., 3 Feb., 2 Apr. 1936.

men elsewhere, for example those on machinery work, were hardly distinguishable from those of the semi-skilled. In the day-to-day industrial relations within the factory, the absence of any substantive links with trends of labour organization in the past was as noticeable as it had been in the sources of union growth.

II. *Morris Motors in the 1930s*

The limitations on the power of shop stewards at Pressed Steel does not hide the fact that their militancy was very different from the behaviour of the Morris workers in the 1920s. Although in the aftermath of the Pressed Steel strike the T. & G.W.U. recruited about 100 members at Morris Motors, neither it nor any other union was able to achieve a more solid position despite persistent efforts. In 1936 the Oxford Trades Council set up a committee to campaign for the recruitment of Morris workers, which was made up of shop stewards from Pressed Steel and a member of the A.E.U. But it achieved very little, part of the problem being the competition for members between the T. & G.W.U. and the N.U.G. & M.W. which created 'confusion amongst the unorganised workers and the consequences are that they do not join up in either union'.[27] The situation worsened later in the year when the A.E.U., which had hitherto confined its attentions to the skilled men (of whom there were very few at Morris Motors), claimed the right to organize all grades of workers.[28]

Much the same was true at the radiator factory in north Oxford. While a number of migrants from the depressed areas found work there, and while some of the workers belonged to the A.E.U., it proved difficult to build up any sort of sustained membership.[29] Although some skilled toolroom men were union members when they moved to the radiator factory they were never properly organized and had little to

[27] C. Bowles, secretary of Trades Council, to Organization Dept., T.U.C., 1 May 1936, T.U.C. TB 406,54.17.

[28] C. Bowles to T.U.C., 29 June 1936, T.U.C. TB 406,54.17.

[29] 'You'd only have to have an incident where somebody was sacked and they'd all drop out.' A. Exell, 'Morris Motors in the 1930's', *History Workshop Journal* 7(1979), 60.

do with the semi-skilled.[30] Not only did the two Morris factories see no recognition of trade unions, they also saw few disputes. In fact there is evidence of only one, a one-day affair at the Cowley assembly plant involving fifty workers in the trim shop, over piece-work payments. It was resolved by an increase in wages, and was not the curtain-raiser for a much longer dispute, as had been the case at Pressed Steel.[31]

There were plenty of good reasons why trade unions should have been so unimportant in Cowley in the 1920s, but fewer for the 1930s. The events at Pressed Steel next door to Morris's showed that it was possible for workers to gain some ground against the opposition of management, and the power of trade unions had recovered in the wider world, after the effects of the General Strike and the Depression. It was also true that the industrial position of Morris Motors was far less happy in the early 1930s than it had been in the 1920s. While Nuffield's position had been unassailed in 1929, his factories were slower to recover from the Depression than others.[32] In the main this was because sales of the 11.9 hp car which earned Morris's most of its profits were harder hit by the Depression, and although a new smaller car was produced in 1931 the financial results of the company were poor. In 1933 Cowley produced one-third fewer cars than in 1929, even though the production of private cars in the UK had increased by 20 per cent; and the company's trading profit fell by 71 per cent between 1929 and 1933.[33] Yet by 1934 there were signs of revival; a new mechanical assembly coincided with the establishment of a smaller car which was to prove successful in later years, and by 1935 trading profit had recovered to the high level of 1928. So the accretion

[30] 'They thought themselves "it", being skilled men, and they didn't mingle with us at all.' A. Exell, 'Morris Motors in the 1930's', *History Workshop Journal* 7(1979), 61.

[31] *Oxford Mail*, 27 Aug. 1935.

[32] William Morris became Lord Nuffield in 1934, and this title is useful hereafter. His factory will still be referred to as 'Morris Motors' or 'Morris's'.

[33] Details of the company's policies and fortunes in this period can be found in Andrews and Brunner, Part IV, II; and R. A. Church and M. Miller, 'The Big Three: Competition, Management and Marketing in the British Motor Industry, 1922–39', in B. Supple (ed.), *Essays in British Business History* (Oxford, 1977), pp. 175–9.

of trade union strength coincided with the revival rather than the nadir of the company's fortunes.

But the healthy firm of the mid-1930s was very different in its organization from that of the 1920s, in that Nuffield himself was far less closely involved in its day-to-day running, or even in the design of cars. The commitment to a high horsepower car at a time when the market was changing towards smaller vehicles, and the departure of some of the individuals responsible for development in the 1920s, were indications that Nuffield was unable to keep pace with the growth of his firm or with progress in the industry. The revival of the firm in the 1930s 'was largely achieved *in absentio* by L. P. Lord and Oliver Boden'.[34] By the early 1930s Nuffield had lost touch with his firm and the force of personal example in the handling of the labour force— 'I work my full weight. I expect my men to'[35]—had consequently been diminished. In the 1930s there was a greater reliance on formal fringe-benefit schemes which Nuffield had in the past tended to decry. A profit-sharing scheme devised by Lord was introduced in 1936, with employees receiving dividend payments from stock; holidays with pay were introduced before the subject was seriously discussed nationally; as well as sick pay, a savings club, and a pension scheme.[36] These schemes indicated a rather different strategy from that of the 1920s, then the emphasis had been on high wages rather than on more complete social provision (Nuffield never built houses for his workers); those introduced by the new managers suggested the view that high wages alone could not provide adequate security.

But whatever the changes within the higher echelons of the firm, Nuffield's influence on the perspectives of his workers had not been seriously diminished and the effect of the fringe-benefit schemes of the 1930s was the same as the high-wage policy of the 1920s—namely to keep ahead of trade union standards of conditions of employment (the

[34] See Church and Miller, 'The British Motor Industry', p. 178. L. P. Lord was managing director, and Oliver Boden a director.

[35] *Oxford Times*, 1 July 1927.

[36] H. A. Goddard, 'Profit Sharing and the Amenities of the Nuffield Factories', in Catherwood and Gannett (eds.), *Industrial Relations in Great Britain* (New York, 1939).

forty-four-hour week and holidays with pay, for example), and to underline how far standards of living were dependent on the firm rather than on labour organization. This can be illustrated by a minor incident which took place in August 1937. The Ministry of Labour refused to pay Morris workers unemployment benefit for three weeks in the summer when they were laid off and for which, as the result of a scheme introduced in May 1936, they were given holiday pay. When the grievance was raised by the Morris workers they appealed initially to Nuffield himself, even though it was through trade union representatives on the Court of Referees that their right to claim benefit was eventually upheld.[37] This episode did show too how the aloofness of the Morris workers tended to be reciprocated by envy of their apparent affluence. When the claim for unemployment benefit in addition to the holiday bonus was made, one worker declared that 'Married employees at Morris Motors already draw out more than they pay in. Other men working for a far smaller wage are paying to help keep them.'[38] And the president of the Trades Council was 'amazed at the Morris workers bemoaning the stoppage of their so-called unemployment pay'.[39]

It was these aspects of employment at Morris Motors, and the still pervasive influence of Nuffield himself, which propaganda on the value of trade union membership tried to confront. In December 1936, the local Communist Party launched 'an open agitation to convince Morris workers and the public of Oxford of the need for trade unionism inside the Morris works', but they were anxious not to fall foul of local sympathy for Nuffield: 'In our criticisms of the Morris Motors industries, and of the foremen and charge hands, we do not try to be vicious. We acknowledge the fact that Lord Nuffield, when he set up the Morris Motors industry at Cowley, made a very big contribution to the prosperity of the city.'[40] Their basic argument—that it was only through trade unions that workers could improve their conditions— came up against profit-sharing schemes and holidays with pay which ran ahead of union demands. This was in sharp contrast to other Oxford industries which had to accede to trade

[37] *Oxford Mail*, 12–13 Aug. 1937.   [38] *Oxford Mail*, 13 Aug. 1937.
[39] Ibid.   [40] *Oxford Mail*, 11 Dec. 1936.

union demands in the 1930s, and where union membership brought specific material gains. The only hope at Morris's, according to Lazarus, was that workers would find that their interests as wage earners would contradict their new concerns as shareholders under the profit-sharing scheme.[41] But given the high output, high wage, low cost 'mix' characteristic of the motor industry, and the healthy position of Morris Motors in the 1930s, it was highly unlikely that increases in dividends would be sought by reducing wages, or that workers would eventually perceive this to be the case. The Communist Party's campaign made little headway.

Despite the intrusion of disturbing factors which upset the 'localism' of the 1920s, successful managerial resistance to unions was still possible, by exploiting the profitability of the firm and the still uncertain position of labour in employment. This sharp contrast in industrial relations clearly makes it difficult to treat the Oxford car workers as a single group, and indeed their separation was a visible characteristic of social life in Cowley;[42] but some general sketch does need to be offered now of life beyond the factory gates in the developing suburbs of south-east Oxford.

III. *The Cowley Working Class*

Pay was an important factor for the 'new men' of the Cowley working class since the motor industry 'a good adult male wage' could be earned by those who had gained familiarity with aspects of assembly-line work, and did not necessarily require the possession of some distinctive skill, as it had before 1914. The weekly earnings of car workers in Cowley came close to those of the skilled printers in Oxford. A high-grade printer in 1936 earned an average of 83s. a week, and the Barnett House *Survey* reported earnings of between 70s. and 80s. a week for those in the motor industry.[43] These earnings were close to those of skilled workers at Pressed Steel: toolfitters there earned in 1938 a minimum of 1s. 9d. an hour, or a weekly wage of 82s. 3d., and the fear had been expressed earlier that they were working at a 'piecework rate

---

[41] Ibid.   [42] Interview with J. B. Clarke.
[43] Barnett House, *Survey*, vol. 1, pp. 87-9.

for time rate pay'.[44] Skilled building workers probably earned less than car workers, with wages of 71s. 8d. in summer and 67s. 10d. in winter. The dominant industry of the 1930s —car production—was just as much a high-wage occupation as the leading pre-1914 industry, printing.

Most of the car workers came from occupations considerably less well paid, for example distributive trades or unskilled building jobs, and so the sense of material improvement— as well, for the migrants, of actually having a job—must have been all the more strong. In such a context the economic function of trade unions at a factory like Morris's must have seemed to be quite marginal.

The main problem with pay lay with fluctuations in earnings. With overtime, perhaps before the October Motor Show when new models were introduced, earnings on the Pressed Steel assembly reached 126s. a week, but in contrast there was the long summer lay-off in July and August as well as short-time working to allow for. In the 1920s such fluctuations were not terribly serious: in June 1926, for example, only 4.6 per cent of the Morris work-force were laid off. By 1930 the Ministry of Labour was reporting that 'There are indications that the trade is becoming more seasonal and the busy season shorter and shorter.'[45] The season began in the early autumn, lasted until December, with a further upswing in sales into the spring, before a summer trough. It was calculated that seasonal unemployment accounted for between 10 and 20 per cent of the industry's unemployment problem.[46] The problem had become sufficiently serious at Pressed Steel for the local union branch to suggest setting up a fund so that members' contributions would not lapse during periods of short-time working or unemployment. The size of fluctuations within the Oxford motor industry can be appreciated from Table 9 which gives the lowest and highest unemployment percentages in a given year.

In 1937 Morris Motors tried to flatten out irregularities by introducing new cars throughout the year and not merely at

[44] A.E.U. Journal, divisional organizer no. 18, report for February 1938; A.E.U. District Committee Minute Book, 6 Apr. 1927.
[45] 'Report and Memoranda on U.K. Car Industry', P.R.O. BT 56/22.
[46] C. T. Saunders, *Seasonal Variations in Employment* (London, 1938), p. 55.

the Motor Show, but this was frustrated in that year through shortage of materials caused by the rearmament programme.

Short-time working, as opposed to temporary unemployment, was also a real problem, since 'waiting time' was not paid for. At Morris's:

It makes very little difference what shop you are in, all are familiar with the system of bringing men in for two, three and four half days a week . . . Men coming from places like Banbury, Reading and Swindon find it expensive to lose half a day regularly, while all workers find it hard to be deprived on the dole to which they would be entitled if work was arranged better.[47]

Table 8. Fluctuations in unemployment in Oxford motor industry (percentages)

1934	2.0 (March)	28.8 (July)
1935	2.4 (October)	26.8 (May)
1936	2.8 (December)	16.9 (October)
1937	2.7 (March)	24.9 (August)

Source: Barnett House, *Survey*, vol. 1, pp. 104–5, tables 20 and 21.

In the post-Second World War period, the combination of unstable but relatively high earnings was a source of unrest; in the inter-war years when even if unions were recognized there was little they could do by way of compensation, fluctuations in work probably underlined more general uncertainties about employment produced by the wider economic situation.[48] They certainly influenced the experience of housing costs, whether in terms of rent or mortgage repayments, as will become clear later.

If, in terms of pay and the strategies of the shop-floor, the car factories were on new ground, the same was true *a fortiori* of life beyond the work place. Descriptions of social life inevitably chart the formation and development of organizations usually found fully formed in more established communities. This was particularly true with regard to the churches: the old village churches of Cowley and Iffley were

[47] The *Spark*, vol. 2, no. 1, 1935.
[48] Which has been emphasized in an interview with Arthur Exell, who worked at the Morris radiator factory in the 1930s.

some distance from the main centres of population growth, and anxieties about religious accommodation were already being voiced at the end of the 1920s.[49] In 1930 the foundations were laid of a new church hall on the Bullingdon estate as a means of meeting those needs.[50] Quite how far the physical provision of churches elicited any strong religious feeling amongst the workers is doubtful. While the Church of England established itself in Cowley with Nuffield's help, he met the hostility of his workers for so doing,[51] and the churchmen found the newcomers indifferent and 'not of a church going class'.[52] Dissent fared better, but while the Congregational Church in Cowley, opened in April 1930, showed obvious vitality, at least in part through its links with the Welsh, the Methodists in Headington were unable to keep pace with the development of the estates, and in this respect there was no suburban parallel to the artisan non-conformity evident in the city and the outlying villages.[53]

Often of course, religious organizations fulfilled a variety of functions beyond access to the supernatural. They provided meeting places and venues for particular activities: those interested in playing football, for example, could conveniently do this through the Temple Cowley Congregational Church. The Cowley Workers' Social Club was opened in 1929 and drew its members from the streets nearby, providing modest enjoyment with beer, skittles, and newspapers—there was no musical entertainment.[54] Unlike the organized social life of the railwaymen, it was only for the men, and since affiliated

[49] According to the Vicar of Cowley, 'The Parish is, in length, about two miles; houses are being built along practically the whole distance, but at the far end from the parish church, and distant from any other parish church is a colony of nearly 3,000 people. If some provision is not made for them immediately, both for worship and for Sunday schools, it means that the church will lose its influence in that district for years to come.' *Oxford Times*, 3 May 1929.

[50] *Oxford Times*, 12 Sept. 1930.   [51] Thomas, *Out on a Wing*, p. 161.

[52] Oxford Diocesan Visitation 1928, fos. 227–8, in MSS Oxford Dioc. c. 388, Bodleian Library. See also the visitation of 1936, reports from Headington, Summertown, and Cowley.

[53] Oxford Methodist Circuit, Minute Book of New Headington (Wesleyan) Chapel, 25 November 1925, in Bodleian Library Oxford Diocesan Visitation 1928 at Stonesfield (fos. 408–10) and South and New Hinksey (fos. 279–80). On dissent in the city before 1914, see Butler, p. 153.

[54] Gambling went on there too, against the wishes of the management. Cowley Workers' Social Club Minute Book, 15 Mar. 1938.

to the Club and Institute Union, formally non-political. It expanded rapidly in the 1930s, the 100 or so who attended the opening night in 1929 growing to 3,000 by 1936. Like the unions and the Labour Party it was not a local creation, the main drive for its formation coming from some vehicle builders who had moved to Cowley from Wolverton and from Lancashire and were keen to establish what they had known elsewhere.

Beyond the club and the churches the other constituents of working-class social life were also free from any local particularity: there were dances organized by the car firms, football, and the cinema at weekends.[55] However, it is not enough simply to indicate the main public activities which went on in Cowley once the factories had closed. It has been argued that forms of social life should be seen not simply as ways of enjoyment or even areas of freedom beyond the constraits of factory employment, but an extension of aspects of the class struggle.[56] There has been a 'creativity in the production of cultural and associational forms',[57] which means that any example of social life or leisure is not necessarily an expression of 'what the people wanted', but the outcome of a conflict between that creativity and the ways in which capitalist groups—the press, the breweries, the cinema chains, for example—have tried to organize 'the masses'. In addition, it is argued, this outcome is not a 'once and for all' result, but a process of struggle never entirely resolved. Nor is this divorced from, or marginal to, the Labour Movement; rather the two interact. And so, according to the Yeos, 'car workers in Oxford had to go to trade unionism through area or community union'.[58]

In the Cowley case, much of the evidence points in the reverse direction: that trade unions and formal organizations generated any wider social cohesion which might have been achieved, and that the 'authentic' working-class recreational

[55] Before 1937, when the Regal Cinema opened on the Cowley Road, this meant a trip into Oxford, *V.C.H. Oxfordshire,* vol. 4, p. 434.

[56] E. and S. Yeo (eds.), *Popular Culture and Class Conflict 1590–1914: Explorations in the History of Labour and Leisure* (Sussex, 1981), esp. chs. 5 and 10.

[57] Ibid., p. 272.

[58] Ibid., p. 150.

form did not necessarily have major implications for class relations. First, consider the tension between organizations of working-class leisure and the aspirations of those for whom they catered. The working men's club in Cowley grew rapidly in the early 1930s, as we have seen, and since it was affiliated to the Club and Institute Union, was non-political and devoted to 'rational recreation'. At its opening in 1929, it was reported that 'for some time past the need has been felt for a club of a non-political character, where men could meet after their day's work and not be bothered with party matters'.[59] As it grew, it went beyond the enthusiasm of the early members, and interest in the running of the club dwindled. But was there any more explicit frustration of working-class behaviour or aspirations? Inevitably, evidence is thin, but the most authentic activity within the club, which also ran against the wishes of the committee, was gambling. While gambling has been shown to express a certain working-class view of the world, it nevertheless had few implications for class relations.[60]

It is not surprising that evidence is short for a cohesive body of working-class cultural aspirations outside conventional social forms, for there is no sign of the social cohesion which was a prerequisite for this. Far from organizations springing from some prior unity, in Cowley they prefaced it. It has already been shown how one of the main problems during the 1934 Pressed Steel strike was maintaining cohesion amongst the strikers, and when Arthur Exell was involved in organizing the tenants on Florence Park, 'the problem was how to form a committee as we did not know each other very well'.[61]

Not everyone was an atom, of course; the incoming Welsh kept together, not least because many came from the same village or region, but their numbers were only a small proportion of the whole. And they tended to be impressed by the dissipation of life outside work, rather than by its creativity or resourcefulness. Tom Harris, the leading shop steward and an ex-South Wales miner (who had none the

---

[59] Oxford Times, 7 June 1929.
[60] Cowley Workers' Social Club Minute Book, 15 Mar. 1938. R. McKibbin, 'Working Class Gambling in Britain 1880-1939', Past and Present, 82(1979), 177.
[61] A. Exell's essay on Florence Park, written in 1975, Ruskin College.

less come to Oxford via the USA), had this observation of
life in Cowley:

Large numbers of young single men are constantly being absorbed into
the motor industry. They have to find lodgings near their work, and
often they get accommodation in rooms that are already overcrowded.
After working hours there is no comfort in such places, and they are
expected to be out during the evenings. They could use this surplus
time with pursuit of knowledge, culture and understanding, or they
may slide into a rut of indifference or worse.[62]

Hence the need for community centres on these new
estates. It is hardly surprising to find little sign in Cowley in
the inter-war period of a cohesive community where working-
class social habits were well developed and to a degree
autonomous from any particular institution or organization.
Voluntary, collective behaviour, expressive of shared attitudes, takes time to develop and requires a particular insularity
or parochialism in which to grow. In Oxfordshire there
were survivals of past customs, such as the occasional appearance of 'rough music' at Witney, and before 1914 Headington
Quarry was the home of a 'rough' proletarian culture which
was hostile to conventional behaviour.[63] However, this was
the product of an inward-looking community free of any
overbearing institution of 'control', although even here these
characteristics were being weakened in the 1920s as better
transport took inhabitants to jobs further afield.[64] To repeat:
it is hard to find any evidence that the Cowley working class
was living in a state of tension with the institutions or
organizations within which social activities were enjoyed, a
tension which pointed to an unsatisfied 'creativity' or a
conflict with conventional society. While the Yeos are right
that historians ought not to regard as finished or decided
what might be unresolved process, it is difficult to avoid the
conclusion that the conditions for a rich communal life, in a
broad sense anti-capitalist, had passed. The disappearance of
such a life in Headington Quarry, as well as its absence in
Cowley, seems proof of this.

[62] *Oxford Mail*, 2 Nov. 1937.
[63] See Samuel, ' "Quarry Roughs": Life and Labour in Headington Quarry
1860–1920'.
[64] Ibid., p. 243.

None the less, cricitisms by the Labour Movement of the nature of working-class activities tended to imply that a more 'cultural' life requiring some voluntary energy would also be more 'political' than was the case with passively enjoyed commercial entertainment. For a small group, of course, there was such an existence, certainly for those involved in running the Labour Party at ward level. For the Communists the experience was probably more intense. 'Left-wing' books were not only read and discussed within the University and Ruskin, but also by the Cowley shop stewards, the most common being Max Werner's, *The Military Strength of the Powers* (1939), E. Snow's *Red Storm over China* (1930), *The Socialist Sixth of the World* (1939) by the Revd. Hewlett Johnson, and George Orwell's *The Road to Wigan Pier* (1937). Those involved in public speaking drew on material in *Imprecorr* and *Labour Monthly*, and there were political and theoretical discussions at weekly party meetings.[65] By and large the Oxford Communists were left to their own devices. There were separate organizations for the town and the University, and the main link with the party for the Cowley group lay with pamphlets from Central Office and the *Daily Worker*. They were left to work out the day-to-day implications of the party line for themselves. This was not always very easy. While it is clearly difficult to re-capture the tone and content of the theoretical and political discussions, uncertainty rather than clarity must often have been the main product. Henry Jones, a local party member, has recalled:

Harry Waterhouse who was a local party organiser reading a pamphlet that dealt with a controversy between Rudas, a writer on Dialectical Materialism, and Professor Carritt of Oxford. One of the main differences being that Rudas said one could only be a Dialectical Materialist if one was a Communist and Professor Carritt disagreed. After reading it three times Waterhouse said he couldn't make up his mind who was right.[66]

Such commitment was not intended only for limited consumption: leaflets and the *Daily Worker* were sold at Pressed Steel, but it is probably impossible to determine how successfully such actions fostered the political aware-

[65] Information from Norman Brown and Henry Jones.
[66] Letter to author.

ness of the labour force. It is doubtful moreover how far such political analyses developed within the small group of activists at Cowley: their viewpoint was essentially industrial rather than political. Even those who recall the Left Book Club publications have been quick to point out that day-to-day organization took much of their time and attention. It was not only that organizing meetings in the factory, supporting strikes, or publishing factory newspapers was time consuming, but also that these were the most immediate and pressing tasks. In such circumstances the industrial perspective was bound to dominate, since union membership had to be built up, and organization established. The fact that many joined the party during the 1934 strike probably reinforced this, as did their rather introverted existence. When wider contacts were made it was usually with small local parties trying to use strikes as a way of increasing their own membership. When the Oxford Communists went over to assist the small party at Banbury with a strike at the aluminium factory there, it never occurred to either group to make contact with Party Centre.[67] Even when events got beyond the group of local parties, as in the case of the 1934 Pressed Steel strike, this did not serve to break the industrial perspective. Abe Lazarus, who was sent to Oxford from King Street as an industrial organizer, was in no sense isolated from political discussion. He spoke at the Thursday Lunch Club in the University, otherwise known as the Pink Dons' Club,[68] and played an important part in the 1938 by-election. But his general view of the working class kept to an industrial rather than a political analysis, since he tended to argue that the standard of living of the working class could be raised by strike action alone.[69] And so, while it is true to say that the Communist strategies of the 1930s were treated in a very narrowly industrial way by the working class, circumstances tended to encourage such a perspective on the part of the Communists. The distinction ought not to be pressed too far; political involvement was to come because of international affairs, but this was in some

[67] Information from Henry Jones.
[68] Information from Professor Christopher Hill.
[69] Letter from Henry Jones.

respects separate from the industrial viewpoint, in that the tactics demanded by the Spanish issue (acceptance of union with moderate parties on the left) did not follow logically from conventional Marxist political interpretations of the industrial struggle (the need for thoroughgoing change of the political system).

IV. *Labour in the Motor Industry—Some Comparisons*

The sharp contrast between the two car factories in Cowley gives no clue as to which was more representative of industrial relations in the industry as a whole. Pressed Steel was clearly affected far more than Morris's by the Labour Movement outside Oxford, and yet the latter was more characteristic of the industry as a whole in that the organization of the semi-skilled and the activities of the shop stewards at Pressed Steel was unusual. Most firms in the motor industry were untroubled by unions before 1939, and if there was any challenge to their position it came from the skilled men.

For British industry as a whole trade union membership and strikes tended to go hand in hand. While, in the inter-war period, union officials tended to try and restrain strikes, and usually played little part in starting them, it was none the less true that organized rather than unorganized workers went on strike.[70] Although in the case of Pressed Steel in 1934 a major strike had resulted in trade union growth, this was not common, the large-scale disputes at Austin's in 1929 and Ford's in 1933 seeing no significant increase in membership. It is therefore not surprising to find that the motor industry was not particularly strike-prone in the inter-war period since union membership was so low. The statistics on which this discussion of strikes is based do not provide a complete record of industrial conflict at any particular firm, not only because absenteeism and labour turnover were alternative forms of dissent but also because the small walk-outs and disputes escaped notice. Thus the very frequent (but probably very minor) strikes at Pressed Steel in 1938 went unrecorded by the Ministry of Labour. The total of

[70] Knowles, *Strikes*, p. 150.

118 strikes in the motor industry between 1921 and 1938 on which the following comments are based may well under-state the degree of conflict, but since the Ministry of Labour recorded disputes of at least one day's duration involving ten workers or more, these give a reasonably informative picture. In terms of the number of strikes which took place, the industry was not noticeably troubled, and became slightly less so in the 1930s compared to the 1920s. While

Table 9. Strikes per 10,000 workers in employment

1923–4		1935–6	
1. Shipbuilding	2.15	1. Coal	11.34
2. Quarrying	1.86	2. Tinplate	3.61
3. Dock and wharf	1.86	3. Shipbuilding	2.4
4. Bricks and glass	1.48	4. Quarrying	2.23
5. Woodworking and finishing	1.39	5. Dock and wharf	2.16
6. Coal	1.27	6. Woodworking and finishing	1.61
7. Tinplate	0.72	7. Other mining	1.44
8. Linen and jute	0.68	8. Boot and shoe	1.14
9. Engineering	0.66	9. Linen and jute	0.95
10. Tailoring	0.58	10. Bricks and glass	0.88
11. Boot and shoe	0.58	11. Printing and bleaching	0.82
12. Iron and steel	0.55	12. Hosiery	0.69
13. Building	0.47	13. Cotton spinning	0.66
14. *Motor vehicles*	0.46	14. Aircraft	0.63
15. Printing and bleaching	0.45	15. Tailoring	0.42
16. Food	0.44	16. Building	0.41
17. Printing	0.42	17. Engineering	0.41
18. Railways	0.34	18. *Motor vehicles*	0.38
19. Wool	0.31	19. Iron and steel	0.2
20. Hosiery	0.29	20. Chemical	0.19
21. Cotton spinning	0.29	21. Railways	0.18
22. Gas and water	0.15	22. Printing	0.15

Source: Ministry of Labour Dispute Books in P.R.O. LAB 34.

strikes in the industry tended to be more frequent when employment was healthiest, especially in 1924–5 and 1933–7, strikes in particular firms did not always reflect a calculative approach in this respect, those at Pressed Steel in July 1934, July 1936, and April 1937 occurring at times of relatively high unemployment locally. Very often strikes in the larger firms directly involved only small numbers of workers, but they could also bring a whole factory to a standstill. At Austin's in Birmingham in 1936, fifty-eight metal workers came out on strike over piece-work prices, and 5,529 others were subsequently affected. As a local newspaper pointed out:

The seriousness of the stoppage lies in the fact that each section of the factory is dependent on the others. In the West Works virtually the entire bodybuilding activity is concentrated, and the hold up in that section will inevitably affect the stream of cars normally issuing from the factory.[71]

The strikes at Pressed Steel over pay tended to follow this pattern; wider solidarities were tapped only when trade union issues arose. The sharp contrast between the strikes at Pressed Steel and the peace at Morris Motors was borne out to a much lesser degree in the industry as a whole by the slight preponderance of disputes on the body building side (60 per cent of the total) as against chassis construction. Some of the larger firms making completed cars found most of the trouble occurring in the body-making departments; this appears to have been the case at Singer's and Armstrong-Siddeley, for example. Variations in body style meant frequent negotiations over piece-work rates which were the main cause of disputes, but this side of production was also more prey to problems of dilution and demarcation than chassis construction. Many of the strikes therefore were defensive efforts by members of the N.U.V.B., to resist the intrusion of semi-skilled workers or to reassert their jurisdiction (against the metal workers) over body construction. These issues did not arise so powerfully at Pressed Steel, where the co-existence of strikes and developing unionism remained highly unusual.

Strikes were episodic indications of industrial relations, and for examination of longer-running trends it is helpful to turn to the motor industry in Coventry.

In Coventry in the 1920s the position of organized labour was far weaker than it had been before 1914; but although it continued to be so in the 1930s, the unions did make some progress. The T. & G.W.U. began to win some members in the 1930s, and although it did not appear to reach the numbers

[71] *Midland Daily Telegraph*, 12–14 Nov. 1936.

recruited previously by the Workers' Union,[72] it did represent workers at the Rover and Humber car firms in the later 1930s.[73] But while the union won some members in Coventry, Cowley became the focus of activities for its Midlands divisional offices, and Coventry tended to be neglected by the full-time officials.[74] The A.E.U. also expanded, doubling its membership by 1937 from the low point of 2,480 in 1933, but ceasing to be a craft union since many of the newcomers fell into the category of semi-skilled workers.[75] The declining fortunes of the N.U.V.B. illustrated further the way in which Coventry was becoming an even less friendly locale for the skilled man than it had been in the 1920s. Having found itself on the defensive in the later 1920s, unable to stop the introduction of new machinery, it lost membership steadily into the 1930s, by 1935 having roughly half the numbers it had had in 1931. Efforts to 'dilute' skilled body-building labour continued into the 1930s with the use of female labour on the trimming of upholstery, and additionally they were unable to prevent the use of efficiency experts for the fixing of piece-rates.[76]

The position of the Coventry car workers in the 1930s was similar to that of the 1920s in that their economic position did not derive from the power of the unions but from the conditions of the labour market. Firms were able to resist union pressure for improvements in basic pay for the three main grades of labour: skilled, semi-skilled, and female. The arguments over the latter two were straightforward enough; in the first case it was to recognize a status greater than that of the labourer,[77] and in the second to improve on a basic rate of only 4*d*. an hour in order to recognize the increasing number of women employed in the Coventry engineering industry. In neither case was the actual level of earnings at stake, since the union negotiators conceded that through piece-work basic rates could be improved upon satisfactorily.

[72] Carr, 'Engineering Workers', thesis cit., p. 451.
[73] C.D.E.E.A. minutes, 15 Nov. 1937, 5 Sept. 1938.
[74] T. & G.W.U. Regional Committee No. 5, 5 Oct. 1935, minute 20.
[75] See the figures given in June issues of A.E.U. Monthly Report.
[76] C.D.E.E.A. minutes, 19 Mar. 1934, 28 May 1934.
[77] For the claim of the T. & G.W.U. for the semi-skilled, see MSS 208/B, TBM 1, Modern Records Centre, University of Warwick.

The employers wished to keep with piece-work systems because they believed these allowed them to economise on labour costs per unit of output.[78] Any moves towards high flat rate payment systems were regarded with much suspicion by other employers. When Fisher Ludlow wanted to begin car body production in 1937, and intended to pay its workers a high flat rate (95s. instead of the usual basic pay of 35s. 6d. to 40s.), it met with the opposition of other employers and was eventually forced to toe the line.[79]

The problem of the skilled men in the toolroom was related to the question of piece-work pay for the semi-skilled. Because of the difficulty of applying incentive systems to toolroom work, the earnings of those setting up machines, a highly skilled task, sometimes fell below those of the semi-skilled workers who operated them.[80] On occasions this led to skilled men going on to production work for higher pay, although the A.E.U.'s solution was to press for higher basic pay instead of relying on lieu rates to make up earnings.[81] It was unable to achieve any formal agreement on this front, although some increases in lieu rates were conceded to increase wages, and to ease problems of wage drift from firms anxious to attract and retain skilled labour.[82]

Earnings generally in Coventry were higher than elsewhere, dropping less sharply during the Depression than in Birmingham, and average wages at 76s. 3d. for engineering as a whole were higher than in the Midlands (71s.). When the Pressed Steel company, on joining the Engineering Employers' Federation, inquired of the Coventry association about pay there, its inquiry was directed to Birmingham for fear of revealing what the Coventry firms were paying their men.[83] However, the employers did not regard the unions as responsible for this, but the 'law of supply and demand, and whilst the present shortage of

[78] C.D.E.E.A. minutes, 18 Nov. 1929.
[79] C.D.E.E.A. minutes, 19 Sept. 1938.
[80] C.D.E.E.A. minutes, 18 May, 1936.
[81] C.D.E.E.A. minutes, 18 June, 20 Aug. 1934.
[82] For complaints about wages above local rates see C.D.E.E.A. minutes, 4 March 1935 (Morris Engines), 14 Oct. 1935 (Armstrong-Siddeley), and 30 July 1936 (Whitworth's).   [83] C.D.E.E.A. minutes, 20 Aug. 1934.

labour continued, very little could be done'.[84] In Coventry for most of the 1930s unions were no more visible than they had been before in 1934 in Cowley. With few shop stewards in factories, and fewer still recognized by management, those who were members of unions would take their grievances to the branch meeting. From here, of course, there was only intermittent contact with officials of the union, perhaps a district officer who might visit an area only once in several weeks, and, because of the need for economies in administrative costs, would be covering more ground than was formerly the case.[85] In these conditions the main drive for increasing membership did not come from the obvious power of unions, but from the commitment of small groups acting on the assumption that, for rather general reasons, 'they ought to be in a union'.[86] Such convictions were historically associated either with particular communities, or with skilled workers; they were bound to be rare in a town like Coventry where there had been little stability of population, and where the skilled man counted for far less than he did elsewhere.

Conditions in Coventry, where a large number of firms competed for labour, were very different from those where only a few factories dominated the labour market; but patterns of pay and organization tended to be similar. At Dagenham, the Ford and the Briggs car body factories dominated the local scene, but the basic division between the skilled men away from the production lines and the semi-skilled assemblers was as clearly drawn as elsewhere:

So far as conveyors are concerned, men actually on the production side where the work was very strenuous, had to work hard. But if you go around into other departments such as the toolroom, electrical maintenance and repair you can say very truly that they are not driven any harder than in any other shop.[87]

At Dagenham the degree to which the conveyor system dictated the pace of work was shown in the method of

[84] C.D.E.E.A. minutes, 22 Sept. 1937.

[85] The A.E.U. amalgamated the office of the organizing district delegates for Birmingham and Coventry in 1930. C.D.E.E.A. minutes, 5 Jan. 1931.

[86] The phrase of Stan Wyatt, a N.U.V.B. member in the 1930s, from a taped interview with Dr S. Tolliday.

[87] Vic Feather's comments in T.U.C. Organization Department file on Dagenham, T 604 57.4(D).

paying high flat-rate wages (roughly 2s. an hour) instead of using a more traditional piece-work system. The need for incentives was seen as irrelevant where there was so little discretion over the pace of work.[88]

Union organization followed divisions of skill: those on the assembly lines were unorganized, whereas in the pattern-making department, the machine shop, and the toolroom a majority were members, as were the electricians.[89] The same was true at Briggs Bodies where in the 1930s only the pattern-makers, the most highly skilled group, were organized.[90] It was usually thought that the best chance of building up member-ship in the 'new' industries lay with the skilled men, and when Briggs Bodies had to recruit 250 tool and die setters through the A.E.U. this was regarded as particularly encouraging, and suggested that recruitment might begin there rather than at Ford's. But such expectations were never realized in the inter-war years; even when skilled men could make their own agree-ments with employers there were few avenues through which these could be transmitted to the production side, even had there been an inclination to do so, which is doubtful.

At Cowley the migrants from the depressed areas had provided the core for organization, though it never took the form of a straightforward commitment to the unions, and was in the early stages simply a bloody-minded attitude towards management. Even this was unusual: at Dagenham the use of labour from the depressed areas was a source of instability rather than a focal point for organization, with a high turnover of young workers from the government training centres having no experience of, or background in, trade unions. This coincided with competitive conditions on the assembly line,[91] and high mobility of labour from job to job, because of extensive subdivision of task. There was a strike at Dagenham in March 1933, which began at the

[88] As Feather put it, 'the belt sees to it that there is not much chance to slack', ibid.; see also M. L. Yates, *Wages and Labour Conditions in British Engineering* (London, 1938), p. 80.

[89] Feather, T.U.C. file on Dagenham, T 604 57.4(D).

[90] Which interestingly enough, was not known by the majority of the work-force for some time, T.U.C. T 602.

[91] 'Men are told that if a man is holding him up to "push him out", and the atmosphere is so tense that men are willing to strike their mates down.' T.U.C. T 604.

Briggs plant over reductions in wages, and also involved those at Ford's. But there was plenty of substitute labour, and the strike did not mark the beginning of more continuous organization at either factory.

Coventry also received migrants from the depressed areas; probably more Welsh went there than to Oxford, and formed a higher proportion of the local working population. Whereas only 10 per cent of those moving into Oxford from outside were Welsh, in Coventry and north Warwickshire, the figure was 21.5 per cent.[92] Some of the characteristics of migration were similar; concentration of origin was as evident in Coventry as in Oxford, in the former most of the Welsh coming from Newport and Cardiff.[93] Within the motor car industry in particular the Welsh were the most prominent group of outsiders, though only slightly larger in number than those from Manchester. Here the similarity with Cowley ends, for shop stewards at the Humber and Standard factories found migrant labour not to be much interested in union organization.[94] In many towns the arrival of such migrants created divisions within the working class because they were seen as competitors for jobs. There was firm opinion in Coventry that local men ought to have priority for jobs, in Slough there was a fairly strong dividing line between the Welsh and the rest, with again little sign that they were a source of organization.[95]

This was hardly surprising; the chief characteristic of labour in the inter-war period was its fluidity. Week by week, month by month, throughout the year, workers suffered temporary unemployment. After the strike at Ford's in 1933 about 500 men were dismissed in the summer when Sorensen, General Manager of Ford's in America, visited the plant to tighten up on discipline.[96] Again, different sources of labour were being exploited, since on simple machinery tasks boys or young women could be employed until they reached

[92] Brinley Thomas, 'Influx of Labour into the Midlands 1920-37', *Economica*, Nov. 1938, 410-34.
[93] O. G. Pickard, 'Midland Immigrations' (Birmingham Univ. B. Com. thesis, 1940), pp. 13-19.
[94] Carr, 'Engineering Workers', thesis cit., p. 435.
[95] 'Religious Bodies and Transfer', P.R.O. LAB 23/102.
[96] Feather, T.U.C. file on Dagenham, T 602.

seniority and became more expensive. Beyond these con-
tinual sources of instability there were the more medium-term
fluctuations in the economy; the shop stewards at Pressed
Steel had proved vulnerable in 1938, when locally unemployment was quite high, and the same was true at Dagenham.
Just as the unions were beginning to focus on the Ford
factory, and the T.U.C. to co-ordinate their efforts, production
slackened off and the unions decided that any campaign would
be fruitless. Feather, interviewing a worker about wrongful
dismissal, put the limitations on union power very clearly:

I pointed out to him that there were a considerable number of people
who were out of work and also that employers had the power of
determining who should work and who shouldn't, even when they
were organised. I asked him if he knew that roughly half the Ford
workers had either been dismissed or were working short-time since
February of this year, and he agreed that the motor trade was not
good.[97]

In such conditions union officials at the centre felt they were
up against an impossible task. But with the absence of 'union
atmosphere' in the factories there was little to be done
locally. As in Oxford, recruitment campaigns organized by
the trades councils were pretty chaotic. Feather again, on
Dagenham:

The meeting commenced at 8.15 and should have commenced at
8.00 p.m. A platform had to be borrowed at the last minute as the
one arranged for had been 'smashed up'. The loudspeaker equipment
was not prepared until 8.45, and after it had been used for the first
speaker, Mr. Evans, the police made a request for the loudspeaker
equipment to be discontinued, as no application had been made for
permission to use such equipment. The meeting was not too well
attended, the audience numbering about 50 people.[98]

However weakly organized a labour force, the keenness of
the Pressed Steel managers to contain the activities of shop
stewards, and the willingness of unions at the centre to assist
them in this, was evident elsewhere. Shop stewards at the
Humber factory in Coventry were brought into line by the
A.E.U. and the T. & G.W.U.,[99] and the employers felt that
'frivolous complaints made direct to trade unions were more

[97] Feather, T. U. C. file on Dagenham, T 602.   [98] Ibid.
[99] C.D.E.E.A. minutes, 25 Apr. 1938.

likely to be "nipped in the bud" than if taken up by the shop stewards'.[100] Wherever recourse was had to the Communist Party for help with organization the union officials tended to be on their guard. At Dagenham Feather was fighting against their influence, getting a particular man elected as a secretary for a recruitment campaign but confessing that 'I think his opposition to the Communists is losing him some popularity.'[101] In general, employers found unions useful for controlling shop stewards, and for actually determining what was a grievance in the 1930s.

In the 1930s the attitude of firms to unions and to the need to contain shop stewards was only just developing: it was to emerge more strongly during negotiations about recognition during the Second World War. Before then there were never enough shop stewards to cause serious problems, and their position in the labour market, even in the relatively prosperous 'new' industries, was always precarious. Dismissal was a straightforward business. At many factories like Morris Motors and Vauxhall, there were never any real difficulties with the labour force, and even at factories which were more volatile, such as those at Dagenham, the noise and activity could not be translated into solid bargaining strength. In this sense Morris Motors and Pressed Steel show, in strikingly dissimilar ways, the basic weakness of labour in the inter-war period.

Very little then was achieved in the 1930s by way of labour organization in the motor industry. From the outside, the major trade unions began to expand their membership by the later 1930s, and it was not until the Second World War that the status of the unions was at all improved compared with what it had been at the end of the First World War. This weakness interacted with conditions in the factories. Unions with scarce funds and inadequate footholds in the 'new' industries pointed to labour turnover, isolation of groups at work, and the recruitment of 'green' or heterogeneous labour forces both

[100] C.D.E.E.A. minutes, 15 Nov. 1937.
[101] Feather, T.U.C. file on Dagenham, T 604.

to explain lack of headway and to justify husbanding their resources.[102] From the local point of view, national unions often appeared distant and unhelpful. Sometimes it was the case that branches, where they existed, had only fleeting contact with officials, and sometimes it was the reverse, the sporadic competition for members by the A.E.U., the T. & G.W.U., and the N.U.G. & M.W. causing confusion amongst potential recruits. In the precarious conditions of the 1930s the efforts of the trades councils did not always inspire confidence or trust; equally, those able to develop some sort of organization on the shop-floor tended to be wary of surrendering what was often mistakenly seen as effective power to full-time officials and the negotiation procedures which they operated. Hence the mixture of acquiescence, apathy, and aggression which characterized different groups of workers in the industry.

[102] These problems were real enough: see J. Parker, 'Trade Union Difficulties in the New Areas', in G. D. H. Cole, *British Trade Unionism Today* (London, 1945). Parker was Labour MP for Romford, Essex, the constituency which included the Dagenham factories.

5

'THE ART OF COMBINATION': TRADE UNIONS IN THE CITY

Within Cowley the impact of the motor industry had been quite dramatic by the 1930s. After a decade or so when it seemed that the main effect of the car factories had been to exert a 'pull' on the low-wage labour of the countryside, rather than to import or to create an untypically militant group of workers, by 1934 it had done precisely this. Oxford, or rather Cowley in particular, became as a result a much more interesting place for the Labour Movement nationally; with a district secretary appointed by the T. & G.W.U. in 1937,[1] it was inevitable that the union would scout around elsewhere in the vicinity for additional members. At the very least then, Oxford was unlikely to remain neglected in the way that it had been in the 1920s. But Morris Motors had proved resistant to any influences or direction from the factory next door, and the industry as a whole illustrated the patchiness of union growth in the 1930s; so the spread of unions to new ground was hardly going to be automatic or certain, and nor was the manner of it. Whether those at Cowley would play an active part in other agitations, or whether theirs would be the indirect role of having attracted an expanding union which in subsequent years was simply to cast its net more widely, was very much an open question.

Before 1934 there had always been a small group of enthusiasts for the cause of labour, who had run the Labour Party and Trades Council in more or less hopeless conditions. With the Pressed Steel strike came the feeling that at last the working class was behaving as it should: 'For the first time the workers of Oxford are being organised to be worthy of the class to which they belong', claimed the president of the

[1] Jack Thomas, from 1 January of that year.

Trades Council.[2] The structure of union membership had undergone some changes since 1914. By the late 1920s there had been growth in the membership of semi-skilled sections of occupations, whose skilled grades were already well organized: the Printing and Paper Workers and the National Union of Railwaymen both recruited members locally in the 1920s, and these new developments were reflected in the partnership of Len Bellinger of the N.U.P.P.W. and Charles Bowles of the N.U.R. as president and secretary of the Trades Council in 1931-5. Although division of opinion within the Trades Council did not strictly follow the lines of who belonged to which union, the members of the N.U.R. put forward a proposal to form a local Council of Action in 1920, which was supported by the other new branch, and opposed by the old guard, the Co-operative Society, the Typographical Association, and the A.E.U.[3]

Figures for the density of trade union membership (actual membership as a percentage of potential recruits) have to be regarded as rough estimates, since trade union and occupational groups rarely coincide with any neatness. By comparison with national aggregates, Oxford unions were stronger in printing and paper but much weaker in metals and engineering. On the railways the Oxford unions were slightly weaker, though in woodworking the position was pretty close to the national one.

There had been various attempts after the First World War to organize other groups of workers, but after some initial success there were no lasting results. An editorial in a local newspaper in 1920 had commented that:

A study of the page or so of matter which we give each week to labour topics must be occasionally surprising to readers who remember the Oxford of some twenty years ago, when, apart from the printers, there was hardly an organised trade in the City. Now there is hardly a trade that is not organised, and all sorts and types of workers are learning the art of combination.[4]

[2] L. Bellinger, *Daily Worker*, 23 July 1934. Much the same happened in nearby Banbury with the arrival of an aluminium factory in the mid-1930s. M. Stacey, *Tradition and Change, a Study of Banbury* (Oxford, 1960), p. 170.
[3] Trades Council minutes, 25 Aug. 1920. This followed the setting up of such a council by the Labour Party and the T.U.C. to prevent the government entering a war against Russia in 1920.   [4] *Oxford Chronicle*, 15 Mar. 1920.

Table 10. Trade union density in Oxford and Great Britain in 1927
(percentage)

	Oxford	Great Britain
Railways	34.0	50.3
Printing and publishing	66.0	46.3
Woodworking	21.0	24.0
Engineering	6.3	30.9

Sources: For Oxford union membership, see Oxford Trades Council Report for 1927 at T.U.C., TC 79. For Great Britain, see G. S. Bain and R. Price, *Profiles of Union Growth, A Comparative Statistical Portrait of Eight Countries* (Oxford, 1980), p. 67, table 2.28; p. 61, table 2.22; p. 59, table 2.26; p. 50, table 2.11.

However, the lesson of the 1920s was that the 'art of combination' could be lost as quickly as it had been gained. By the middle of the 1920s the ground which had been won earlier in the decade had been surrendered, largely because the unions could not withstand the pressure on wages exerted by employers during the downturn in the economy.

One of those to expand most rapidly in the immediate post-war period was the Amalgamated Society of Gas, Municipal, and General Workers, the local branch of which was formed in June 1917. In 1920 it was reported to have nearly 500 members, which made it the largest union branch in the town.[5] When the Society amalgamated with the National Federation of General Workers in 1920 it had established a foothold amongst gas and municipal workers, even though the attempt to organize the college servants had, rather predictably, come to nothing. The leadership provided by the union was far from aggressive, and when wage reductions were threatened in 1920 the union organizers tended to be conciliatory. Members had 'to recognise the employers' difficulties' and to 'guard against men being discharged on account of high wages'.[6] By 1921 many of the corporation workers had dropped out of the union on the very reasonable grounds that it had done little to protect them, and by 1922 the membership of the union had roughly halved from the high point two years earlier.[7]

[5] *Oxford Chronicle*, 28 Jan. 1921.   [6] *Oxford Chronicle*, 22 Oct. 1920.
[7] *Oxford Chronicle*, 23 Dec. 1921 and 29 Sept. 1922.

For the brewers and busmen it was the same story, some activity but little real achievement. Wherever particular individuals tried to organize within a firm, or newly recruited members attempted to improve their conditions by striking, they were usually dealt with quite easily by their employers. A strike by the busmen in May 1920 for higher wages and shorter working hours achieved nothing, and those who had started a union branch at the brewery were dismissed.[8] While in 1919 the National Amalgamated Union of Shop Assistants was recruiting members and pressing for the application of a national wages scale and a reduction in hours, by 1922 organizers were complaining of indifference and apathy.[9] A particularly sensitive problem for local working-class leaders lay with the Co-operative Society. The rhetoric of the Society stressed its close links with the trade unions: 'they were twin movements'.[10] In general it was felt that the Co-operative Society's obligations lay in two directions: to pay better wages than other local firms and to give some representation to workers on management committees.[11] But in 1920 a motion to allow employees on to the management committee was lost, and it was also argued that to pay over the 'going rate' locally would mean increased prices, loss of trade, and decline in dividend, clear evidence of contemporary views that 'the Co-op is more capitalistic than the F.B.I. or the Prudential'.[12] There was also a more simple problem, namely the very few trade union members among the Co-op workers. Although the management was hostile,[13] a union organizer 'was amazed at the attitude of the staff towards the trade union movement' when he visited them in 1930.[14]

The short burst of activity by trade unions, which had appeared so impressive in 1920, had, by 1922, burnt itself out with few traces left. There was a tendency to blame the

[8] Trades Council minutes, 16 June 1920; *Oxford Times*, 20 Jan 1922.

[9] *Oxford Chronicle*, 28 Mar., 18 Apr. 1919; Trades Council minutes, 24 May 1922.

[10] *Oxford Times*, 17 Sept. 1919.

[11] G.D.H. Cole, *A Century of Co-operation* (Manchester, 1944), p. 335.

[12] *Oxford Chronicle*, 13 Aug., 6 Aug. 1920; A.E.U. Journal, Sept. 1923, 'Influence of the Co-operative Movement on Capitalism'.

[13] *Oxford Chronicle*, 25 Nov. 1921.

[14] Trades Council minutes, 16 Mar. 1930.

apathy of the Oxford workers, and to criticize them for regarding 'a weekly contribution to the Trade Union a waste of money'.[15] But the rank and file could hardly be blamed for this; the unions had done little to upgrade wages and conditions and had not been able to withstand pressures for cuts in wages. 'Apathy' was a measured reaction to exaggerated claims. The cynicism towards the rhetoric of 'the Movement' which the experience of the 1920s had bred was expressed most clearly by the busmen during the General Strike in 1926. During a meeting on 7 May which was intended to bring the busmen out on strike:

The Chairman began to allude to the miners who were on strike, but this was objected to by the busmen who attended in large numbers as they understood that the meeting was called for busmen, and they wanted to hear nothing whatever about the miners.

The Chairman began to talk about the Trade Union supporting the busmen if they came out on strike, but the busmen's reply to this was that they well remembered the last strike when they were promised support by the unions and got none.

The Chairman appealed to all busmen to 'down tools and strike', but the busmen wanted to know why they should. To this no reply was given. Thereupon the busmen began to sing 'Land of Hope and Glory' which was heartily joined in by the crowd.[16]

There were, of course, equally intense reactions to the strike on the other side: the printers were solidly in favour, all except a handful of the Typographical Association members coming out, and there was 'complete desolation' at Oxford station.[17] The building workers joined in too. The strike was also the occasion for a brief liaison between the University Left and the local Labour Movement. A University Strike Committee was set up to assist the Trades Council, mainly through propaganda and providing transport to and from London. The results of this collaboration lay with the University rather than with the town: the strike provided an opportunity for left-wing undergraduates to meet some of the major figures on the Left, and the Committee was the nucleus of the 'Cole group' which continued to meet at

[15] Trades Council minutes, 28 Feb. 1923.
[16] Oxford Daily Strike Bulletin, 8 May 1926.
[17] Typographical Association minutes, 4 May 1926; *Oxford Times*, 6 May 1926.

Holywell.[18] Besides the impressive display by the printers (who, being pensionable, had much at stake), there were others too small to have much influence on events: the engineers fell into that category. The local District Committee of the A.E.U. awaited developments before taking action, and in the end only eleven joined the strike.[19] A similar line had been taken during the 1922 lock-out.[20]

Despite the efforts at organization at the end of the First World War, relations with employers were in many cases unchanged, and a sense of belonging to a wider 'Labour Movement' conspicuously lacking. Industrially, Oxford was still the introverted and small world that it had been before 1914. Predictably, three things happened in the 1930s. Some groups became solidly organized for the first time; some, already union members, became more aggressive when bargaining with employers; and some continued as before.

Where those workers who became more solidly organized in the 1930s than hitherto were concerned, the analysis is not straightforward, for it is necessary to disentangle the impact of a purely local event, the 1934 Pressed Steel strike, from a more wide-ranging phenomenon, namely the expansion in membership of the two general unions, the T. & G.W.U. and the N.U.G. & M.W. The T. & G.W.U.'s membership increased by 83 per cent between 1933 and 1939, and that of the N.U.G. & M.W. by 94 per cent.[21] Local increases in membership might, therefore, merely reflect the national expansion of these unions, and not be particularly revealing about local attitudes. It should also be borne in mind that the growth of these unions did change the possibilities open to workers to organize in industries in which previously the wisdom of so doing must have seemed doubtful. However, as was shown in the case of Pressed Steel, local social change could still play a part even when the policies of a union formulated at national level were important.

The busmen provide a good illustration of the forces of

[18] M. Cole, *The Life of G. D. H. Cole* (London, 1971), pp. 155-6.
[19] A.E.U. District Committee Minute Book, May 1926; Council of Action Register of Strike Pay, 1926.
[20] A.E.U. District Committee Minute Book, 29 May 1922.
[21] H. A. Clegg, *General Union in a Changing Society* (Oxford, 1954), p. 143.

union and social change taking effect. After 1935, the activities of the busmen were representative of the 'new' city, just as they had expressed the attitudes of the 'old' city in the 1920s. In the earlier period they had been parochial, and, with some justification, cynical towards the claims of the trade unions. In the 1930s they became more aggressive in their claims, impatient with their union, and aware also of the common interests they had with busmen in other districts.

From 1929, the T. & G.W.U. was anxious to establish national negotiating machinery for the privately-owned bus companies outside London, because concentration of ownership was outstripping the regional coverage of the union's trade groups in the country.[22] The City of Oxford Motor Services Company was itself part of the larger British Electric Traction undertaking, which along with T. Tillings Ltd. controlled most of the provincial bus services. The City of Oxford Company was one of those unorganized in 1928, and to remedy this was a necessary preliminary to national negotiations. There was a sense of grievance over the effect of operating schedules on working hours after a rearrangement of duties in 1930-1,[23] but this did not mean automatic support for the trade union. Meetings were held in St. Giles in September 1934, at which Abe Lazarus, the Communist Party organizer who had made such impact during the Pressed Steel strike earlier in the summer, and Stan Tombling, a busman and member of the union, did most of the talking.[24] But the busmen were unimpressed and stayed away from the St. Giles' meetings; and when balloted they voted decisively against joining a union.[25]

Clearly, to win over the busmen, something more was required than speeches by local sympathizers at a familiar left-wing meeting ground. In July 1935 the Trades Council decided to make a fresh effort, with a systematic canvass of all the busmen; since many of them lived in the surrounding countryside this was no easy matter. The Council's committee was led by Tom Harris, the chief shop steward at Pressed

---

[22] T. & G.W.U. Passenger Transport Trade Group minutes, 30 Mar. 1928, Appendix ix.
[23] *Oxford Mail*, 3 and 4 Dec. 1934.
[24] *Oxford Mail*, 17 Sept. 1934.   [25] *Oxford Mail*, 4 Dec. 1934.

Steel; and Dai Huish, another leader of the Pressed Steel strike and chairman of the T. & G.W.U. branch there, held meetings at his house for the members of the Communist Party involved in the campaign.[26] It was only through this more intensive recruiting effort that a strike over pay and hours could be used as a realistic threat to force union recognition.[27] The new arrivals from the depressed areas who had played an important part in changing industrial relations at Pressed Steel had not remained an isolated enclave at Cowley but had made a real contribution where more conventional methods had failed. While the bus industry in Oxford had absorbed proportionally more workers from outside the area than the car factories (56.2 per cent of its labour force in 1936, compared to 46.7 per cent) most of these men came from the South of England.[28] They had been very different from and less disruptive than the new arrivals at Pressed Steel.

Once the question of union recognition had been settled the busmen became more aggressive and troublesome. The framework within which this changing behaviour took place was provided by the efforts of the T. & G.W.U. to establish national negotiating machinery for the private bus companies. If the union was to achieve this by negotiation it had to be able to hold its members to agreements signed on their behalf. But the provincial busmen were difficult to handle, particularly if they were newly unionized and wished to achieve parity with other bus workers. Bevin, general secretary of the T. & G.W.U., found their behaviour exasperating: 'It is really a very difficult and peculiar section to deal with. We work away to get them organised and immediately we secure a measure of organisation the first thing they want to do is strike.'[29] The main thrust in the employer's arguments against national negotiations was that the union had no control over its membership and unofficial strikes merely underlined this point.

Industrial relations in the provincial bus companies in the 1930s were hardly smooth or ordered. There was no powerful

[26] Trades Council minutes, 4 July 1935; interview with Henry Jones.
[27] *Oxford Mail*, 15 July 1935.
[28] Barnett House, *Survey*, vol. 1, p. 54.
[29] In his quarterly report to the G.E.C., Aug. 1935.

reason why things in Oxford should have turned out any differently; the busmen were aware that their conditions were less satisfactory than those elsewhere. Compared with those in the Midlands they worked longer for less money: 1s. 3d. for each hour of a fifty-four-hour week compared to 1s. 4d. for a forty-eight-hour week.[30] Although the terms were agreed in November 1935,[31] dissatisfaction arose in 1936 with the way schedules were implemented because labour shortages had extended the working week.[32] During the strikes and negotiations which took place over these and other issues, two local men emerged as leaders of the busmen, Jackson and Lawson, president and secretary respectively of the T. & G.W.U. branch.

It took time for the local branch to become fully absorbed into the formal system of industrial relations favoured by the union. In May 1936 the branch officials agreed to return from an unofficial strike over the dismissal of a conductor when the case was put to an inquiry carried out by local academics. This had been set up by the Mayor and Chief Constable: trust in local dignitaries still counted for more with the branch officials than any help they could get from the union machine. Bevin was displeased.[33] Conflict with the union nationally broke the surface far more dramatically early in 1937, because of disagreements with the union by many provincial busmen about how a national agreement could best be achieved. In April of that year the Oxford busmen were anxious to yoke their claims for better conditions to a strike which began at Maidstone Bus Company and spread to depots in Bedford, Cambridge, and Northampton. Some of the shop-floor leaders at the Pressed Steel factory made an appearance in the early days of this dispute, three of them speaking at a meeting of strikers in Aylesbury.[34]

The two Oxford men not only led their own followers, but also the main provincial strike movement; Jackson

[30] Trades Council minutes, 28 Oct. 1934; *Oxford Mail*, 31 July 1935.
[31] *Oxford Mail*, 27 Nov. 1935.   [32] *Oxford Mail*, 8 Jan. 1936.
[33] 'It would have been much better if the matter could have been dealt with by the union in the first instance, and it is quite clear from the enquiry that the strike was ill-advised.' Bevin's report of August 1936 to G.E.C. on the Passenger Services Group.
[34] *Oxford Mail*, 24 Apr. 1937.

became chairman of the Central Committee organizing the
strikers, and when its headquarters moved from Chelms-
ford to Oxford it met at Lawson's house in Headington.
It was Lawson who met Papworth, leader of the London
busmen's rank and file movement.[35] The union's area
organizer argued that such a strike merely played into the
hands of the employers, who claimed that the union had no
control over its membership; Jackson replied that the Executive Council 'were not in touch with the conditions under
which the men had to work'.[36] The parallels with the Pressed
Steel strike went further than the opposition to the national
union, for just as the car workers had established contacts
with other factories beyond Oxford, so the busmen's leaders
became involved in a wider movement imposed by the logic
of ownership within the industry. But the staying power was
not there, and the strikers eventually agreed on a return to
work with no victimization, and resumption of local negotiations.[37] This essay in grass roots militancy ended in failure
with the management in Oxford rejecting any increase in
wages, though they agreed to a reduction in the working
week from fifty-two to fifty hours; the busmen also had to
agree not to embark on any unofficial strikes in the future.[38]

Three points can be made about the experience of the
busmen in the 1930s. First, the initiative required to win
union recognition, which flowed from the same sources as
the militancy at Pressed Steel, was purely local. Secondly,
the effect of union membership was fundamental, and also
irreversible, because of the much greater strength of the
T. & G.W.U. in the 1930s compared to that of the N.U.V.W.
in the early 1920s. Thirdly, once the union was launched,
and once the pressures on busmen arising from the concentration of ownership within the industry came into play, the
relations between employers and workers reflected any
purely local circumstances much less. Workers' attitudes now

---

[35] *Oxford Mail*, 3 May 1937. Papworth derived little benefit from the strike
in the provinces; see H. A. Clegg, *Labour Relations in London Transport* (Oxford,
1950), p. 121.

[36] *Oxford Mail*, 1 May 1937.

[37] Clegg, *Labour Relations*, p. 121; *Oxford Mail*, 10 May 1937.

[38] Report of meeting of national officer with company, T. & G.W.U. Passenger
Transport Trade Group minutes, 30 Dec. 1937.

showed a sense of common interest with busmen in other regions, and were no longer so firmly bounded by the locality. An impressive indication of this was the way in which the association between militant attitudes and a particular section of immigrant labour no longer obtained by 1936. By then, two local men had come to the forefront, Jackson and Lawson, who took a leading part in the dissident movement for a national agreement. Their behaviour reflects particularly clearly the supersession of community by industrial pressures.

Much the same point can be made about the workers in the municipal, gas, and distributive industries who also 'learnt the art of combination' more soundly in the 1930s than they had done in the early 1920s. More so than the examples of the bus industry or Pressed Steel, this growth derived from trade union expansion nationally, and did not rely so heavily on local initiatives.

The National Federation of General Workers had become absorbed into the National Union of General and Municipal Workers and this union grew with the economic recovery after 1933. Its Oxford branch had not closed down completely after the loss of membership in the early 1920s, and in 1927 it had ninety members;[39] but this was a poor showing in view of its strength earlier in the decade. During the latter part of 1933 some members were made among council employees, and in January 1935 a meeting was held to celebrate the revival of the branch, when it was commented that 'during the last year or so applications for membership have greatly increased with the rapid commercial development of the City'.[40]

One of the major benefits of this growth was that the Oxford corporation was persuaded to join the West Midlands Non-Trading Joint Industrial Council, from which wage increases for various groups of workers followed.[41] With the inclusion of the gas workers in the branch, its membership in June 1936 stood at 800.[42] They also used the national negotiating machinery to press for higher wages,[43] and to move away from discretionary methods of wage payment,

[39] Return of union branch in Oxford Trades Council file at T.U.C.
[40] *Oxford Mail*, 9 Feb. 1935.   [41] N.U.G. & M.W. Journal, May 1935.
[42] *Oxford Mail*, 1 June 1936.   [43] *Oxford Mail*, 8 Dec. 1936.

the members wanting 'modern pay packets so that the amount of wages and deductions may be clearly seen'.[44]

In the distributive trades, the most contentious field for union organization in the 1920s had been the Co-operative Society, and it continued to be so in the 1930s. The attitude of the Management Committee had not changed greatly by then: they still refused to make trade union membership compulsory, or to allow trade union organizers to canvass workers during working hours.[45] When a union branch was established which catered for these workers, it was felt that an important gap in the local Labour Movement had been filled.[46] But, once again, the drive came from the union nationally. In February 1936 organizers were working in Oxford as well as in other towns in the South of England, and when demands for wage increases were presented to the Oxford Society the same was being done nearby at Chipping Norton.[47] As a result, the frame of reference for wage bargaining was no longer constrained, as it had been in the past, by the arguments of the Oxford Society that it had to keep prices locally competitive, but was opened up to comparisons with wages paid by other societies. In brief, the Oxford Co-operative Society offered the same wages as were being paid at Brighton, but the membership rejected this in favour of the higher Reading scale.[48]

A further example of an increase in wages following on union recognition also shows how trade union growth in a major industry enabled district organizers to make new members in the nooks and crannies of the occupational structure. This particular case concerned the coalmen at a wharf on the Oxford canal. In the early 1920s the local labour leaders had been unable to make any headway among the small group of casual, poorly paid labourers. It was not possible to get any of the men permanently employed, although a register of unloaders was kept.[49] In the 1930s they were an obvious inheritance from the past, gaining an uncertain and poorly paid living in the twilight world of those

[44] *Oxford Mail*, 11 Nov. 1936.
[45] Trades Council minutes, 6 June 1935.
[46] *Oxford Mail*, 21 Mar. 1936.
[47] N.U.D.A.W., *New Dawn*, 8 Feb., 22 Aug. 1936.
[48] *Oxford Mail*, 16 Dec. 1936.   [49] *Oxford Chronicle*, 30 Mar. 1923.

who belonged to no organization. But in 1938 a radical change was effected. Following a recruitment drive by the district organizer of the T. & G.W.U. and an officially sanctioned strike, the coal merchants agreed to recognize the union. As a result, working hours were reduced from fifty-six hours to forty-eight, and wages raised from 45s. to between 53s. and 57s. a week.[50] This brought coalmen close to the conditions of similarly employed manual workers in the Co-operative Society, with whom the T. & G.W.U. had had an agreement since 1936.[51]

This completes the survey of the first groups of industries, namely those in which union recognition itself was a major problem in the 1920s, or in which membership had been very weak. While the workers in these industries usually experienced, as a result of unionization, marked improvements in wages, negotiations about pay were not affected by the location of the high-wage motor industry at Cowley. Rather, the limits of wage bargaining were set by the rates within the particular industries, by national or regional negotiating machinery.

In the engineering industry the situation was different. This forms the second category of firms, namely those already organized by the 1920s, but in which relationships were significantly changed in the later 1930s. In the engineering industry, of which Pressed Steel was considered a part, workers already belonged to a union, but the high wages paid at the car factories led them to demand parity. The two firms involved were Lucy's in west Oxford and John Allen's in Cowley. Both were small firms, and both members of the London Association of the E.A.E.F. Although the A.E.U. and the Foundry Workers' Union had members at both firms, they were not strongly established, and, particularly at Lucy's, workers had no complaints against their employer. Relations between management and labour approximated to the harmonious ideal of the small-scale establishment. J. R. Dick, managing director of the firm since 1905, was opposed to piece-work payment systems, because 'good relations lay

---

[50] *Oxford Mail*, 28 Feb., 4–5 Mar. 1938. Meeting of G.E.C. of T. & G.W.U., Mar. 1938, minute 219.
[51] G.E.C. meeting, Aug. 1936, minute 750.

in paying proper wages in a straightforward manner'.[52] Apparently this paid off, for in 1919 during a national strike by the ironworkers, it was pointed out that there was no local grievance, and that 'Messrs. Lucy and Co. have always been the best of friends with their employees, a fact that the workers themselves admit, and which becomes very evident on entering the works and the offices.'[53]

While both firms were members of the London Association, and while their wages were undisturbed by any local comparisons, these mutually trustful relations were hardly threatened. Because of the small number of skilled workers employed at Morris Motors, and the absence of union organization there, the early expansion of the motor industry at Cowley did not disrupt this situation. Pressed Steel was another matter, for in the early 1930s it was employing about 200 skilled machine-shop workers and millwrights.[54] But the disturbing effect was not felt immediately, for union organization was still weak at that firm in the early 1930s. The situation changed after the 1934 strike, from which the A.E.U. improved its membership. This led to a redoubling of efforts at the other engineering firms and at Lucy's. In October 1936 the A.E.U.'s national organizer reported that:

Where previously it has been impossible to arouse interest, we were able to get a meeting on each occasion, and a number of recruits from the firm attended an evening meeting. The absence of organisation in the past has meant financial loss to the men as we found in coming into contact with them, that the firm, though members of the London Employers' Federation, had not observed agreements.[55]

But it was not only a question of paying the rates obtaining within the London Association, but of bringing the wages at John Allen's and Lucy's up to those paid at Pressed Steel, which happened to be a member of the Birmingham Association. The Pressed Steel toolroom workers probably earned as a minimum between 71s. and 78s. a week, that is, between 1s. 6d. and 1s. 8d. an hour.[56] When the matter came up at the

[52] P.W.S. Andrews, *The Eagle Ironworks of Oxford* (Oxford, 1965), p. 27.
[53] *Oxford Chronicle*, 26 Sept. 1919.
[54] Return in Pressed Steel file at E.E.F., Tothill Street, London.
[55] Divisional organizer's report for Area 18, A.E.U. Journal, Oct. 1936.
[56] A.E.U. Journal, Sept. 1934. These are basic hourly rates and do not take account of lieu rate earnings.

Central Conference which was part of the disputes procedure
operating in the engineering industry, the way in which wage
expectations had been transformed by the arrival of the high-
wage motor industry was succinctly outlined by the chairman:

They [i.e. Lucy's and John Allen] have been, and still are, really
Oxford. Then along comes the Pressed Steel Company and put down a
big place very highly specialised—not general engineers at all. They
make a lot of money and they pay very high rates of wages. They go
to the Birmingham Association and apply to them for membership,
and since they are paying substantially higher rates than the Federation
are normally able to afford, being poor people, there is some discussion
as to what the recognised rates of pay shall be in certain departments.
As a result of that the rates of pay being paid by the Pressed Steel
Company to the skilled men in the die department are recognised as the
minimum rate applicable to that department.
There is not the remotest hope of these two firms engaged in general
engineering work, beginning to pay specialised rates such as are paid to
the men at Pressed Steel—not a hope.[57]

Subsequent negotiations tended to establish the chairman's
point. The offer from the two firms was an increase from 61s.
to 62s. a week at John Allen's, and an increase to the same
amount (by two shillings) at Lucy's. This did not match the
rates existing at Pressed Steel; and the gap was widened
further by an increase at Pressed Steel in June 1937, which
brought many workers up to 1s. 8¾d. an hour as a minimum,
way above the 1s. 3d. which was paid by the two smaller
firms.[58] Even though the differential remained, perception
of it had altered the temper of relations between management
and labour at the two firms. Once again, the most graphic
illustration of this comes from Lucy's. Having lost some of its
credibility as a fair employer, it also had to abandon one
method of maintaining a compliant work-force, namely a
discretionary bonus of 1s. a week which was occasionally
distributed to the men. This method of periodically under-
lining the good faith of the employers was criticized for evading
a commitment to pay a proper wage: 'The feeling was that
what was given away with one hand was being taken back with
the other, at least as far as the 1 shilling was concerned.[59]

[57] Central Conference minutes, 9 Apr. 1937, p. 18.
[58] Divisional organizer's report for Area 18, A.E.U. Journal, June 1937.
[59] Central Conference minutes, 9 Apr. 1937, p. 18.

The Cowley Iron Works of John Allen carried out less skilled work than Lucy's, although it did have contracts with Pressed Steel for certain skilled operations, and the T. & G.W.U. recruited members there in 1937.[60] For the labourers the result was a wage increase of 4s. a week to 52s., and the firm agreed to pay overtime rates in accordance with established practice in the engineering industry. The 'levelling up' in this case was more successful than it had been with the skilled workers, although actual parity with the semi-skilled assemblers in the car factories was out of the question, and not sought.

This completes the survey of the two categories within which change took place in the 1930s. Clearly, an obvious statement about industrial relations in a 'mature' economy— that the industry in which a worker made his living was more important than where he lived—now applied to Oxford more comprehensively than it had done in the early 1920s. This was an inevitable consequence of the application of national or regional agreements, and the willingness of local officials to negotiate about wages within the limits which these imposed. For many workers in Oxford this brought a fundamental gain, even though the monetary dimensions of this may appear to have been modest. Wages no longer reflected the weak bargaining position produced by local conditions, and implementation of national agreements invariably brought an upgrading of the wages of the men concerned.

But the local trade unionists, fired with enthusiasm during the 1934 strike, had hoped the gains in future years were not going to be purely sectional. In a document circulated after the 1934 strike, its importance was seen to lie not only in the establishment of trade unionism in the factory but also in the alliance between various industrial and political groups in the early stages of the strike, which proved that 'with this kind of leadership the trade unions can be made again the fighting organisations they once were'.[61] By 'this leadership'

[60] Central Conference minutes, 9 Apr. 1937, p. 18; and Dalgleish's report to Metal, Engineering, and Chemical Trade Group, Sept. 1937.
[61] 'The Significance of the Pressed Steel Strike', typescript by C. Bowles and H. Waterhouse, Oct. 1934, in correspondence file, Abe Lazarus Library.

was meant the joint involvement of the Labour Party, Trades Council, and Communist Party with the strike committee. It was not simply a question of fund raising, but that 'through such a united body the mass of workers can be drawn into activity'.[62] The 'activity' of the 'mass', of course, is evidentially elusive and probably beyond investigation, but it is clear from the foregoing that the energies of the Pressed Steel group in connection with Morris Motors and the busmen made them more wide ranging than conventional trade unionists.

While some outsiders regarded the Pressed Steel strike as convincing proof of the efficacy of a 'united front' of all organizations on the Left, the Labour Movement nationally was bound to regard such activities with suspicion. In 1933 the General Council of the T.U.C. had rejected proposals presented by the Communist Party and the I.L.P. for a United Front,[63] and in 1934 Walter Citrine saw the sole object of the policy being 'to permeate the working class movement at every point and destroy completely the influence of the British Labour Party and the British T.U.C.'.[64] In view of the Communist Party's policy in the 1920s of attempting to set up independent trade union organizations under the Minority Movement, these suspicions were well founded. The T.U.C. issued a circular in 1934 advising Trades Councils that if they participated in United Front movements in which the Communist Party was involved they would be removed from the list of affiliated organizations. Many Trades Councils, particularly in the Home Counties, refused to operate this circular, and the Oxford Council took a leading part in the campaign to have it withdrawn. The Council reacted strongly to the circular, accusing the T.U.C. of being out of touch with the situation in Oxford. In a resolution passed unanimously in April 1935, the Council wished:

To impress upon the T.U.C. the fact that the council has a long and exceptionally fine record of trade union activity and that its strength has never been greater than at present. It desires also to explain to the

[62] Ibid.
[63] Conference Report, 1933, p. 174.
[64] Conference Report, 1934, p. 350.

T.U.C. that this strength and activity is due in no small measure to the presence on the council of members of the Communist Party and what the T.U.C. calls its ancillary organisations. In our daily experience Communist Party members have, so far from showing disruptive tendencies, thrown themselves into the work of strengthening the Trade Union movement as well as the best of us.[65]

A committee was set up to organize opposition to the circular,[66] and representations were made both to the T.U.C. conference at York in 1935 and to the Home Counties Federation of Trades Councils. But, all too obviously, power lay with the T.U.C., and in September 1935 its organization committee 'intimated' to the Oxford Council that they wished to form a new body in accordance with T.U.C. regulations.[67] After a local conference in March 1936, the Council agreed to accept the circular.[68] In the meantime, a member of the Communist Party and delegate from the Pressed Steel branch of the T. & G.W.U. had been obliged to resign from the Council.[69]

Attempts to use the alliance with the Communist Party to unite the various local working-class groups were further frustrated by the divided attitudes of local unions to the Communist Party. While the local branches of the A.E.U., A.S.W., N.U.D.A.W., T.A., and N.U.G. & M.W. accepted the circular, the Pressed Steel branch of the T. & G.W.U. chose to ignore it;[70] and the busmen were willing to accept the help of local Communist Party members in the campaign for recognition in 1935. It was with these two groups that the penetration of the Communists into local trade union organizations was most in evidence, and the success in involving other organizations in industrial disputes most obvious. During the 1934 Pressed Steel strike, £197 was collected by the Council of Action (into which the Trades Council had formed themselves),[71] and £50 was collected for the busmen in 1936 during a short strike over the

---

[65] Trades Council minutes, 11 Apr. 1935.
[66] Trades Council minutes, 4 July 1935.
[67] Trades Council minutes, 16 Sept. 1935.
[68] T.U.C. file on disruptive organizations, TC, JCC 3/1.
[69] Trades Council minutes, 27 Feb. 1936.
[70] Trades Council minutes, 6 Dec. 1934.
[71] Bowles and Waterhouse, 'Pressed Steel Strike'.

dismissal of a conductor.[72] During the provincial bus strike in 1937, for which Oxford acted as a headquarters, meetings were organized by the Trades Council, with the Communist Party and Labour Party in support. The local Communist Party was also willing to carry out many of the more mundane tasks of labour organization. It published and printed propaganda material, such as factory newspapers and hand-outs dealing with particular strikes, as well as performing the more onerous tasks, like the drawing-up of the names and addresses of busmen in the outlying districts to be canvassed about union membership in 1935.[73]

It was the willingness of the Communist Party to carry out these chores, and the energy which its members brought to local campaigns, which won them a place in the local Labour Movement, even though members of the Trades Council (for example, the president, Len Bellinger) were not noted for their left-wing political sympathies. Because the activity of the Communist Party in Oxford never went beyond this politically innocuous participation in immediate issues, the division of opinion over matters of principle never seriously asserted itself. As the secretary of the Trades Council put it when writing to the T.U.C.: 'All members of our council, *whatever their political affiliations*, are able to work together unanimously in building up the trade union movement in Oxford.'[74] This view was perfectly legitimate within Oxford, since political opinions were defined in a national and not a local context; and the basic chores of industrial organization carried no specific political overtones. Indeed, the willingness of the Communist Party in Oxford to accept a strongly industrial perspective meant that its involvement in trade union organization served the aims of the local Labour Movement far more than it served its wider ambitions. But from the centre the position was inevitably seen differently, and the local movement was in trouble. Local 'democracy', in both the forms it took—the freedom of action by local alliances of union branches, Trades Council, and Communist

---

[72] Trades Council minutes, 7 May 1936.

[73] Interview with Henry Jones.

[74] C. Bowles to T.U.C., 23 Dec. 1934 (emphasis added) in T.U.C. file on disruptive organizations, TC, JCC 3/1.

Party, or of union branches by themselves—was limited by
the power of central organizations. When the Trades Council
tried in 1938 to take up the case of the Pressed Steel shop
steward who had been sacked,[75] it was told by the union
to mind its own business, and the area secretary of the
T. & G.W.U. was given powers to withdraw the Pressed Steel
branch from the Council, because of the latter's sympathy
for the shop stewards at the factory.[76] This experience, and
the 'unofficial' action of the car workers and the busmen,
showed that the power of local 'democracy' was quite
limited. In this respect, the tension between the two products
of the 1934 strike—the local united front operating hori-
zontally across various organizations, and the growth of trade
union membership incorporated vertically into centralized
institutions—was inevitably resolved at critical points in
favour of the latter.

At a more modest level, the experience of the 1934
strike and the active part taken by the Communist Party had
bred a greater awareness of the changes which industrial
organization could effect in working-class lives. In the
enthusiasms of the 1930s there was little of the cynicism
towards the 'Movement' which had been apparent in the
1920s. There were, of course, still limits to this: when the
N.U.G. & M.W. tried to organize the college servants in
1937, around a 'charter' of uniform pay and hours, it was no
more successful than its predecessors had been. Union
membership was still believed to be the badge of the factory
worker, and inapplicable to the college servant. While they
were not uniformly traditional, since one of their number,
H. S. Richardson, became president of the Labour Party in
1938, their attitudes had in general changed little. At a
meeting held by the union to recruit members, one of the
servants stated that theirs 'was one of the finest jobs in the
world', and he was loudly applauded.[77] Their refusal to
compromise their status was as strong as it had always been.
The only lesson drawn from the motor industry was the

[75] See above, ch.4, part 1.
[76] Trades Council minutes, 18 Dec. 1938; and T. & G.W.U., Area 5 commi-
tee minutes, Apr. 1939.
[77] *Oxford Mail*, 12 Apr. 1937.

fundamental dissimilarity between work in the colleges and the more intensive effort at Cowley: to press for specified hours of work during term and vacation was therefore inappropriate.

Within the local hierarchy of trade unions, the Typographical Association had lost the dominant position it had enjoyed before 1914 and no longer determined the direction of the local movement. But its members continued to protect their craft position: they maintained their exclusive right to man certain machines, and prevented the use of female labour on certain jobs.[78] The attempts of certain firms to control more closely the use of time in their establishments were frustrated by members ignoring devices installed to clock them on and off jobs.[79] Because skilled printers had achieved control over new machines in 1911, the increase of machine compositors in the inter-war period (to outnumber the hand compositors, from being only a handful in 1911) carried no threat to the craft position.[80] In control over working conditions and strength of unionism the printers had some affinities with the highly-skilled craft groups in the motor industry, such as the patternmakers, and both were markedly different from the 'mass' of semi-skilled assemblers in Cowley. The distinction between craftsmen and the semi-skilled was underlined by the success of the Association in overcoming resistance to unions at Morris Motors, where a chapel was formed for the printers in the publicity department. This was the sole example of union recognition at the firm, but it had no wider repercussions since these men had no connections with the main production process.[81]

Besides these two examples of the persistence of 'tradition', the gains made by trade unions had been quite fundamental, releasing many workers from locally imposed constraints on their standards of living. It would be a great over-simplification to attribute the advances in every

[78] Typographical Association minutes, 21 Dec. 1932, 16 Oct. 1933.
[79] Typographical Association minutes, 14 Sept. 1925.
[80] See J. Zeitlin, 'Craft Control and the Division of Labour: Engineers and Compositors in Britain 1890–1930', *Cambridge Journal of Economics*, 3 (1979), 264.
[81] Typographical Association minutes, 13 Oct. 1930, 16 Feb. 1931, 9 Mar. and 13 May 1937.

occupation to the Pressed Steel strike of 1934. The expansion of the two general unions during the economic recovery after 1933 provided a radically different national context from that of the 1919-22 period when attempts to organize workers were unsuccessful. While life for many employers in Oxford was therefore far different from what it had been before 1914, and their freedom of action over pay was restricted, the power of the unions did give industrial relations some stability. By 1939 the local dimension of trade union growth in the 1930s (the attempt to launch a militant trades unionism on the alliance between the Communist Party and the Trades Council) had been contained by the institutions of the wider industrial society. It is in this subordination of the specifically local dimension that the 'modernization' of Oxford's industrial relations lies.

The effects of the high-wage motor industry on the labour market were not transmitted solely through the trade unions: the result of their negotiating procedures was to separate industries from one another, not to bring them into closer relation. The easiest form of improvement lay through individuals moving into the motor industry; as in Coventry, many of the newcomers began in the distributive trades before going on to the Cowley factories.[82] Women benefited especially, one sign of this being the decline in the supply of domestic servants for north Oxford. The balance never swung completely the other way: the traditional employers of female labour, namely the binding section of the printing press, and the marmalade factory, were never short of labour even though wages were below the average of 45s. a week to be earned trimming the upholstery in the car factory.[83] However, the differences compared with Edwardian Oxford were clear enough. While Oxford remained a city 'full of odd jobs', the car factories nevertheless produced a condition close to 'full' employment.[84] The motor industry, besides its own need for labour, was also responsible for a high demand

[82] Barnett House, *Survey*, vol. 1, p. 289.

[83] Barnett House, *Survey*, vol. 1, p. 86.

[84] L. R. Phelps, Provost of Oriel, chairman of the Public Assistance Committee, letter to Nicholson, 15 July 1933, Phelps Papers, Oriel College. In 1936 he wrote: 'Our work is light as Morris Motors are "going strong" and unemployment is almost negligible', letter, 21 Sept. 1936.

for housing. The house building of the 1920s and 1930s stimulated employment, to such an extent that in the 1920s 'difficulty was experienced in obtaining locally a supply of men suitable for work as navvies'.[85] In the 1930s unemployment in the Oxford building trade tended to be lower than for the South-Eastern region as a whole, where the house building 'boom' took place.[86] Despite the efforts of some firms building the Cowley estates to keep out union members, some growth in membership was achieved in Oxford.[87] More generally, a significant economic effect of the greater demand for labour was that the vagrant posed the main social problem in the inter-war period, instead of the unskilled casual building labourer, who had done so in the Edwardian years. The market for motor cars, rather than the demands of the University, was now the chief influence on economic life in Oxford, and in this respect the town had become more fully a part of the national economy by the end of the inter-war period than it had been at the beginning.

[85] *Oxford Chronicle*, 20 Mar. 1925.
[86] Barnett House, *Survey*, vol. 1, p. 107, table 23.
[87] Report of national secretary to T. & G.W.U. Building Trades group, Dec. 1935; A.U.B.T.W. Monthly Report, Feb. 1938.

6

POLITICS IN THE 1920s

Politics in Oxford in the 1920s differed little from in the pre-1914 period. The Labour Party was essentially powerless, left-wing activity in the University for the most part unrelated to any local context, and the main connections between the town and the colleges forged through the relief of poverty or unemployment. The housing market had been inherited from the pre-1914 period, and the nature of unemployment and the unemployed was typical of a small, essentially non-industrial town in a country region. A technical change was responsible for altering this picture at the end of the 1920s, namely the incorporation into the city of areas of recent population growth. This brought Headington and Cowley into the local government area, with their problems of suburban development and their largely working-class populations, but the benefit for Labour was not immediate: it was not until 1935 that the developing periphery began to return Labour councillors with any regularity.

The parliamentary constituency excluded the Cowley and Headington areas for the whole of the inter-war period. The car workers, therefore, did not make a political impact *en bloc*. As these were spread residentially over the town, the suburbs, and the countryside, there was much doubt over how many actually lived within the parliamentary constituency. Their influence in the 1923 free trade election was therefore hard to assess, but probably not decisive. As the car factories grew, and the suburbs with them, their main impact was on municipal elections, once Cowley and Headington were brought into the city for purposes of local government. The 1918 Representation of the People Act had little effect upon the class composition of the electorate. While the Act brought in many of those previously excluded from the franchise—those in lodgings, paupers, and those who moved frequently—and had a dramatic effect on the size of

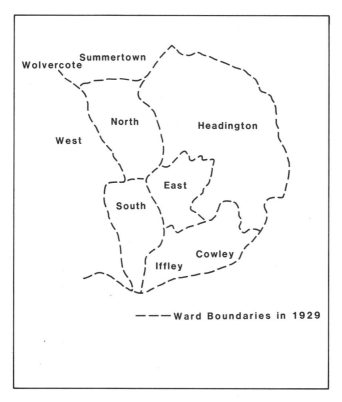

Map 2. Ward Boundaries in 1929

the electorate in many industrial towns, it did not do so in Oxford. Most of the increase came from the enfranchisement of women.[1] Both the Liberals and Conservatives brought women into their organizations, but mainly to help return men to political office.[2]

But Oxford was not politically quiescent for the whole of

[1] 81 per cent of the increase in the electorate was due to the enfranchisement of women. The electorate increased from 9,827 in 1911 to 25,093 in 1921.

[2] A Women's Liberal and Progressive Club was formed in 1921 and Conservative women were active at ward level, particularly Lady Oman in the West ward. *Oxford Chronicle*, 7 Apr. 1922; *Oxford Times*, 24 Mar. 1920. At the Conservatives' AGM in 1927 it was claimed that 'very much of their success as a party in Oxford resulted from the capital work that had been put in by the women's associations and clubs throughout the wards of the city', *Oxford Times*, 25 Mar. 1927.

the 1920s, thanks to the success of the Liberal, Frank Gray, in breaking a long run of Conservative dominance at the 1922 parliamentary election. Gray's success typified that of the Liberals nationally, who were able to do well against the major party but unable to hold on to a seat for very long.[3] The swing from Conservative to Liberal and back again is shown in Table 11.

Table 11. Parliamentary elections in Oxford

	Percentage turnout			Share of vote (percentage)
1918	55.7	J. Marriott	Coalition Cons.	70.7
		G. Higgins	Liberal	29.3
1922	83.8	F. Gray	Liberal	59.0
		J. Marriott	Conservative	41.0
1923	83.5	F. Gray	Liberal	56.1
		R. Bourne	Conservative	43.9
		— election void on petition		
1924	80.3	R. Bourne	Conservative	47.8
		C. B. Fry	Liberal	39.1
		K. Lindsay	Labour	13.1

Source: F. W. S. Craig, *British Parliamentary Election Results 1918-49* (Glasgow, 1969).

According to Michael Kinnear 'the above average swing to the Liberals in Oxford and Southend may be attributed to the large nonconformist vote in both places'.[4] Although the local Liberal Association has been closely allied with nonconformity before 1914, it would be surprising to find a habitual vote like this (which is what it had become by the 1920s) having a short term, but very marked, effect when there was no particular issue around which to mobilize it. It would be difficult to argue that the nonconformist vote could have had such an impact in 1922 and 1923 when it had failed to do so in 1906;[5] and it is clear from the reports of Gray's campaigns

[3] To be fair to Gray he was unseated by petition for technically exceeding his election expenses. He was judged not guilty of corrupt practice. C. Fenby, *The Other Oxford: the Life and Times of Frank Gray and his Father* (London, 1970), ch. 14.   [4] *The British Voter* (London, 1968), p. 129.

[5] In 1906, during the Liberal landslide, Oxford had been held by the Unionists,

that he made no effort to bring out a slumbering nonconformist vote.

What is interesting about Gray's success is the way it
followed from a strongly populist campaign. Rather than
acting as a conventional Liberal and setting out the issues
so that reasonable men might decide for themselves, Gray
covered the poorer streets of Oxford to put over a sympathetic, but essentially non-political identity. Marriott, the
Conservative candidate, was quite clear about the reasons
for his defeat:

I made a grave miscalculation. Although I spoke constantly in the
constituency at weekends, and attended many meetings and dinners
and entertainments of all sorts, work in committee rooms at West-
minster did not compensate for absence from smoking concerts and
football grounds in Oxford.[6]

He was consoled only by the report that 'all "the better sort"
went into mourning after my defeat'.[7] Gray realized that the
more densely populated slum areas and cheap eating houses
yielded a better return for his electioneering than north
Oxford, where 'the aristocratic dignity of Lord Valentia and
the academic haughtiness of Mr. J. A. R. Marriott' were more
suitable.[8] To get at this vote in the lower half of the social
structure Gray attempted to place himself in people's lives,
although in a non-political way. It was all a matter of flower
shows, sport, and the avoidance of political opinion.[9]

Gray was by profession a solicitor, and son of one of
Oxford's more important Conservatives, William Gray. He
had been encouraged to see himself as an effective public
speaker, or leader of the mob, by his part in Morris's attempt
to run motor buses in Oxford in 1912 against the wishes of
the corporation. This aroused much popular excitement in
whose development Gray played a leading part.[10] The war

and Kinnear, in contradictory vein, comments 'few seats remaining Unionist
had an appreciable number of nonconformists'. Kinnear, p. 30.

[6] *Memories of Four Score Years* (London, 1946), p. 174.

[7] Ibid., p. 175.

[8] F. Gray, *Confessions of a Candidate* (London, 1925), p. 32.

[9] 'The man who can get to 100 flower shows, 50 football matches, 20 cricket
matches and make 150 after-dinner speeches without disclosing a political opinion
must be a strong candidate.' *Confessions*, p. 94.

[10] Fenby, pp. 121 ff., provides a useful account of this episode.

—in which he served by choice as a private soldier—pushed him towards Liberalism, as did a visit to Ireland after the Treaty of 1921.[11] The Oxford Liberal Association was Asquithian, its president, John Massie, hoping of Lloyd George that 'the contents of his head may "gush out" with the swelling thereof'.[12] Gray was adopted in 1920, and his identity was avowedly 'progressive'. As the secretary of one of the ward associations put it, 'We have in the person of Mr. Frank Gray one who, whilst fighting under our auspices, yet embraces in his beliefs the best elements of the Labour Party's gospel.'[13]

In Gray's campaign the working class—and not only the artisan—began to count for something in Oxford politics and he met with an enthusiastic response from certain groups. The railway workers gave him their support, as did those from the parts of the town where Conservative interests had, in the later nineteenth century, attempted to manipulate the popular vote:

The most remarkable scenes occurred behind the brewery where Squire Hall (its Conservative owner) once decided to fight Harcourt. Here there were hordes of children with mouth organs, tin whistles, trombones and an old drum. The band formed up, Frank came next, and then a mob of people, who all marched up to the Town Hall.[14]

Beyond the active personal involvement lay a hazy presentation of certain issues relevant to labour. He side-stepped the question of workers' control and hoped for 'the happy co-operation of the one party and the other' in industry.[15] He was against nationalization in practice though not in theory, and on unemployment thought that 'workers in conjunction with master men in their own trades will find the most likely solution in self-help'.[16]

This ambiguity and evasion was quite deliberate. It was carried beyond electioneering into an effort to 'de-politicize' the local Liberal newspaper, the *Oxford Chronicle*. The paper

[11] Fenby, p. 134.

[12] J. A. Massie to Gilbert Murray, 20 Dec. 1918, Murray MSS, Bodleian Library, Box 38, fo. 106. Massie had been until 1903 Yates Professor of New Testament Exegesis, and formerly chairman of the Council of the Congregational Union. He died in 1925. Murray was Regius Professor of Greek.

[13] *Oxford Chronicle*, 19 Mar. 1920.   [14] Fenby, p. 138.

[15] *Oxford Chronicle*, 24 Sept. 1920.   [16] Ibid.

was in the hands of Liberals from both the town and the University, principally Massie, president of the Association, and Alderman Salter. They undoubtedly found Gray's views rebarbative, since he denied the political intelligence of the electors on which their own interpretation of Liberalism, as rising above partial or material interest, depended.[17] But Gray's analysis of his position is worth reporting, since it was a highly unusual view of Liberalism and the working class in Oxford. It is reported here by Massie in a letter to Gilbert Murray dealing with Gray's plans for the *Chronicle*:

> He [Gray] was elected by the votes of a large number of people who care nothing for Liberalism or the Liberal Party and he is anxious to do nothing to antagonise them . . . The paper must therefore support him personally but not politically. It must give itself to sport and such like matters, and keep clear of politics as far as possible, and boost him but not his [ostensible] principles.[18]

But however nebulous Gray's Liberalism might have intentionally appeared, and however much it eschewed the language of class, local trade unionists found that it was what they wanted.[19] According to one, there was 'no man for whom Labour would have a warmer welcome and he only wished Labour had more men like the City member'.[20] Even those who wished to field a Labour candidate felt it wise to hold back in 1923 in view of Gray's ability to attract working-class support: 'We shall not even get the support of our own people. Our people worked for Frank Gray last time. They signed his nomination papers and they voted for him. Members of the party had even said now that they were going to vote for him again'.[21]

The Labour Party in Oxford had been formed in November 1921 after that year's municipal elections, and reflected the collusion of local enthusiasts with national party organizers.[22]

[17] See Massie's views at Gray's adoption, *Oxford Chronicle*, 16 Jan. 1920.

[18] Letter of 22 Apr. 1923, in Murray MSS, Box 46, fos. 210-12.

[19] Namely, spreading the burden of unemployment insurance, reduced military expenditure, free trade and 'a direct interest in the control of industry in which they are engaged'. *Oxford Chronicle*, 10 Nov. 1920.

[20] F. J. North, National Federation of General Workers, *Oxford Chronicle*, 22 Feb. 1922.

[21] Frederick Ludlow, a printer, Labour's only city councillor in the 1920s, *Oxford Chronicle*, 23 Nov. 1923.

[22] At that time G. R. Shepherd, a district organizer for the party, had been

The local party was as much a product of an expanding organization as of ineluctable social forces at the grass roots, the majority in favour of forming a party being the narrowest possible, five unions in favour and four against.[23] The Typographical Association, which had been the most important union locally since before 1914, was mainly Liberal,[24] and the strongest support for Labour among the local working class had come from the railwaymen. In 1923 in the West ward 'all that was done was attributable to the railwaymen'[25] when there had been very little support from other members. They were a socially cohesive group. During the national railway strike of 1919 they went with their families to St. Ebbe's Church to hear speeches, complete with biblical rhetoric, defending their action, and they held a concert to celebrate the end of the strike.[26] According to a printer in the west of the city, where most of the railwaymen lived, 'The unity, solidarity, and determination of the railwaymen was almost solely the result of a number of concerts and social gatherings in which the men, their wives and children all joined together in one united family.'[27] The railwaymen were rather unusual, both in their evident solidarity and in their commitment to the Labour Party.[28] Yet it still made sense for them to vote for Gray in parliamentary elections, since there was little possibility of a Labour candidate winning a seat like Oxford in the inter-war period, and much certainty of attracting hostility by actually opposing him.

But Gray was an unusual figure, and after the 1923 election had been declared void there was no obvious person to follow him who could cultivate the populist appeal as he had done. For the Liberals, C. B. Fry and R. O. Moon, a London doctor, were rather innocuous, and as late as 1930, when the

'instrumental in starting Labour parties in Hitchin, Hertford, Oxford, Windsor, and Canterbury', minutes of N.E.C. District D, 29 Nov. 1921.

[23] Trades Council minutes, 21 Oct. 1921.

[24] Minutes of Typographical Association branch, 23 Sept. 1921, and *Oxford Chronicle*, 9 June 1922.

[25] *Oxford Chronicle*, 19 Apr. 1924.

[26] *Oxford Chronicle*, 10 Oct. 1919.

[27] *Oxford Chronicle*, 30 Jan. 1920.

[28] For the most part the Labour interest locally 'had never got a majority of the votes of trade unionists. That was the plain truth.' F. J. North, *Oxford Chronicle*, 17 Sept. 1920.

party was discussing possible candidates, 'the only name mentioned was that of Frank Gray'.[29] But Gray declined the candidature, arguing that the day of the Liberal Party 'as the chief agent of progressive reforms is over', and advising 'progressively minded young people' to make their contribution to the right wing of the Labour Party.[30] In a sense Gray's demise opened up the field for Labour but there was some disagreement as to the type of candidate most suitable to exploit this. Some members of the local party claimed that 'it was absurd to say that Oxford was different from other places' and they wanted working-class candidates rather than wealthy carpet-baggers.[31] But the view from Eccleston Square was different:

The best type to do good in Oxford was one of the professional classes. He [G. R. Shepherd, district organizer] referred to Mr. Kenneth Lindsay, an Oxford blue and ex-President of the Union.
   Another possible man was Mr. Markham, at present secretary to Sir Sydney Lee. This was a man of the working classes who had worked up through the University and there was the possibility that such a candidate would attract people's support where another might not.[32]

The idea that a candidate like Markham, who had used the University to improve upon his working-class origins, would in some way straddle both those worlds was one example of the frequent misconception of working-class views among those from the Labour Party's head office: the Oxford Trades Council was, in fact, suspicious of those drawn away to other occupations after further education.[33] Lindsay, the candidate adopted, did not attempt an assiduous cultivation of the popular vote. He based his campaign on the need for more secondary schools and a class-less Labour Party derived from the camaraderie of the trenches.[34] He probably received the votes of those in the University who were sympathetic to Labour, such as Carlyle, Professor Soddy, and Godfrey (later Lord) Elton of The Queen's College.[35] The by-election to replace Gray did show that Labour could win enough

[29] *Oxford Times*, 7 Feb. 1930.   [30] *Oxford Times*, 21 Feb. 1930.
[31] *Oxford Chronicle*, 2 Sept. 1921.   [32] *Oxford Chronicle*, 21 Mar. 1924.
[33] Trades Council minutes, 14 July 1914.
[34] *Oxford Times*, 23 May 1924.
[35] A. L. Smith, Master of Balliol, also appeared on Lindsay's platform during his campaign, as did G. D. H. Cole.

votes to prevent the Liberals winning the seat[36] but Labour
could never take enough of the Liberal vote to remotely
challenge the Conservatives, who after Gray's rude interruption, reverted to their familiar position as owners of a safe
seat.

A different tack was pursued in 1924 at the General Election when Ludlow, a local working-class figure and Labour
councillor, lost his deposit and fell foul of middle-class
groups, like the teachers, over Labour's support for Russia.
J. L. Etty, a Ruskin College teacher, fought the seat in 1929
with a campaign which stressed that Labour was not a class
party, and which recommended international co-operation to
solve territorial and economic problems. But it was all rather
insipid and distant compared to the excitement of Gray's
campaigns, and there was little hope of the party effecting
any major change in allegiance. For Labour to do well in a
town like Oxford, attention had to be paid to both middle-
and working-class opinion.[37] Gray had been able to carry the
former, probably because of commitment to free trade,
while assiduously cultivating the latter. The Labour Party in
Oxford was not a socially isolated organization: while its
executive was essentially dominated by trade unionists, they
did not regard it as a purely working-class organization and
welcomed the involvement of those from the University and
Ruskin College.[38] Additionally, a branch of the I.L.P. was
formed in 1920 to engage political issues and people outside
the trade unions, with several of the key figures drawn from
Ruskin.[39] But by 1926 the Oxford I.L.P. was floundering,[40]
and although the Labour Party had some support within the
University, its position there was still weak, 'a raw and hostile

[36] Labour took 13.1 per cent of the Liberal loss, and the Conservatives only
3.9 per cent.
[37] Kinnear in *The British Voter*, p. 122, includes Oxford among the middle-
class constituencies in 1921.
[38] As W. Hyde, a member of the Workers' Union, commented in 1922: 'In the
Party were men and women of all social circles including Dr. Carlyle, Mr. J. L.
Stocks and the Vice-President of St. John's, the principal of Ruskin and Mrs.
Sanderson-Furniss. He had always considered that the accession of these persons
was a considerable service to the local Labour Movement.' *Oxford Chronicle*,
29 Sept. 1922.
[39] *Oxford Chronicle*, 26 Mar. 1920. A branch had been formed in 1905 but
it had ceased operating in 1910.
[40] *Oxford Times*, 5 Feb. 1926.

antithesis to the rich scholarship, the glowing mahogany, the shaded candles and the fine eighteenth century silver of the common room'.[41]

In the 1920s an interest among undergraduates in any dimension of politics was much less than it was to be in the later 1930s. According to Gaitskell, 'Politics, to tell the truth were rather at a discount', but there was no conscious effort by the Labour Party to change this: J. L. Etty, campaigning in 1929, refused undergraduate help for fear that it would damage his chances.[42] In the 1930s this was to change, and undergraduates trooped off to the Cowley housing estates to see the problems of an industrial working class.[43] As Osbert Lancaster has described it, 'Martinis and champagne had given way to sherry and beer', and Crossman as a political don became a more seriously regarded figure than he had been as an undergraduate.[44] But until local affairs could be placed firmly within a wider context (as they could in the later 1930s), for those in the University politics in the town was sandwiched between national and international concerns and the 'congenial underworld' of their own institution.[45] While Murray was an important figure in Oxford Liberalism,[46] his main concerns were with the League of Nations on the one hand, and the recherché calculations of University politics on the other. It is not surprising, therefore, that the main energy for political activity in the town came from outside the University. Before 1914, as we have seen, the move to Labour representation after 1906 was generated from within the working class, despite the earlier efforts of University and Ruskin members; and after 1918 the decisive change for the Liberals came from Gray, whose attitude to politics was rather different from that of Murray and Massie.

Other connections outside parliamentary politics were also less than wholly successful. G. D. H. Cole had taken up the

[41] G. Elton, *Among Others* (London, 1938), p. 173.

[42] P. H. Williams, *Hugh Gaitskell: a Political Biography* (London, 1979), p. 13. J. Parker, 'Oxford Politics in the 1920's', *Political Quarterly*, XLV(1974), esp. p. 216.

[43] Exell, 'Morris Motors in the 1930's', p. 53.

[44] O. Lancaster, *With an Eye to the Future* (London, 1967), p. 94.

[45] The phrase is Michael Bentley's, in *The Liberal Mind 1914–1929* (Cambridge, 1977), p. 172.

[46] Ibid., p. 176.

newly-created Readership in Economics in 1925 and attracted
a following of devoted students many of whom belonged to
the loosely-knit 'Cole group' which met in Holywell Street.[47]
This group was a survivor of the committee set up in Oxford
to help organize the General Strike, but it drew more on the
University and Ruskin than on the town. For Cole, Oxford
was never as attractive or interesting a base for political
activity as London: there were simply not enough people of
sufficient weight on the Left to make permanent residence
there worthwhile, hence the move to Hampstead in 1929.[48]

The main link Cole had with the local working class was
forged by extra-mural teaching, but this was not terribly
successful. In the 1920s Cole was much interested in working-
class education, seeing it as a crucial prerequisite for the
successful revival of the demand for workers' control.[49] He
taught economics in a University extension class, but found
his group 'hard going' and the students not very good; overtime amongst the printers diminished their attendance and
active trade unionists found that industrial matters robbed
them of the hours needed for study.[50] Cole also gave
economics classes for the W.E.A., but in the main they drew
in clerks (especially from the railways) rather than manual
workers.[51] The way in which adult education could shape the
culture of small numbers of often significant individuals
within the working class was not therefore much in evidence
in Oxford.[52]

In the late 1920s then, Cole was less typical of the Univer-
sity interest in the local working class than was L. R. Phelps,
Provost of Oriel, and chairman of the local Board of
Guardians. Phelps's concern with the casual poor was not

[47] The Cole group is discussed in M. Cole, *The Life of G. D. H. Cole*, ch. 14;
and in Parker, pp. 216 ff.

[48] M. Cole, p. 171.   [49] Wright, *G. D. H. Cole*, p. 144.

[50] Reports of Oxford University Extension Classes Tutorial Committee,
1927–8; 1928–9.

[51] The report for the Berks., Bucks., and Oxon. region for 1929 explained that
'The predominance of clerks over manual workers is largely attributable to the
considerable number who are in Oxford. This matter is deserving of some attention, because it seems to indicate a lack of success in attracting the industrial
worker in this area.'

[52] See S. Pollard, *A History of Labour in Sheffield* (Liverpool, 1959), p. 263,
for a town where it did fulfil this function.

simply an Oxford pursuit: he had been a member of the
Royal Commission on the Poor Law of 1909, and in 1929
chaired a departmental committee on the casual poor.[53]
But while Phelps could easily relate Oxford's problems to his
wider interests, it was more difficult for Cole to do so. Cole
was essentially concerned with labour in aggregate, and with
shifts in the national economy. In the conditions of the
1920s his outlook was less optimistic than Phelps's, the latter
being reasonably satisfied with the 'strong and sound committee' which he chaired in Oxford.[54] When Cole gave evidence before Phelps's committee of inquiry he

drew a gloomy picture of the future—he foresees a great increase in
unemployment and a general state of unrest. He himself has changed
his position amazingly: everything is now to be controlled not worked
by the State—such is the sum of his book on *The Next Ten Years*.[55]

But if Cole's interest in the working class did not assign a
strategic place to the traditional Oxford worker, he was none
the less very much alive to what was happening in the 'new'
industry areas, including Cowley. In this respect the different
views of Phelps and Cole no longer implied that one was
interested in Oxford and the other was not. Cole's book *The
Next Ten Years in British Economic and Social Policy*
(1929) had a chapter on the 'New Capitalism' for which he
used the motor industry as one of his immediate examples.
The techniques of assembly-line production, the use of
semi-skilled rather than skilled labour, the displacement of
craft unionism and of particular occupational identities were
all delineated with some accuracy if not originality. While
America provided the source for these developments, there
was evidence of them nearer home, even though the manner
of Cole's description does not suggest first-hand knowledge:
'We have no Mr. Ford, but we have Mr. Morris; and Cowley,
I *understand*, is not very different from Detroit on a smaller
scale.'[56]

Perhaps Cole's chapter begins the period when University
interest in Oxford was moving away from social service for

[53] Unfortunately the minutes of evidence taken by this committee have not
survived.
[54] Letter to Boyce, 15 July 1933, Phelps Papers.
[55] Letter to Boyce, 3 Apr. 1930, Phelps Papers.
[56] *The Next Ten Years* (London, 1929), p. 98 (emphasis added).

the poor towards the political cultivation of a more independent working class. For most of the 1920s however this
was still in the future, and the only case of a University
member trying to represent Labour electorally occurred at a
municipal election in the West ward in April 1923. Godfrey
Elton, fellow of The Queen's College, failed to win the ward
where Labour had its most realistic chance of success
(although it was never remotely a 'safe' seat). Elton's experience revealed quite plainly the difficulties of the party
locally: the doubtful allegiance of the working-class vote and
the problems of using effectively a sympathetic interest in
the University. The drink interest was more powerful than
Elton's programme for the provision of open spaces, public
works to relieve unemployment, and 'securing the best conditions for motherhood':

There were no meetings in the election campaign. I issued an eloquent
address and was introduced to a small gathering of supporters as 'a
member of an historic Oxford family' on the grounds, apparently, that
one of my grandfathers had been the last Rector of Carfax.
   My opponent was a publican who confined his activities to driving
around the district on polling day in an open car and fur coat. Needless
to say, he was elected.[57]

Labour had very little success in municipal elections in the
1920s:

Table 12. Municipal election results, 1919–27

	North	West	South	East
Conservatives	23	23	0	6
Liberals	4	2	27	21
Labour	0	2	0	0

Source: Oxford Times.

In comparison with the pre-war period, the Conservatives
had held on to the residential North ward, strengthened their
position in the West but given up the South and East to the
Liberals. As a local paper commented quite accurately in
1926: 'We are outside the main current of the fight between

[57] Elton, p. 163. Elton was defeated by 381 votes.

private enterprise and socialism and we can indulge in the harmless pastime of a boxing match between Liberals and Conservatives.'[58] After the fall of Frank Gray and the success of R. C. Bourne in parliamentary elections, the Conservatives tried to break into Liberal municipal successes. They saw their main obstacle in the South and East to be working-class Liberalism, organizing street campaigns in 1926 to try and erode this, and putting up a chimney-sweep in the South ward, whom they regarded as 'A Conservative working man in the best sense of the term'.[59] Through street meetings and smoking concerts local Conservatives urged on their audiences some familiar themes: the interdependence of capital and labour, the perversion of legitimate trade union functions by Soviet interference, and the futility of the Liberal position now that 'the alternative to a Conservative government was a Socialist one'.[60] The Conservatives derived no benefit from such campaigning, and even when there were complaints in the South ward of the lack of working men on the council this did not mean a break with Liberalism, but simply a gardener from Hinksey standing against a dentist.[61] When Labour campaigned in the East ward, it was conscious that old battles with working-class Liberalism still had to be fought, the most compelling argument in their campaign in 1930 being 'Follow Frank Gray's advice—vote Labour.'[62]

The success of the Liberals in the 1920s was quite remark-able in view of what was happening elsewhere, namely the almost continuous decline of Liberals in municipal elections. They lost a substantial number of seats in 1923-6, just when the Oxford Liberals were showing themselves resistant to Conservative attacks upon their working-class supporters.[63] Although the Liberals in Oxford remained important right up to the end of the 1920s, some of the vitality within ward

---

[58] *Oxford Times*, 5 Nov. 1926.

[59] *Oxford Times*, 24 Sept., 29 Oct. 1926.

[60] *Oxford Times*, 29 Jan., 26 Feb., 24 Sept. 1926.

[61] *Oxford Times*, 20 Mar. 1931.

[62] *Oxford Times*, 4 Apr. 1930. The Labour candidate was unsuccessful at this by-election.

[63] C. P. Cook, *The Age of Alignment: Electoral Politics in Britain 1922-29* (London, 1975), p. 67; and 'Liberals, Labour and Local Elections', in C. P. Cook and G. Peele (eds.), *The Politics of Re-appraisal 1918-39* (London, 1975), pp. 167, 169.

parties began to disappear when the parliamentary seat was lost. H. A. L. Fisher, Warden of New College, and one of the key figures in Oxford Liberalism, resigned the presidency of the Association in 1928 owing to other commitments. A year later its newspaper, the *Oxford Chronicle*, was merged with the *Oxford Times*, and in 1932 Fisher was reporting that the Association had failed to keep Liberalism going: 'It has not been successful in raising funds, or in appealing to the youth of the City.'[64] But this was in the future, when Labour began to exert some sort of influence on local alignments. In the 1920s there was still something to cheer about.

Within this rather uninspiring local context, of an essentially non-industrial town whose small working class was as much Liberal as Labour, the connections between the University and the working class were made as much over social problems as over politics. L. R. Phelps, who had been chairman of the management committee of the Charity Organization Society before 1914, was also chairman of the Board of Guardians in the 1920s. Unemployment in the city was not serious.[65] In the early 1920s it included the returning ex-soldier,[66] but by 1925 the winter unemployment of the building workers had come to dominate the pattern, although at 6.3 per cent of the work-force, at its worst, it was not striking. The Board of Guardians was as concerned as the C.O.S. had been to discourage indiscriminate giving to vagrants, but in the 1920s working-class leaders tended to be far more critical of those administering relief than they had been before 1914.[67] The unemployed themselves were no sort of threat to stability: local working-class leaders found them difficult to organize, lacking in any sense of cohesion, and always vulnerable to the key men in their organizations

[64] Letter of 21 June 1932, H. A. L. Fisher MSS, Bodleian Library, Box 29.
[65] In September 1923 the Unemployment Grants Committee of the central government did not think that the level of unemployment in the district warranted any assistance from its funds. Oxford City Council Unemployment Committee Report, 21 Sept. 1923.
[66] *Oxford Chronicle*, 23 Aug. 1923.
[67] F. Ludlow, Labour city councillor reported that 'on the Board of Guardians he had got some insight into the feelings of some of the people who waved the Union Jack and talked so loudly about the Empire. Unemployed men who applied for relief were often told they must "go into the house" and take their wives and families with them.' *Oxford Chronicle*, 28 June 1923.

leaving when they found work elsewhere. The occasional confrontations at the meetings of the Board of Guardians were
more ludicrous than dangerous.[68]

Housing was of more continuous interest in the 1920s than
unemployment but again there was little political advantage
to be gained from it. The pattern of ownership and cost
remained similar to that of the pre-1914 period: a large
number of landlords with very little owner-occupation, and
rents following pretty closely the hierarchy of earnings with
the engineers, printers, and railwaymen paying more than the
less skilled, irrespective of family size.[69]

Table 13. Working-class rents (averages)
by union membership, 1926

A.E.U.	11s.
Typographical Association	9s.
N.U.R.	8s.
Paper Workers	7s. 6d.
Workers' Union	5s.

Source: Trades Council, Council of Action
ledger of strike pay, 1926.

In the East ward, in St. Clements, where houses were
spacious and in good condition with little evidence of overcrowding, lived the college servants, shop salesmen, carpenters, and clerks; while the labourers, corporation workmen,
and casual labourers lived to the north of them, where housing
was poor, with lack of ventilation and shared sanitation.[70]

There was a housing shortage in 1919 of 802 houses,
needed to meet unsatisfied demand and to rehouse tenants
from substandard housing in St. Ebbe's, St. Aldates, and St.
Clements. By 1923 there were 1,600 applications for houses

[68] When a member of a deputation before the Board of Guardians claimed that
'revolution is brewing fast in Oxford', Phelps replied that 'I am quite sure that if
there is a revolution in Oxford the Guardians will not be responsible for it.'
Oxford Times, 7 Apr. 1922.

[69] In a group of working-class streets in the West ward, 4.6 per cent owned
their own houses, and in the South ward 2.9 per cent. Oxford City Rates Books
for 1921.

[70] Revd M. Bradyll Johnson, 'An Enquiry into Housing Conditions in the
Parish of St. Clements' (unpub. MS, Oxford City Library, 1924), vol. 1, pp. 82, 87.

on the council's list, including about 250 from those living
outside the city because of the shortage of adequate housing.[71] In the main houses for the working class were provided
by the council, but often rents were too high.[72] Although the
Addison Act of 1919 was generous in so far as central government met all expenses in excess of a penny rate, the Oxford
council was slow in getting its programme under way, and
when it did so met resistance from the Ministry of Health
which was beginning to find the Act expensive. The rents
of the houses built under the Act were still high for the less
skilled workers, ranging from 11s. to 14s. a week for a three-
bedroomed house, compared to the 7s. to 8s. 6d. a week
being paid in the 1920s for houses built before 1914 in the
South and East wards.[73] Even the Wheatley Act of the
Labour government which permitted council houses to be let
at lower rents did not prevent rehoused slum tenants from
taking in lodgers and perpetuating overcrowding.[74]

It was difficult for the Labour interest to turn the housing
question to good effect, and it tended to fight the battle with
the same arguments which had been used before 1914. The
Trades Council said that houses should not be built along the
Cowley Road (to the south-east where the population was expanding most rapidly), but in the west for the railway
workers and in the south for the labourers.[75] Not only did
this argument overlook the changing nature of population
growth in Oxford, but there was also little suitable building
land to the south and west. When the Labour Party organized
ward meetings on the housing question in 1925 it failed to
derive any benefit from them at the municipal elections in
November, losing its only councillor to a Conservative
in the West ward.[76]

[71] Oxford County Borough General Housing Scheme in records of Ministry
of Housing and Local Government, P.R.O. 48/174.
[72] In 1919-29 private builders were responsible for 436 houses compared to
1,556 built by the local authority.
[73] Commenting on the overcrowding in parts of the city, the Medical Officer
of Health remarked in 1922 that 'The new housing schemes have been of little
assistance in this respect, owing to the fact that the rents charged are beyond the
means of the poorer people.' Report for 1922 in Oxford City Library.
[74] MOH Report for 1925.
[75] Minutes of Housing and Town Planning Committee, 20 Oct. 1921.
[76] Trades Council minutes, 17 June, 1 July 1925.

Within the realm of conventional politics Labour leaders had very little scope, and their only other initiative was to set up in 1923 the Oxford Housing Guild 'to provide, improve, manage, let or sell houses for the working class' because of the 'shortage of houses and the slow rate at which new houses are being built'.[77] Run by trade unionists and financed by the Trades Council, it achieved very little, being wound up in 1925 because of loss of contracts and lack of capital.[78]

The Oxford working class had changed little from its Edwardian appearance. While the Labour Party had some active supporters in the trade unions, the working class for the most part was not deeply committed to the party. When politics meant something to the people of St. Ebbe's or St. Clements it was in the form of Frank Gray's populism, from a candidate who flung himself into the canvassing of the casual poor, and tried to experience at first hand life in the workhouse or on the road. The idea of identification with politics alone was not enough: Lindsay, the ex-president of the Union, was too distant to mean very much, and trade unionism was never strong enough to encourage people to turn towards the Labour Party. The wider issues affecting labour as a political force meant very little in Oxford at this time, since industrial growth at Cowley had hardly impinged upon the city. And so what mattered to the unskilled labourers was involvement in their life, rather than an effort to link them up with what was happening in the industrial society, which at that stage had little relevance for labour in Oxford. In that sense the apathy of which the local Labour Party leaders complained was as sensible a response as their own enthusiasm. Labour leaders from outside tended to mis-judge the local working class. When Walter Citrine and Marion Phillips visited Oxford in March 1925 they attracted only a small audience, and the meeting was transferred from the Town Hall to Ruskin College. Phillips admitted they were not doing much by way of organization in Oxford and then,

[77] *Oxford Times*, 25 Feb. 1925.
[78] According to the Receiver, 'it did not appear that the persons in this company were qualified by knowledge and experience to engage in the business of builders'. *Oxford Chronicle*, 2 Oct. 1925, *Oxford Times*, 25 Sept., 2 Oct. 1925.

perhaps by way of pique, added that she 'did not think Oxford workers had a sense of class; they did not like to think of themselves as a class, and they had not got the pride of workers, but had the feelings of the servants of the rich'.[79] This was wide of the mark, since there was no shortage of hostility to the rich; it was simply that the Labour Party was not an immediate beneficiary.[80]

In these difficult conditions all that the local Labour Party could hope for was to keep itself in existence, maintaining interest and raising funds by various social activities. In the West ward, where Labour had its only municipal success in the 1920s, this was always rather difficult. Usually only six or seven members turned up at meetings, and there were often not enough when officers had to be elected. Whist drives and dances at Ruskin brought in little money.[81] In the East ward there was more activity with a Labour orchestra, choir, and dramatic society in addition to the usual fund-raising gambits. But this vitality was deceptive, there always being some doubt as to whether it served any real purpose: 'Whilst we are in hearty agreement with these attractions however, we do feel that there is a real necessity for more efforts to be made to educate us in the principles of Labour politics.'[82] Efforts to establish a local Labour paper or to form a 'Daily Herald' committee also came to nothing.[83]

The Co-operative Society too could never be brought into a closer relationship with the Labour Movement. While some 'expected, as they had similar aims and similar objects, that they should work together [towards] a Co-operative Commonwealth',[84] with a much larger membership than the number of Labour supporters, these wider ambitions were

[79] *Oxford Times*, 26 Mar. 1925.

[80] At a college ball in the 1920s 'the young gentlemen in their white ties and flowered buttonholes had been jeered by rows of angry workers shouting "enjoy yourselves while you can, it won't last much longer"'. Williams, *Hugh Gaitskell* p. 17, citing of J. B. Orrick, a friend of Gaitskell's at Oxford.

[81] West Ward Labour Party Minute Book, 5 Dec. 1924, 11 Sept. 1925, 9 July 1929.

[82] *East Oxford Clarion*, Oct. 1928; *Oxford Times*, 21 Sept. 1928, 19 Jan 1929.

[83] *Oxford Chronicle*, 25 June 1924, 18 Apr. 1924.

[84] E. King in *Oxford Chronicle*, 19 Sept. 1919.

frustrated. Labour's nominees failed to get elected to the management committee.[85] Since a large number of the Oxford Society's members were Conservatives or Liberals, there was no wish to be integrated into the Labour Movement; on the contrary, it was argued that 'co-operation is the very antithesis of socialism . . . Now the co-operative idea is to make every man or woman a capitalist.'[86] At the Society's Jubilee in 1922, J. A. R. Marriott, the Conservative MP, had commented that 'If he thought the Co-operative Movement was a menace to the private trader, he would not have come.'[87]

The ambiguity in the identity of the Co-operative Society was therefore resolved in favour of the 'capitalist' rather than the 'socialist' interpretation. While in itself this was unsurprising, given the political views of its membership, it is worth noting the efforts of the local Labour leadership to change this, to give the Society a political definition, to use its funds for supporting strikers, to place its workers in a trade union. Here was a struggle over whether what was ostensibly a working-class organization should have that identity precisely defined in a political and industrial way, or not.

But there were aspects of life away from the more formal Labour Movement where the 'dilution' of political purpose was not seen as in any way threatening. Attempts to give fund-raising events an exclusively working-class character were resisted. When a committee raising money to build a Trades Hall invited the wife of the Liberal MP to give away the prizes at a fête it was pointed out that 'The Trades Hall movement was a working class movement, and in their endeavours they should have people at the head of affairs who were of the working class.'[88] This suggestion was overruled by one of the most influential of the working-class Labour group, who observed to its proposer that the fête was being held in grounds owned by a Conservative and yet 'I have no doubt that you will go as a supporter of the Socialist Party.'[89] Political attitudes were believed to be

---

[85] *Oxford Chronicle*, 5 Nov. 1920.   [86] *Oxford Times*, 3 Feb. 1933.
[87] *Oxford Chronicle*, 13 Oct. 1922.   [88] *Oxford Chronicle*, 21 July 1922.
[89] Ibid.

resistant to the possible implications of social patronage. But local Labour politicians had to recognize the non-political nature of social life: activities on the social side could not bring politics into areas where it might be unwelcome. When the party in east Oxford formed a dramatic society, it was careful to stress that the first play, by a Ruskin lecturer, 'was not a party play, and indeed, Mr. Schofield has not had anything to do with political propaganda of any kind'.[90]

Until the developing south-east was brought into the city, the Labour Party in Oxford was unlikely to improve upon its weak position. But since neither trade union organization nor industrial militancy followed inevitably from the location of the motor industry at Cowley, the precise way in which Labour voting followed on from economic change deserves to be more closely described, as does the changing relationship between the University, Ruskin, and the local working class.

[90] *Oxford Times*, 28 Sept. 1928.

7

THE LABOUR PARTY IN THE 1930s:
DONS AND WORKERS

The Labour Party nationally had gained considerable ground in the 1920s, doubling the number of seats it won between 1922 and 1929 (from 142 to 289), but Oxford was not the sort of town where it could have hoped to do well, either in municipal or parliamentary elections. The weakness of Labour locally was compounded by the débâcle of 1931, but in the years after 1934 the party became more important in local politics (through municipal elections) than it had been at any previous date. This improvement in the 1930s was based on two sources of political orientation. The first, on the local scene, was the growth of trade union membership and the problems of life on the new housing estates around which the Labour Party was able to construct a programme for municipal elections. The second lay in international affairs, and concerned the threat of Fascism and what course of action should be pursued in domestic politics to oppose it. This prompted interest in Popular Fronts of moderate left-wing groups which were intended to combine and defeat the national government.

These two movements tended to be the preoccupation of different groups in the Labour Party. Recruitment or attachment to the Labour Party via trade union membership or the housing estates concerned in the main the working class. By comparison, intellectuals from outside the working class took the leading role in the movement for a Popular Front, which, in the way it brought Liberals and Labour together, ran against traditional Labour loyalties and Labour Party policy. In this respect the two sources of orientation conflicted. In a town like Oxford, where the University was faced with a growing industrial sector, such a clash of interests would have struck with particular force. In turn, this posed the question of who ruled Oxford Labour politics, the

University members or the working class? Did the social changes on the periphery of Oxford carry all before them, or could the old city still dictate terms?

I. *The Labour Party and Municipal Elections*

The strength of local Labour Parties in the 1920s was heavily dependent on trade union branches. It is inconceivable that the Labour Party[1] could have been successful in Oxford in the 1920s because trade unions did not count for much in local society. This is to make no allowance either for the un-yielding pockets of working-class Liberalism with which the Labour leadership had to contend. But in the 1930s the fundamental changes in Oxford's economy had shown through in the widespread expansion of trade union member-ship, particularly among the general unions. This had been accompanied by noticeable changes in the temper of in-dustrial relations. In many cases, the trust which employers had been able to elicit from their workers in the small, intro-verted world of Oxford industry had been broken for ever.

The benefits of the technical changes in local government boundaries in 1928 had not been immediately grasped. Soon after the débâcle of 1931 the Labour Party organiza-tion in the two new south-eastern wards of Headington and Cowley ceased to operate. Before 1931 neither party had been deeply affected by the growth of the local motor in-dustry. Headington had received most support from the Ruskin College connection of Sam Smith and Frederick Smith, and the working-class element had been drawn from the building trades. At Cowley, a boilermaker employed on the railways, Harry Uzzell, and his wife Ruth, an organizer for the National Union of Agricultural Workers, had been responsible for the formation of the party in 1929, and its secretary had been a typewriter mechanic.[2] Among the small membership were carpenters, printers, and insurance sales-men. The membership lists of the Headington Party closed

[1] In this chapter 'City Labour Party' refers to the party which covered the four inner wards—North, South, East, and West—the Cowley and Headington Parties operating only in those wards. The term 'Labour Party' is used where no such differentiation is required.

[2] Interview with G. Currill, secretary of Cowley Labour Party 1929–30.

in 1930, and the only thread of continuity between its demise and its refounding in 1935 was an active women's section. The Cowley Party dissolved after the collapse of the Labour government in 1931, and did not run a candidate for the next three years; members simply stopped paying subscriptions.

There was little vitality either in the City Labour Party in the period 1929-33, and candidates were conscious that old battles with working-class Liberalism still had to be fought. In 1931 the Party did not put up a candidate for the General Election, and contested the West ward only at municipal elections; none were contested in 1932. One consequence of the lack of vitality in Labour's organization was the large number of uncontested elections in 1930-3; only eight out of a possible twenty-eight. In 1931 the Conservatives were able to propose a compromise with the Liberal Party to avoid contests in all wards, and in 1932 this was 'spoilt' only by two 'Progressives' standing in Cowley and Iffley.[3] The Conservatives had been more prepared than Labour for the growth of Cowley. Although Nuffield had turned down the offer of the Conservative candidacy in 1923, he was president of the Cowley Conservative Club, and one of his directors, S. G. K. Smallbone, was a vice-president.[4] The Conservative agent organized a series of smoking concerts, a familiar social activity of trade union branches, to increase support for the party.[5] Both he and Nuffield used political meetings to reiterate the benefits of protection for the motor industry. But the Conservative candidates in Cowley reflected the party's past not its present—they were connected either with the military or the Law—and it is doubtful too whether it was pre-empting Labour Party success by cultivating the working-class vote. The very low turn-out at elections— 15 per cent in 1930 and 21 per cent in 1932—suggests that Conservative campaigning had left many sectors of the electorate untouched.

By the early 1930s then, the material conditions of Oxford politics had begun to shed their pre-1914 inheritance. On the south-eastern fringe, where social investment lagged behind

---

[3] Oxford Conservative and Unionist Association minutes, 28 Sept. 1931.
[4] *Oxford Times*, 27 Feb. 1931.   [5] *Oxford Times*, 1 Feb. 1929.

industrial growth,[6] more favourable conditions were being created for labour, and the motor industry as an employer had begun to affect the market for labour in the city.[7] But political advantage could not be taken in any automatic way, and the task of reconstructing basic organization had yet to be tackled in 1933.

By 1935, after what was later described as 'a vacuum as far as political life was concerned',[8] both parties had been revived and had won seats during the municipal elections in November of that year. But the parties did not share a common relationship with the breakthrough in union organization achieved during the Pressed Steel strike of 1934. The Cowley Labour Party was much more of an offspring of this event than the Headington Party. The question of forming a Labour Party in Cowley was first raised late in 1934 by Emrys Williams, a migrant from South Wales.[9] It was taken up by Rowland Garrett and Harry Hamilton (who had both been on the Pressed Steel strike committee), and they became president and vice-president of the new party. A list of those present at the original meeting reads like a roll-call of the Pressed Steel strike committee: Mick Murphy, John Welsh, Harry Crooks, Dai Huish, and Emrys Williams.[10] Some continuity was maintained with the attendance of the leading members from the old Cowley Labour Party, but they did not provide the initiative for its revival. The key event had been the 1934 strike, which had brought together for the first time in Cowley those immigrants with some experience of the Labour Movement, and which was to serve as a point of reference for many later campaigns. The Cowley estates did not present particularly fertile soil for the Labour Party.

[6] In November 1930 a group of Cowley householders complained that: 'The roads and pavements are unsafe, filthy, and a great danger to all inhabitants. May we urge that immediate steps be taken to give us light, decent pathways and roads, before the winter is upon us.' Oxford Times, 7 Nov. 1930.

[7] See the comment of Provost Phelps, chairman of the Board of Guardians: 'I am beginning to get rather tired of providing at the expense of the taxpayer a reservoir of labour for Morris Motors and the Pressed Steel Co. to draw upon when they are pleased to work full-time.' Letter to Nicholson, 15 July 1933, Phelps Papers.

[8] Kathleen Lower, secretary of the Headington Labour Party, in the Gazette, June 1939.

[9] Interview with R. Garrett.   [10] Ibid.

Conditions were far from unsympathetic in that it was a one-class, one-industry suburb, but there were few internal links between tenants from which a sense of cohesion might have developed. The keenness of the strike committee at Pressed Steel to establish a local Labour Party was therefore crucial, particularly as the leadership of the old party had shown no signs of doing so.

No such direct connections with the Pressed Steel strike explain the revival of the Headington Party. Here the links with the past were more obvious. Sam Smith of Ruskin College had made several attempts to restart the party when he finally succeeded in setting up a provisional committee in January 1935.[11] Frederick Smith was another member of the old party who reappeared on this committee, filling the same post, as treasurer. C. F. Abbott and H. J. Franklin were other committee members who had been in the party in the 1920s.[12] In all, twenty-two of those who were among the eighty-eight members in 1935 had been members of the party between 1925 and 1929. Beyond the continuation of members, the occupational identity of the party officials shows how the party had emerged broadly unchanged in the 1930s. They came either from education (Ruskin, the W.E.A., and the University) or from well-established Oxford industries, in particular printing, building, and the railways. Comparing the officials of both the new parties, it was not simply that Headington was a more middle-class party than Cowley (though it did have a higher number of 'white-collar' members in its leadership), but that they were not drawn so exclusively from the motor industry. Of the Morris workers in 1936, 785 lived on the council estates in Marston, on the London Road in Headington, and in Iffley, and many did take up tenancies on the privately built Great Headley estate.[13] None of their number, however, figured among the leadership or sat on the parties' committees.

It would be wrong to write about developments in Oxford Labour politics solely in terms of the emergence of the Cowley and Headington Parties, for the changes of the 1930s

[11] Headington Labour Party Minute Book, 22 Jan. 1935.
[12] From H.L.P. membership lists 1924–38.
[13] Liepmann, *The Journey to Work*, p. 154.

also affected the older wards in the inner city. One way of showing this is to consider the candidates who stood for Labour in municipal elections in the period 1934-9. The 'new' forces operating in Oxford working-class society could express themselves in three associations: with one of the expanding general unions; with the Pressed Steel car factory; with the long-distance migrants from South Wales or the North of England.

Of the twenty-three Labour candidates who were put up, eleven showed some association with the forces of economic and industrial change, and their impact was not confined to Cowley and Headington. Eight working-class candidates representing the 'new' forces campaigned in the 'old' city wards, but there was little dramatic improvement on the position in the 1920s. Attempts to win the East ward, or to improve representation in the West, came to nothing; the only success lay in the South ward, where officials of the General and Municipal Workers' Union derived some benefit from their union's success in recruiting workers in the gas company or on the corporation.[14] This was the only new development. When these candidates tried their hand in Headington and Cowley they were more successful: Evan Roberts, who had failed to win a seat in the West ward, was successful in Cowley in 1937; and Lawson, who had made no impression on the East ward, was returned unopposed with Crossman for Headington in 1938.

In the Labour group of ten councillors which met in 1939 four were from manual occupations, and three of these were members of the N.U.R. Their predominance was not surprising: council meetings were held during the day, and it was particularly difficult for working-class councillors to attend meetings regularly if they could not make up their loss of earnings. W. Hawley, an electrician at Pressed Steel, received no financial support from his union, and did not stand for re-election in 1938 because of the damage done to his domestic finances.[15] Those councillors from the N.U.R. had their earnings made up by their union, hence their importance in the Labour group, and hence the persistent demand

---

[14] G. W. Clarkson in 1934 and W. J. Wiltshire in 1935.
[15] Interview with W. Hawley.

for council meetings to be held in the evenings. Those from the 'intellectual' Left, from Ruskin and the University in the main, could use their time more flexibly than most, and their contribution was important. University members were far more prominent in local Labour affairs than they had been in the 1920s. For that decade it has been possible to describe only the forlorn attempt of Godfrey Elton in the West ward; in the 1930s Richard Crossman, Frank Pakenham, and Patrick Gordon-Walker were more obviously to the fore.

This was not a complete break from the past, in the sense that, despite some prodding from a Marxist in Ruskin, the Oxford Labour Party had not regarded itself as socially exclusive, nor had it been opposed to having non-working-class members. Hand in hand with politics, the social investigation had continued, bearing fruit impressively, but incompletely, in the two-volume *Survey of Social Services in the Oxford District* (1938–40) whose production had been overseen by a committee working from Barnett House. This survey included very thorough treatment of the economic changes affecting Oxford since 1914, but inevitably the relationship of the authors to their subjects was more detached and academic, and the combination of investigation and service far less marked in the inter-war period, compared to the work of A. J. Carlyle and Miss Butler before 1914. Then members of the University had been faced with a relatively small working-class society, which they could understand and make contact with fairly easily, a prerequisite for successful voluntary work. In the 1930s the observers from the University were regarding a town which they saw as replicating the features of nineteenth-century growth. It was less amenable to charitable influence, partly because of size, partly because of intention: the Trades Council kept clear of the Oxford Council of Social Service when it was formed in 1933, and offered 'steady resistance to well-meaning but patronising persons in official positions whose "sympathy" not being prompted by knowledge or experience of working class conditions is sometimes obnoxious if not nauseating'.[16] Not only were there new aspirations towards full maintenance by

[16] Trades Council minutes, 22 June 1933; Trades Council Annual Report for 1931 in T.U.C. TC 79.

the state, which had taken over local relief of unemployment, but the growth of the motor industry had eased the problem of unemployment attached to a pool of unskilled, casual labour in the late nineteenth and early twentieth centuries.

To the extent that the declining influence of social service reflected a more independent core in the local working class, this affected the political relationship too. Before 1914 the University members had made all the running in the encouragement of a working-class Labour interest, and, initially, had received little encouragement.[17] By the 1930s the working-class element was inevitably stronger, and could even frustrate the intentions of the 'white-collar' membership. In 1938 Kathleen Lower, secretary of the Headington Labour Party, lost the candidacy for that ward when Lawson, the busmen's leader, packed the nomination meeting with his own supporters.[18] The changing balance between the middle-class Left and the local working class was caused to a great extent by the Labour Party's dependence for their success on the two new wards of Cowley and Headington, which is brought out by this summary of municipal election results:

Table 14. Results of contested elections, 1934–38

North	South	East	West	Headington	Cowley and Iffley	Summertown and Wolvercote
5 Cons.	7 Ind.	6 Cons.	8 Cons.	6 Lab.	6 Lab.	4 Cons.
1 Ind.	2 Lab.	2 Lib.	2 Lab.	3 Ind.	3 Cons.	2 Lib.
	1 Cons.			1 Cons.	1 Ind.	1 Ind.

Source: Oxford Mail.

Besides the Labour successes in Cowley and Headington, the other main development of the 1930s was the way in which the Liberals (who also fought as non-party Independents) lost out to the Conservatives in the 'old' city wards, with the exception of the South. This was to be expected: the Liberals had a lot to lose after their unusually successful period in Oxford in the 1920s, and the trend nationally was for the Liberals to give ground to both parties in the 1930s.[19]

[17] See above p. 20.   [18] Interview with Mrs Lower.
[19] Cook, 'Liberals, Labour and Local Elections', p. 67.

Cowley and Headington bore the brunt of the population increase, and as well as creating wards of safe Labour voters they harboured the problems of suburban development around which Labour councillors could formulate a coherent critique of council policy. Labour's opposition to the two other parties developed over the provision of services to the expanding south-east. The Conservatives and Liberals had established their place on the city council on the 'old' city wards which made up the wealthy and undemanding municipality. Growth was unequal: the number of children attending school in the newly developing eastern parts of Oxford increased very markedly, whereas in the older wards which supported Conservatives and Liberals numbers had remained much more stable.[20]

Education was only one area of need; in Headington and Cowley the whole social infrastructure had to be built for a growing population. As one writer put it in 1938: 'The bones of a modern urban community are its roads, its drains, its water mains, parks and open spaces; the most pressing problem of local finance is to find the means to insert them before, and not after, the flesh has grown.'[21] To provide adequate facilities and services demanded planning and expenditure beyond immediate needs. Oxford City Council was no longer governing a static, relatively small residential town whose inhabitants were not particularly demanding, but facing one which, through its fastest growing sector, was becoming a moderately-sized industrial one. If the industrial town is more expensive than the residential one, to face the transfer from one to the other is more costly still.[22]

It was the Labour Party's contention that the Conservative and Liberal councillors were unable and unwilling to meet the challenge of Oxford's growth. As Crossman put it, with reference to Headington, 'We are cast together as certain outlying areas which no one ought to trouble about', and he claimed that 'The Council, under the control of the Conservative-Liberals, paid no heed to the bitter experiences of the industrial north.'[23] Here was some overstatement of

[20] Barnett House, *Survey*, vol. 2, p. 7.
[21] R. F. Bretherton in Barnett House, *Survey*, vol. 1, p. 241.
[22] Ibid., pp. 214–5.
[23] In *Oxford Mail*, 5 Dec. 1935 and in *Labour Versus the Caucus* (Oxford, 1936), p. 4.

the case; spending on local services did increase markedly in the inter-war period compared to what it had been before the war (even in real terms). Expenditure increased four and a half times between 1913/14 and 1935/6, and capital expenditure by the later date was higher than in most county boroughs of a similar size.[24] The amounts spent on education, roads, and lighting increased fourfold. However, Oxford still remained one of the lowest-rated county boroughs; rates had been kept low by borrowing to finance capital projects instead of relying solely on income.

But while the council recognized obvious needs—for example, to provide infant schools on the new estates—there were still sufficient lags in the building of such institutions, still enough examples of piecemeal land purchase, or reluctance to take over services from private companies, for the Labour Party to base its policy on the need for more action at local government level in the outlying districts. In housing policy, for example, the council lost valuable building land by selling off from 1932 onwards land which it had bought in Headington.[25] With regard to electricity supply, this had been in the hands of a private company up to 1931 when the council exercised its right of purchase.[26] The council took in only the inner city wards (North, South, East, and West), and the supply of electricity to the growing fringe was still left under the control of the private company, whose prices and efficiency were far below that of the municipal enterprise.[27] It became part of the Labour campaign throughout the 1930s to get corporation ownership of electricity supply extended to these areas.[28] In 1936, Dr H. T. Gillett, the Liberal councillor for the South ward who had been involved in the original purchase of 1931, claimed that it was the key question in municipal politics.[29] The extension of municipal ownership was, however, not achieved before 1939.

Electricity was not the only issue arising from Oxford's growth. The Headington Labour Party began in 1935 by forming a subcommittee to survey the footpaths and roads

[24] *V.C.H. Oxfordshire*, vol. 4, p. 243.
[25] Oxford City Council Housing Committee Minute Book, 7 July 1932.
[26] Barnett House, *Survey*, vol. 1, pp. 365-7.   [27] Ibid.
[28] See *Labour Versus the Caucus*, p. 4.
[29] *Oxford Mail*, 26 Oct. 1936.

in the ward, and by complaining about the high bus fares charged to children over twelve.[30] When Crossman campaigned successfully for the ward for the first time in 1935, he did so on the need for more adequate footpaths and lighting, evening meetings of the council, and the extension of municipal electricity supply to take in Headington.[31] The Cowley and Iffley Labour Party complained about the lack of attention being given to the roads and footpaths on the Bullingdon and Rose Hill estates,[32] and the reluctance of the council to construct paths was heavily underlined by Pakenham in a Cowley and Iffley election in 1937.[33] In 1936 the Rose Hill estate had no school, community centre, or recreation ground, and the same was true of the Cutteslowe estate in the north of Oxford.

The differences between the parties were most clearly stated during the 1936 municipal elections. The Labour Party, with Crossman taking a prominent part, produced a five-point programme: the building of 500 working-class houses over the following two years, provision of public baths in the city, housing estates to be planned to incorporate schools and open places, evening meetings of the council, and aldermen to be elected on merit rather than by length of service.[34] In reply the Conservatives and Liberals proclaimed a pact against Labour, by which they were to pool resources and support each other's candidates in preference to Labour.[35] The formal pact merely showed that the two parties took Labour seriously, since they stopped short of the logical step of allocating wards between them to prevent a split in the vote. There were some grounds for this action, for by the middle of 1936 Labour had seven members on the council. Such an accretion of numbers never caused the *frisson* amongst the Oxford employing class that the Labour Party had done in Coventry. There were no signs of local businessmen entering council politics to counter the 'Socialist'

[30] H.L.P. Minute Book, 2 May 1935.
[31] *Oxford Mail*, 26 Oct. 1935.
[32] *Oxford Mail*, 17 Mar., 5 Apr. 1937.
[33] *Oxford Mail*, 29 Oct. 1936, letter of Evan Roberts.
[34] *Labour Versus the Caucus* and *Oxford Mail*, 22 Oct. 1936.
[35] *Oxford Mail*, 1 Oct. 1936.

threat,[36] and no alternative proposals to the Labour manifesto. Rather, it was claimed, politics had no place in municipal affairs, which were seen largely as problems of administration.[37]

The Labour Party councillors went to the trouble of organizing themselves as a group, both inside and outside the council chamber; but they were aware of the limited possibilities of action in local government, and of the way in which political affiliations were correspondingly less precise. According to Crossman, they did not believe that: 'The municipalization of transport, electricity, gas etc. is the introduction of socialism. We recognise that the job of the Labour Party in local government differs from its job in parliament, and that many who are with us in municipal policy may part company with us in national affairs.'[38] The Labour Party did succeed in bringing into its ranks some of those interested in social reform locally. A group of Independents used to meet in the mid-1930s to discuss proposals which later became part of Labour's policy, for example, the need for public baths in certain districts; but they had no sustained organization and their two leading members eventually joined the Labour Party.[39]

While the Labour Party had been able to put some pressure on existing political alignments, it would be wrong to overemphasize the increase in strength over the 1920s. Labour had not captured a ward in the inner city, although it took seats on both the West and South wards; its only solid base was on the developing fringe to the south-east. This was not sufficient to enable Labour to take the council by storm. In 1936, the Conservatives (30) and the Liberals (17) both had more councillors than Labour (12). This minority position was translated into weakness on most of the committees for much of the 1930s. The situation in 1937 was hardly

[36] The industrial interest was hardly represented on the council. From a sample of 168 councillors who sat between 1901 and 1938, 64 were retail traders, 26 were retired, 18 were professional men, 11 were builders and 7 were lawyers. Barnett House, *Survey*, vol. 1, p. 191.

[37] Alderman Bennett, Conservative, in *Oxford Mail*, 23 Oct. 1936.

[38] *Labour Versus the Caucus*, p. 11.

[39] Minute Book of the Independent group, 11 Jan. 1935, 17 July 1935. M. Yeatman joined the Labour Party in September 1937 and R. Gibbs one year later. *Oxford Mail*, 27 Sept. 1937, 10 Oct. 1938.

encouraging on those committees in which Labour was most interested. They had two members out of fourteen on the Education Committee, none on the Highways Committee, and only one on the Public Assistance Committee. In these cases the Labour Party acted as an external pressure group rather than exerting leverage from within. Most significant of all, since the argument of the Labour Party with the Liberal and Conservative Parties was about expenditure on services, Labour had only one representative on the Finance Committee in 1937. The influence of the Labour Party in such circumstances was inevitably limited. Crossman was unable to make any progress on the question of evening meetings,[40] and Smewin's proposal to give educational grants to deserving children over fourteen was also lost.[41]

It was not a case of complete ineffectiveness. At the very least the council was made aware of the need to provide more lampposts, public lavatories, and roads. Alliances with sympathetic non-Labour councillors could give committees a lead on certain problems. Smewin allied with G. W. Clarkson, to propose that the council return to its policy of building houses for the working class, over and above those required to deal with slum clearance.[42] This was accepted, and the council applied to the Ministry of Health to build 250 non-parlour, three-bedroomed houses to be let at not more than 10s. a week.[43] A proposal originating from a minority Labour interest had become declared Council policy. But this was deceptive, for the Labour Party was unable to intervene effectively in the housing market on behalf of the working class. The council's hands were tied by the attitude of central government: the Ministry of Health was adamant that local councils should not build to meet 'normal' working-class demand but devote their resources to relieving overcrowding, of which there was comparatively little in Oxford.[44]

[40] *Oxford Mail*, 6 Apr. 1936.
[41] Printed report of Oxford City Council meeting 20 Mar. 1939, p. 422.
[42] *Oxford Mail*, 4 Mar. 1935.
[43] Letter of Town Clerk to Minister, 15 Apr. 1935 in P.R.O. HLG 48/175.
[44] Letter to Town Clerk from Minister of Health, 20 May 1935 in P.R.O. HLG 48/175.

II. *Housing, the Working Class, and Political Parties*

In the 1920s the main responsibility for building houses for the working class had lain with the city council. In the 1930s central government policy directed local authorities to build houses to rehouse slum tenants (by the Act of 1930) and to relieve overcrowding (by the Act of 1935).[45] Just as Oxford's population was beginning to grow because of industrial development, the responsibility for meeting that 'normal' demand was shifted to private builders. In the 1930s, as a result, private enterprise made a much larger contribution to the housing stock than it had done in the 1920s: during the period 1930–7 it built 4,336 houses against the local authority's 944, whereas in the previous decade the figures had been 436 and 1,551 respectively.[46] The same story was repeated wherever population was growing with industrial expansion: in Luton, home of the Vauxhall Motor Company, the local council built only 196 houses compared to 7,174 by private builders during the boom in population during the 1930s.[47]

Reliance on private enterprise had two consequences as far as working-class housing was concerned; a large number of houses for sale, and high rents for those built for letting.[48] At the lower end of the market, that is houses below £13 in rateable value, the proportions nationally of houses built for sale and for letting were about equal.[49] This departure from past practice deserves some explanation. The crucial factor was the lending policy of building societies, rather than the fall in interest rates in 1932 (the conversion to 'cheap money'). The growth of privately built houses around Oxford's fringe was beginning to take shape in 1930, and houses were being offered for sale in Cowley in September 1931.[50] Building costs were already coming

---

[45] D. H. Aldcroft and H. W. Richardson, *Building in the British Economy Between the Wars* (London, 1968), pp. 179, 185.

[46] Barnett House, *Survey*, vol. 2, pp. 352, 341, 344, 353.

[47] E. D. Smithies, 'The Contrast between North and South in England 1918–39: Economic, Social and Political Problems with Special Reference to Burnley, Halifax, Luton and Ipswich' (Leeds Univ. Ph. D. thesis, 1974), p. 192.

[48] Aldcroft and Richardson, *Building*, p. 100.

[49] M. Bowley, *Housing and the State* (London, 1945), table xiv, p. 172.

[50] *Oxford Times*, 4 Sept. 1931.

down by 1930,[51] but the significant factor in opening up house purchase to the less well-off was the reduction in initial deposit required, from roughly 20 per cent to around 5 per cent.[52] This reduction in deposit was usually achieved by a builder providing security for advances made to the buyer beyond 80 per cent of the purchase price.[53] For the working man faced with the opportunity (or necessity, if rented accommodation was scarce) of home ownership, this made a considerable difference. Houses on the Cowley estates in Oxford were being sold at £695 freehold, and a deposit on a 95 per cent mortgage was £35 compared to £139 on a conventional mortgage. The building societies in Oxford did most of their business at the lower end of the market,[54] and home ownership by lower income groups was far higher than for the country as a whole. In the Ministry of Labour's survey of 1937 of the budgets of those earning not more than £250 a year, only 17.5 per cent owned their houses, compared with 46.7 per cent of a sample from the Cowley estates.[55]

Interpretation of this development is not straightforward. It is possible, for instance, that house ownership was suffered as a burden and not as a relief from paying rent. The Barnett House *Survey* noted that many of the new householders were car workers,[56] but according to the Sanitary Inspector for Oxford 'such a practice is to be deplored'.[57] A car worker earning between £5 and £6 during a busy week could easily meet the weekly repayment of 21s. on a £695 house in the early 1930s.[58] The difficulty came with irregular earnings; as the Barnett House *Survey* argued, house ownership for the motor car worker 'is attended with too great a risk, as prolonged ill-health, or unemployment, or an ever-increasing family, may prevent him fulfilling his obligations'.[59] Some

[51] Aldcroft and Richardson, *Building*, p. 203.
[52] Bowley, *Housing*, p. 175.
[53] Aldcroft and Richardson, *Building*, p. 205.
[54] Barnett House, *Survey*, vol. 2, p. 355.
[55] Ministry of Labour *Gazette*, Dec. 1940, p. 304. Figure for Cowley from a sample of 800 houses extracted from the city rate book for 1933. In the South ward of the 'old' city in the 1920s, only 2.9 per cent of the sample owned their houses. [56] Barnett House, *Survey*, vol. 2, p. 355.
[57] *Oxford Mail*, 11 Dec. 1937. [58] *Oxford Times*, 4 Sept. 1931.
[59] Barnett House, *Survey*, vol. 2, p. 355.

car workers may well have become unwilling owner-occupiers because the supply of housing by private builders left them little choice. The register of applications for council houses in 1937 contained several from roads exclusively peopled by owner-occupiers.[60] These applications were usually refused because of the high earnings of the applicants, but they do point to some dissatisfaction with house ownership.

Although the market for selling houses had widened considerably by the early 1930s, it was still a worthwhile investment to build houses to let. Costs were falling and returns on other investments were poor.[61] But this did not mean that private builders let houses at rents which the Cowley workers could easily afford. The rent considered suitable for working-class tenants by the Oxford City Council was 10s. a week for a three-bedroomed house, and the Political and Economic Planning Group used the same level in their report *Housing England*.[62] Rents paid by council tenants were less than 10s. a week, and much less than those paid by tenants of private landlords. While it can be said that all private tenants in the 1930s were paying 15s. a week or more for a three-bedroomed house, a similar council house in Cutteslowe in 1931 cost 6s. 8d., and in Headington 5s. 6d.[63] Oxford rents in the private sector were also high by national standards: the average rent in the Ministry of Labour survey was 10s. 7d.[64] They did, however, fall in line with those paid by workers in other 'new' industry towns; in Luton, for example, rents in 1937 ranged between 14s. and £1.[65]

The experience and responses of the private tenants were similar to those of the unwilling owner-occupier. They applied for council houses because they thought their rents were excessive, but usually failed because their earnings were too high in relation to the qualifying scale.[66] Again, the car

[60] Housing subcommittee on allocation of council houses, minutes, 9 Dec. 1937.

[61] Aldcroft and Richardson, *Building*, p. 102.

[62] Report of Housing Committee for February 1931, and *Housing England* (London, 1934), p. 8.

[63] P.R.O. HLG 49/1 086. See Appendix, Housing Committee minutes, 29 June 1934.

[64] Ministry of Labour *Gazette*, Dec. 1940, p. 304.

[65] Smithies, 'The Contrast', thesis cit., p. 144.

[66] Housing subcommittee on allocations, 15 Oct. 1936, 9 Dec. 1937.

worker probably accommodated a rent of one-fifth of his
income with some ease; the difficulty arose with short-time
working when, as one worker put it, 'their main worry was
to find £1 a week for rent'.[67]

The political implications of the housing market were not
in any specific way helpful to the Labour Party, even though
general grievances about housing might have been so. Clearly
the aggrieved house owner, perhaps anxious to move to a
council house, was not necessarily a 'rate-conscious voter'.
But as far as the tenant of a private landlord was concerned,
the Labour Party was not immediately helpful. Because the
council could not build extensively, it was difficult for the
Labour Party to present itself as an active agency through
which the working class could exercise some control over
housing. It could set out a programme for building houses for
the working class, even manage, from a minority position, to
get it adopted by the council, and yet because of central
government policy such houses would not be built. The
Labour Party could do nothing either to ease the problem of
high rents in the private sector, hence the growth of tenants'
associations in wards which were strongly Labour. In the context of Labour strength in these wards they might appear as
unnecessary appendages to the more mainstream working-
class organizations. But their role becomes understandable
once the marginality of the Labour Party to a housing
market dominated by private enterprise is recognized.

The tenants' associations grew up around the problems
of the rented sector, and they owed much of their organization to the local Communist Party. Through these associations the Communists were able to develop a political as
well as an industrial role in Oxford. There were two main
campaigns, in 1935 on the Florence Park estate in Cowley
and in 1939 on the Great Headley estate in Headington, both
aimed at reducing rents, though in the former case this was
linked closely to the poor quality of the houses.[68] Both
campaigns ended in failure, with tenants being taken to

[67] Daniel, 'The Movement of Labour', p. 174. The same complaint was made
by tenants in Luton, Smithies, 'The Contrast', thesis cit., p. 195.
[68] See the *Oxford Rent and Housing Scandal*, published by the Florence Park
Tenants' Committee; and Wogan Phillips, *The Englishman's Home: the Story of
the Struggle for Fair Rents on the Great Headley Estate* (Oxford, 1939).

court for refusal to pay rent,[69] but certain of their features deserve comment. They do show the connection between factory and estate, and not only in their rank and file, who were chiefly car workers. Many of the officials in both tenants' associations were trade union members at the car factories, and Tom Harris, a senior shop steward at Pressed Steel, spoke at many of the meetings of the Cowley association. Apart from the participation of the trade unionists, the members of the Communist Party were particularly active in Cowley, organizing meetings and distributing leaflets and so overcoming the paucity of social contacts on the estate.[70] The Communist Party also tried to give its protest some coherence, defining its attitude to the city council and drawing parallels with the Pressed Steel strike. A working-class city council would not solve everything, so the argument ran; the virtues of 'direct action', after the example of Pressed Steel, were obvious. In Headington much more of the basic organization was done by the Labour Party, Pakenham, Redvers Opie, and Crossman acting as trustees of the fund into which rents were paid.[71]

If in Cowley the Communist Party was particularly active in the campaign to lower rents, it was there also that it tried to develop its publicist's role in particular campaigns into a successful strategy for local elections.[72] Initially there was some support locally from the Labour Party for sharing the two seats in the ward with the Communist Party. The enthusiasm for a 'united front' was real enough after the summer of 1934, and at the Labour Party's annual conference at Southport, in October, F. J. Heath from Oxford moved a reference back (which was heavily defeated) on the

[69] Oxford City Labour Party, General Management Committee (hereafter O.C.L.P., G.M.C.) minutes, 15 Jan. 1936; *Oxford Mail*, 12 Aug. 1939.

[70] See Arthur Exell's essay on Florence Park, 1975, held by Ruskin College.

[71] The *Gazette*, July 1939, a short-lived newspaper produced by the Oxford Labour Party.

[72] Abe Lazarus, the most important of the Communitsts locally, was also involved in the Cutteslowe Walls dispute in north Oxford. The dispute concerned two walls built across roads running from a council estate through a private estate to join one of the main roads leading into Oxford. The owners of the private estate did not wish the council tenants to have access to the main road by going through their estate. However, the main pressure on working-class tenants in Oxford was exerted by the cost of housing not by efforts at residential segregation. See P. Collison, *The Cutteslowe Walls* (London, 1963).

rejection of overtures from the Communist Party and the
I.L.P. for a United Front. Heath reported of the Communists
that 'we have found them extremely anxious to find a
common basis for unity'.[73] Given the weak organization of
the Labour Party in Cowley, and its lack of money, there
were practical arguments in favour too.[74] It was not difficult
to draw up a common programme, but the leaders of the
Labour Party in Cowley (in contrast to those in the city)
became lukewarm, trying to end the agreement in 1935 and
1936.[75] While arguing that such an arrangement would harm
them in a General Election, they also resented the loss of a
safe Labour seat: they took both places on the council in
1935 and 1938, giving up one seat in the intervening years to
the unsuccessful Communist Party candidate.[76] Among the
Cowley Labour Party candidates and officials there was,
therefore, considerable resistance to any co-operation with
the Communists. Since the Cowley Party was regarded by the
City Party as essentially a ward committee without real
autonomy, there was little that could be done.[77]

Rank and file opinion is harder to evaluate. Some sympathy for the Communists is evident from the support of the
Pressed Steel branch of the T. & G.W.U. for the Communist
Party's application for affiliation to the Labour Party in
1936.[78] The Communist candidate Lazarus was only twenty-
one votes short of a seat in 1937, but since the Labour Party
had given him a clear run this indicates very real limits
to Communist Party strength.

To sum up: trade union growth had clearly provided a significant source of Labour voting in the south-eastern fringe,

[73] *Conference Report*, p. 137.
[74] O.C.L.P., G.M.C. minutes, 3 June 1935.
[75] They had a nine-point programme which included specific proposals on the
reduction in cost of private houses, cheaper electricity and more schools, as well
as general declarations about the need to bring more workers into trade unions.
O.C.L.P., G.M.C. minutes, 7 July 1935.
[76] O.C.L.P., G.M.C. minutes, 7 July 1935. The clearest example of a split vote
occurred in a by-election in December 1935:

Nelson	(Cons.)	1,104 (elected)
Hamilton	(Lab.)	748
Brown	(Com.)	453.

[77] O.C.L.P., G.M.C., minutes, 11 Dec. 1935.
[78] O.C.L.P., G.M.C. minutes, 19 Jan. 1936.

around the motor industry. It had done so to a much more limited extent in the southern part of the 'old' city where union membership had spread amongst the gas and corporation workers. The Labour Party had not been able to monopolize the political effects of social change, largely because of the opportunity presented to the Communist Party by a privately rented housing sector which prevented the Labour Party concerning itself directly with the provision of council housing. Even more so than in the industrial sector, the Communist Party failed to win any tangible results from the tactic of 'direct action'.

III. *Spain, the 'Intellectual' Left, and the 1938 By-Election*

There was a second source of political orientation in the 1930s, namely international affairs. The years when the University members of the Labour Party achieved some prominence in municipal affairs coincided with a period when politics in the wider world (the threat of Fascism) tended to distort conventional political alliances, and in Oxford this raised the key question about the relationship between left-wing political groups in the University and the newly-arrived supporters of Labour near the car factories. Those concerned about the threat of Fascism were also anxious to defeat the strongly entrenched national government whose foreign policy over Spain had come in for heavy criticism. The national government could not be trusted to rearm or to resist Hitler. But since the Labour Party alone could not achieve this, alliances with other parties or groups were justified if they brought a greater chance of success. Such a policy had obvious attractions in non-industrial constituencies like Oxford,[79] where Labour had no real hope of winning the seat by itself, and was pursued in October 1938 when there was a by-election, post-Munich, caused by the death of the city member, R. C. Bourne. In 1935 Bourne had easily defeated the Labour candidate, Patrick Gordon-Walker,

[79] The parliamentary constituency in the 1930s still excluded the new wards which contained the car factories and most of their work-force. However, most of the prominent members of the three Labour Parties contributed to the debates on the Popular Front, and so the political argument went beyond the confines of the constituency.

of Christ Church. Although the Liberals announced that they were going to run a candidate in 1938 (as they had not done in 1935), they agreed to withdraw if Gordon-Walker did the same, in favour of a non-party 'peace' candidate. Pakenham and Crossman both took this up and approached Lindsay, Master of Balliol, who agreed to stand.[80] Although Gordon-Walker and the national agent of the Labour Party were opposed to the withdrawal of the Labour candidate, the weight of opinion in the city party was in favour, and Lindsay ran as an Independent, losing to Quintin Hogg, but reducing his majority by just over 12 per cent.

Gordon-Walker claimed that the whole affair had been orchestrated by the University members, and that in its concentration on foreign policy it represented the indulgences of the well-off:

The whole thing was initiated in middle class and University circles. There has been no stint of money in a most lavish campaign. The programme of this Democratic Front to a large extent reflected the views of people who are rich enough to afford the luxury of ignoring everything except foreign policy.[81]

Lindsay's campaign certainly gave the impression that the University had 'run away' with the City Labour Party. Lindsay himself was not a convincing candidate outside University circles, since 'over half the Oxford electorate didn't know Lindsay from Adam'. Fellow dons who talked with reverence about 'The Master' were regarded with incomprehension.[82]

If Lindsay was an improbable candidate (even though a member of the Labour Party and W.E.A. lecturer) it was clear that the middle-class members of the Labour Party believed that foreign affairs should dictate what action was taken locally. As G. D. H. Cole argued, 'In the tremendous emergency created by Munich we felt it imperative that there should be a solid opposition demonstration against the Government'; and according to the secretary of the

[80] *Oxford Mail*, 2–3 Sept. 1938; and see also I. McLean, 'Oxford and Bridgwater', in C. P. Cook and J. Ramsden (eds.), *By-Elections in British Politics* (London, 1973), pp. 146 ff.
[81] *Oxford Mail*, 28 Oct. 1938. See also his comments in the *New Statesman*, 5 Nov. 1938.
[82] *Picture Post*, 5 Nov. 1938.

Headington Party 'for the immediate future the problems of the international situation override and condition all matters of domestic policy'.[83] It was from this analysis that the Oxford Labour Party recommended the Labour candidate to withdraw from the Aylesbury by-election, to give the Liberals a better chance of defeating the Conservative candidate, an action which the national agent thought 'not the sort of thing to be done by an affiliated organisation of the Labour Party in its fight against capitalism'.[84]

It was also true that some of the key figures in the by-election campaign for Lindsay did not see the Labour Party as a purely working-class organization. Pakenham had only recently joined the party, becoming a member after Mosley had held a meeting for the B.U.F. at Oxford Town Hall on 25 May 1936. This was a disorderly affair, with speakers from the floor being roughly handled by Mosley's stewards, and Pakenham himself being injured.[85] He had not therefore joined the party out of sympathy with the problems which the working class was facing in the developing areas of Oxford, or out of the conviction that through the Labour Party an egalitarian social policy might be achieved. He joined the Labour Party primarily as a reaction to Mosley's Fascism which also appeared to be linked with developments abroad. It is not surprising that Pakenham believed that the policies of the Labour Party should not be defined solely by the interests of the working class. At a meeting of the Didcot W.E.A. he claimed that there had been a gradual shift in social structure from the working to the middle class. This, for Pakenham, invalidated any Marxist assumptions about the increasing poverty of the working class and, 'it raises the question of whether a working class party can ever get a clear majority in England, or whether it will not take in other elements and tend to move to the Right'.[86]

Pakenham was not alone in this view: Crossman, for example, believed that the Labour Party would never succeed in gaining power unless it abandoned its narrow appeal to

[83] *New Statesman*, 12 Nov. 1938; *Oxford Mail*, 7 Apr. 1938.
[84] Letter of G. Shepherd to secretary of Oxford City Labour Party, 9 June 1938.
[85] *Oxford Mail*, 26 May 1936; Pakenham, *Born to Believe*, p. 83.
[86] *Oxford Mail*, 12 Feb. 1936.

the working class.[87] But Crossman was far less willing than Pakenham to pursue the implications of a moderate, 'classless' view of the Labour Party towards co-operation with those outside it. While Pakenham had supported the running of a 'Progressive' Liberal candidate in a municipal election in the East ward in 1937,[88] Crossman was more qualified in his support for Lindsay. He seems to have followed Cole's view that a Lib–Lab pact which drew on Communist Party support was worth while for a by-election which was essentially a demonstration of opinion. Any national agreements would lose Labour electoral support; loyalty to the Labour Party was more important than alliances with those on the Left of the party.[89] But even these limited concessions to a Popular Front were not entered into lightly or without cost. When the Lib–Lab agreement was being discussed in October 1938 it was suggested by R. F. Harrod, the Christ Church economist, that Labour would have to give up specific policies, such as the nationalization of land and of the Bank of England.[90] So Gordon-Walker's view that the Popular Front represented the maverick behaviour of intellectuals had some substance. The moves for such an alliance had originated from the University, not from Cowley, from people whose perspective was essentially international. They ran right against Labour Party policy that the Labour Movement was sufficiently representative to meet all emergencies facing the Left. To the extent that the Labour Party's working-class strength derived from 'an implicit consciousness that the Labour Party stood for them in a way which no other party did',[91] indulgence with 'broad left' alliances which seemed

[87] *Oxford Mail*, 18 May 1935.

[88] The candidate was Miss Honor Balfour. See O.C.L.P., Executive Committee minutes, 29 Apr. 1937; G.M.C. minutes, 13 May, 24 May 1937. She was defeated by a Conservative.

[89] Crossman expressed these views when the question was raised of Gordon-Walker signing the Unity Manifesto, which had been issued by Stafford Cripps (Labour Party), James Maxton (I.L.P.), and Harry Pollitt (Communist Party) and which recommended closer links between the three groups. See O.C.L.P., G.M.C. minutes, 18 Feb. 1937. For Crossman's views at the time of the by-election see R. Eatwell, 'The Labour Party and the Popular Front Movement in Britain in the 1930's' (Oxford Univ. D. Phil. thesis, 1975), p. 250.

[90] *Oxford Mail*, 10 Oct. 1938.

[91] R. McKibbin, *The Evolution of the Labour Party 1910–1924* (Oxford, 1975), p. 243.

to involve, at least ultimately, some specific sacrifices by Labour, seemed to threaten local unity and the mobilization which had been achieved as a result of trade union growth in the motor industry. Put crudely, was there, as Gordon-Walker had suggested, a working-class view of politics concerned with social policy and class loyalty, and a middle-class perspective which took its orientation from a national or international framework, and which had little time for a view of the Labour Party as a mainly working-class organization? Were there essentially two areas of local politics, operating at different levels, which in turn rested on different social backgrounds?

This distinction, drawn by Gordon-Walker, was more apparent than real. One difficulty for an analysis which tried to explain everything in terms of middle/working class, 'intellectual'/trade union dichotomies was the solid voting in favour of withdrawing Gordon-Walker,[92] who was also defeated by Pakenham 43-11 for the parliamentary candidacy after the by-election.[93] But this was not a party with which the University members could do as they pleased: in 1936, Gordon-Walker was defeated in the contest for the chairmanship of the party by F. Jackson, the busmen's leader.[94] The committees and activities connected with international affairs were never purely middle-class or University dominated affairs: the Oxford Spanish Democratic Defence Committee had representatives from Pressed Steel as well as from the City Labour Party.[95]

Concern about international affairs was not confined to Spain. The signatories of a letter published in December 1937 demanding a boycott on Japanese goods because of that country's aggression towards China read like a roll-call of the local trade union leadership.[96] Hitler's invasion of Austria in March 1938 prompted a meeting between the Labour

[92] Resolutions were carried 46-12 and 109-34. O.C.L.P., G.M.C. minutes, 15 Oct. 1938; N.E.C. by-election report, 26 Oct. 1938.
[93] O.C.L.P., G.M.C. minutes, 20 Jan. 1939.
[94] O.C.L.P., G.M.C. minutes, 27 May 1936.
[95] *Oxford Mail*, 17 Aug. 1936.
[96] They were Gomm (Trades Council secretary), Loynd and Lawson (T. & G.W.U.), Richardson and Wiltshire (N.U.G. & M.W.), and Foster, Smewin, and Roberts (all N.U.R.). *Oxford Mail*, 16 Dec. 1937.

Party and the Trades Council which set up a Co-ordinating Committee for Peace and Democracy 'to embrace all working class and progressive organisations prepared to work for the downfall of the Chamberlain Government'.[97] This committee was particularly active, holding ward meetings and a May Day procession which included Communists, Liberals, trade unionists, and Labour Party supporters.[98] Harrod's proposals[99] for a Lib–Lab alliance at the time of the 1938 by-election received the support of three leading trade unionists who were on the Left rather than the Right of the Labour Party.[100] In short, there is no evidence of any marked divergence in view between the University members and the working-class leaders on the advisability of a Lib–Lab agreement at local level, in part at least because of the active agency of Lazarus and the Communist Party. The views of the leadership locally were echoed by the voters. By and large, Lindsay received the support of the working class and there appears to have been a temporary increase in membership and ward activity.[101] The main opposition to such Popular Fronts tended to come from those who saw their main loyalties as lying with the Labour movement nationally rather than locally; Jack Thomas, district secretary of the T. & G.W.U., was one of those who had opposed Lindsay's candidature, and he was subsequently excluded from a committee set up in 1939 on the organization of the local party.[102]

Much of the change in balance between middle and working class in Labour politics had of course remained internal to the Left, in the sense that the increasing vote for the party had not made a great deal of difference to the way the city was run. The changes in city finance caused by suburban growth were not a direct product of Labour's new political strength, simply because its councillors were never in a majority. However, within the Left, Oxford politics could now be integrated into a political life with

[97] O.C.L.P., G.M.C. minutes, 13 Mar. 1938.
[98] *Oxford Mail*, 2 May 1938.   [99] See above p. 173.
[100] E. Roberts and C. Bowles (N.U.R.), and W. Lawson (T. & G.W.U.).
[101] McLean, 'Oxford and Bridgwater', p. 156; O.C.L.P., AGM minutes, 2 Mar. 1939.
[102] O.C.L.P., G.M.C. minutes, 22 June 1939.

a national perspective in a way that had not been true in the 1920s or before 1914. Yet this did not mark the arrival of political activism amongst the working class outside the small group of their leaders who have been the subject of the foregoing pages. Whilst it was true enough that the busmen could be brought out to challenge Mosley at Oxford Town Hall, there is little sign that the party counted for much in working-class lives beyond the ballot box. May Day celebrations were poorly attended, and a local newspaper, the *Gazette*, attracted little interest.[103] While the Headington and Cowley parties had more members in the 1930s than in the 1920s, 'the satisfactory increase in party membership has not unfortunately been accompanied by a corresponding growth in activity; it might in fairness be said that activity had actually declined'.[104]

In the 1920s there had been efforts 'to cultivate the social side of things', but it was only late in the 1930s that the Labour interest realized that it had to come to grips with sport. A branch of the British Workers' Sports Association was established in 1937 'because it was felt that it would be a great advantage if sport could be organised inside the Labour Movement in its broadest sense'.[105] In the 1930s most working-class sport in Oxford was organized at work. The corporation, the gas works, the electricity company, the Clarendon Press, the bus company, in addition to the car factories, all had their sports clubs.[106] Such aspects of 'the human touch' in management were much in vogue in the inter-war period.[107] They had obviously not impeded the spread of union organization, but in Oxford, as elsewhere, they had prevented Labour from using sport as an entrée to an ulterior purpose. The reliance on municipal elections to arouse enthusiasm was correspondingly greater. Even then it

[103] O.C.L.P., G.M.C. minutes, 13 May 1937, 31 Mar. 1938, 22 June 1939. Few copies of the *Gazette* have survived, and even fewer memories of it.

[104] H.L.P. Minute Book, 5 Sept. 1938.

[105] *Oxford Mail*, 24 May 1937.

[106] *Oxford Chronicle*, 28 July 1922 (gas workers), 25 Aug. 1922 (corporation), 21 Oct. 1926 (Clarendon Press).

[107] For a representative example see 'Human Problems of Management', *Works Manager*, Mar. 1938. A report of a sports meeting for the employees of the Oxford Electricity Co. was headed 'Cementing Relations between Employers and Employees', *Oxford Times*, 17 May 1929.

was not terribly impressive, at best between 30 and 40 per
cent of all possible votes were cast.[108] In north Oxford it was
reported that outside municipal elections 'it is practically
impossible to make these people take an active interest in the
Party'.[109] When the secretary of the Headington Party wrote
to Transport House about the electoral truce which was
called in 1940, its predicament was described with some
force:

We wonder if you fully appreciate the difficulty we have in maintaining interest in the Party and the necessary financial support. Under
existing circumstances [the electoral truce] the voter cannot see the
Labour Party either as an effective opposition or as an alternative
government, because it does not fight elections which give the opportunity for propaganda and securing an expression of popular opinion.[110]

Beyond the local 'Movement', therefore, lay a working class
without the internal ties of the railwaymen who had sustained
the party in the West ward in the much bleaker days of the
1920s. The car workers of the 1930s were not yet an occupational group, but still best described as ex-miners, building
workers, tradesmen, or agricultural labourers. By the time
they had become so, political life no longer seemed to
bear the imprints of industrial identities in the way that it
once had.

[108] Barnett House, *Survey*, vol. 1, p. 198.
[109] O.C.L.P., organizing secretary's report for 1939.
[110] Letter to J. Middleton of Transport House, 20 Feb. 1940, in H.L.P. records.

8

THE SECOND WORLD WAR AND BEYOND

In the Second World War organization from above replaced agitation from below as the main source of union growth. Before 1934, as the preceding chapters have shown, it was very difficult for unions to make much headway in organizing the semi-skilled, and even where the shop-floor asserted itself against hostile employers, as at Pressed Steel, it had been subdued by the end of the 1930s. The cyclical downturn in the economy in 1937–8 had underlined the instability of employment in the motor industry which had made union organization so difficult. Wartime conditions not only improved the supply position of labour—in making it more scarce—but also elevated the status of trade unions whose officials became intimately involved in the direction of labour under Ernest Bevin, as Minister of Labour and National Service.[1] Specific legislation helped too: the Essential Works Order of 1941 which aimed to prevent skilled labour searching for its highest price also provided reciprocal benefits by restricting management's right of dismissal, and establishing minimum standards of pay and conditions. 'Skill' was interpreted as much by economic necessity as by more traditional criteria; those having familiarity with important tasks tended to be classified as 'skilled' even though their lack of all-round engineering capability did not warrant this.[2] The vulnerability of shop stewards, so transparent and limiting before 1939, was to some extent reversed.

The stronger position of labour was shown by the way in which several car plants where management had successfully resisted unionization ceased to do so during the war, and joined the E.A.E.F. as part of recognizing trade unions;

[1] H. Pelling, *A History of British Trade Unionism* (Harmondsworth, 2nd edn., 1971), p. 243.
[2] Ibid., pp. 214 ff. See A. Exell, 'Morris Motors in the 1940's', *History Workshop Journal*, 9 (1980), 90, for such definitions of skill in wartime.

Morris Motors, Ford's, and Vauxhall were the most important. The chief purpose from the union side was not usually
to improve the welfare or conditions of the workers—which
were not any worse and were usually better in the non-
federated firms[3]—but simply to establish negotiating procedures to secure their own position. To employers the union
officials offered the possibility of orderly industrial relations;
as Deakin of the T. & G.W.U. pointed out to Ford's when
negotiating over union recognition in 1944,

After considerable strife and disturbance in that industry [tyre manu-
facture] one employer after another had come into line with the
established custom and practice and the result now was that relationships within the industry were good and amicable and industrial disturbance had been reduced to a minimum.[4]

Ford's had been brought to the conference table in stages.
The first stage was in 1941 with the holding of a Court of
Inquiry into a dispute at the Briggs factory which supplied
bodies for Ford's, which led to agreements on procedures for
the avoidance of disputes. Ford's refused to follow this
example, but suffered an occupation of the manager's office
wihich was ended only when Feather arrived and calmed
the situation by discussing cricket.[5] Meetings between Citrine
and Perry of Ford's eventually led to a conference in 1944.
The main anxiety on the company side was that minor
officials could not control the shop stewards, although as
Feather remarked, 'even from a union's point of view the
suggestion of Ford's that there might need to be stricter
control over shop stewards may not be unhelpful'. Some of
the stewards Feather found difficult: 'Every issue they raise
is a political one, or inspired by political motives, and they
appear satisfied not to get things put right, but to be able to
point to further inequities of Ford's.' In other words they
were Communists, impatient with the traditional distinction

---

[3] When Morris Motors applied to join the Engineering and Allied Employers'
Federation problems were envisaged because the firm worked a forty-four-hour
rather than a forty-seven-hour week; it was thought that this might prove
'a dangerous precedent'. The firm was admitted none the less to the Federation.
Meeting of the Management Board, 29 July 1943.

[4] T.U.C. file on Dagenham, T 602 57.4.

[5] Ibid. Unless otherwise stated, the evidence for what went on at Dagenham
is drawn from these papers in the T.U.C. organization department.

between industry and politics widespread in the Labour Movement. Ford's was also wary of popularly-elected district officials (like those of the A.E.U. but not the T. & G.W.U.) who shared the political outlook of such shop stewards: workers wanted national officials, preferably the general secretary, to 'vet' shop stewards. They were also anxious to maintain the mobility of labour around the shop-floor, and again the T.U.C. supported them in this. In sum, the T.U.C. did nothing to support shop-floor organization which would in turn have impeded the firm's productivity.

The only way in which the negotiations can be said to have had this result was as an unintended consequence of including a large number of unions—eleven in all—in the 1944 agreement. Not all of these unions catered for the same groups of workers, but some did, and competition between unions through the efforts of one to surpass pay deals struck by the other clearly had damaging results for industrial performance in the 1950s and 1960s. This was probably a result of union recognition derived from above, or from the centre, which gave more weight to the claims of each union to be included in the final agreement than the much more haphazard conditions of union growth in the 1930s had done. At Pressed Steel before the Second World War unions had to win members how they could, with no support from management, and relying heavily on the shop-floor. This tended to favour the strong against the weak, and to reflect very sharply the ambitions of the T. & G.W.U. to recruit semi-skilled industrial workers, and the reluctance of the A.E.U. and N.U.V.B. to 'dilute' their membership by turning themselves into 'industrial' unions. The belated efforts of the N.U.V.B. to increase its membership met with firm resistance from the T. & G.W.U.[6] The T. & G.W.U. had a clear field amongst production workers at Pressed Steel; in the post-war period when industrial relations there were more peaceable than at Morris's, one of the main causes of volatility at the

[6] Bevin was unwilling even to concede some demarcation between the two unions on the basis of skill—as he noted on Deakin's report proposing such a division: 'In view of all these unions becoming general unions I have great doubts about this proposal.' Notes of a conference between N.U.V.B. and T. & G.W.U. at Transport House, 3 Apr. 1939.

latter was held to be competitive piece-work bargaining between unions.[7] Not all car firms negotiated with unions in quite the distant manner adopted by Ford's; Vauxhall's agreements embraced the shop-floor more positively, and in this respect gave shop stewards less ground for grievance.[8] But how did the wartime conditions affect the variable state of industrial relations in Oxford? The upsetting of labour supply as factories changed over to wartime production and men were called up had the potential for disrupting existing shop-floor organization or spoiling tentative efforts being made in that direction. At the outbreak of the war there was considerable unemployment, accounting for virtually the entire labour force at the two car factories, and even when demand picked up there were complaints at Pressed Steel that preference was being shown to women and to new workers, rather than to the old guard.[9] The same effect, if not the same intention, was evident at Morris's; a small branch of the T. & G.W.U., about fifty strong, had been started there in 1938 (although not recognized by the firm), but it fell apart at the beginning of the war with the call-up of key individuals.[10] But there were gains as well as losses; labour moving from east London to the aircraft repair factory run by Morris's included committed trade unionists who formed the nucleus of organization. The same was true at the radiator factory in north Oxford where some sheet metal workers had arrived from the railway workshops at Wolverton who insisted on retaining union membership and levels of pay. This demand, which could be sustained given their relative security, in addition to their earning more than non-trade unionists, helped to win over many of the other workers to the virtues of union membership.[11] The use of individual piece-work systems, which inhibited the development of any sort of collective view, and the effects of relatively high pay on a labour force

[7] Interview with Jack Thomas, T. & G.W.U. district secretary. See also H. A. Turner, G. Clack, and G. Roberts, *Labour Relations in the Motor Industry* (London, 1967), p. 350.

[8] Turner, Clack, and Roberts, p. 194.

[9] Trades Council minutes, 16 Nov. 1939, 22 Feb. 1940.

[10] Interview with Jack Thomas.

[11] Exell, 'Morris Motors in the 1940's', pp. 91-3.

recruited in the main from the locality, had both proved an obstacle to the recruitment of union members in the 1930s. Then the few committed trade unionists had had little effect on the rest; for one thing they had appeared to be all too vulnerable to dismissal. In wartime, with jobs more secure through legislation, the position was quite different. At the other Morris factories legislation played its part; efforts to get rid of trade unionists at the MG car factory in Abingdon, which in the 1930s had been successful, fell foul of the Essential Works Order when they were repeated in 1941.[12] More positively, certain regulations governing fire-watching relied upon the representation of workers through trade unions, which provided a useful incentive for gaining such representation where none had existed before, and was exploited to good effect in the radiator factory in north Oxford.[13] This was the prelude to the granting of union recognition and the formation of an A.E.U. branch for that factory.

The war was not only a period which presented unusual opportunities for recruiting unorganized workers into trade unions, but also one which the Communist Party tried to exploit to yoke together industrial and political perspectives. In the 1930s party members themselves often had an essentially industrial perspective. At the very least, the alliances across the Left supported in their political strategy did not follow in any obvious way from a more class-conscious industrial outlook. During the war the Communist line changed sharply in July 1941 when Germany invaded the Soviet Union; instead of denouncing the imperialist war, support was now to be given to the Red Army as part of the general war effort. Industrially this meant no stinting of effort; the Communist Party group at the radiator factory insisted on 'no interruption of production or transport under any circumstances'.[14] This did not simply mean the acceptance of existing industrial power since, as Dr Hinton has argued, 'they sought to channel working class feeling and

[12] *Oxford Mail*, 10 June 1941; southern region Conciliation Officer's report, 17 May 1941, P.R.O. LAB 10/383.

[13] Interview with Norman Brown.

[14] *The Communist Party (Morris Radiators Group)*, by Norman Brown (n.d. [1944]), p. 2.

initiative into an offensive against managerial power—but one designed to increase rather than to restrict production'.[15]

The newly-organized workers at the radiator factory joined the A.E.U. which during the war acted on its intention expressed much earlier to recruit semi-skilled workers. The A.E.U. was also regarded as more politically sympathetic than the T. & G.W.U. by the local Communist shop stewards.[16] From 1941 onwards the emphasis was very much on shop stewards in the local factories working to improve production; conferences were held by the Trades Council,[17] some stewards formed 'shock brigades' to alleviate any immediate problems,[18] and Joint Production Committees were set up at the radiator factory and at Pressed Steel.[19] Those who were not keen on the intensive labour required were left with no one to represent them,[20] the only solution being the absenteeism with which the J.P.C.'s had to grapple.[21] The achievements of these committees in encroaching on managerial discretion were probably little comfort while the promise to raise women's wages commensurately with those of the men remained unfulfilled.

The efforts to develop a political perspective out of this industrial activism, which had been made before 1939, were if anything intensified during the war. The fifty or so members of the party at the radiator factory held discussion groups, ran a library, as well as an 'unofficial' bookshop.[22] Several of the Communist Party shop stewards wre also members of the Labour Party, although the latter was facing the considerable problems it had anticipated it might during the electoral truce.[23] As Hinton has put it, 'Part of the reason for the decline of Labour Party membership was

[15] J. Hinton, 'Coventry Communism: a Study of Factory Politics in the Second World War', *History Workshop Journal*, 9 (1980), 97–8.

[16] In 1946 the radiator branch of the A.E.U. supported the affiliation of the Communist Party to the Labour Party.

[17] Trades Council minutes, 21 Aug. 1941.

[18] Exell, 'Morris Motors in the 1940's', p. 96.

[19] Interview with Norman Brown; Trades Council minutes, 15 May 1942.

[20] As Dr Pelling has suggested, this might well have been a factor diminishing the number of disputes during the war; see *Trade Unionism*, p. 215.

[21] Exell, 'Morris Motors in the 1920's', pp. 94–5.

[22] Interview with Norman Brown; Exell, 'Morris Motors in the 1920's', p. 98.

[23] See above p. 177.

the leadership's inability to find anything for the member-ship to do.'[24] In Oxford the ward parties ran down, after a reasonable level of activity had been reached at the end of the 1930s, though this might well have reflected the excite-ment generated by the 1938 by-election. By February 1940 ward parties were finding it difficult to maintain their activities, and by 1941 they had been further depleted by the calling up of members.[25] The party was also in debt as its various social activities failed to raise any money.[26]

But the Communists were unable to exploit either the weakness of the Labour Party or the sympathetic hearing it had received in the 1930s. The Labour Party became suspicious of the Trades Council's support for the local Communists, and steered clear of any co-operation with them. The unease engendered by the Communists' hostility to the war before 1941[27] was not removed by the change of policy after that, or by support given by Communists to Conservatives at by-elections.[28] Fears were also expressed that the Communists would try to win offices in the Labour Party and prove to be disruptive. Rejection of overtures by the Communist Party in 1943 meant that the refusal to discuss electoral co-operation with them in 1944 was in-evitable.[29] The attempt to yoke together politics and industrial matters by the Communists made them appear far less innocent than they had done in the 1930s, when locally it had been possible to hold the two in separation. But it was not simply a question of changed attitudes towards the Communists; given that the Liberals were slipping further from the political stage, the Labour Party was bound to search for potential voters amongst the Conservatives, and collusion across the Left appeared *passé* or irrelevant; 'success was more likely to be forthcoming if attention was directed to that part of the electorate who had supported the Conser-vatives in the past rather than with those who had voted I.L.P. or Communist'.[30] When a Communist candidate did stand in

[24] Hinton, 'Coventry Communism', p. 91.
[25] O.C.L.P., AGM minutes, Feb. 1940, 20 Aug. 1941.
[26] O.C.L.P. minutes, 4 Jan. 1940.   [27] O.C.L.P. minutes, 9 May 1940.
[28] O.C.L.P. Executive Committee minutes, 23 Mar. 1943.
[29] O.C.L.P. minutes, 21 Mar. 1944.
[30] O.C.L.P., Executive Committee minutes, 2 Nov. 1944.

1950 (by which time factors in the wider world had begun to work against them), he polled only 0.4 per cent of the total vote and a quarter of the number won by Lazarus in the Cowley ward alone in the municipal elections of the 1930s.

The Communists had been quite willing during the war, and in its immediate aftermath, to work within the framework of political discussion set by the Labour Party, which meant discussions of the Beveridge Report, and committees to consider Oxford's post-war industrial structure. This was argued to be seriously imbalanced as a result of growth in the inter-war period being confined to the motor industry. Before 1914 Oxford had not been a particularly backward or impoverished town; it had simply been a non-industrial one. By 1945 industrialization in the intervening period had exposed it to fluctuating patterns of demand, and therefore brought it within the scope of a newly emerging regional policy designed to prevent serious unemployment in the future. Keynesianism and regional policy went together; if measures to draw industry to depressed areas were not to arouse anxieties in the more prosperous regions that they were losing what was rightfully theirs, these regions would expect 'an effective policy to eliminate the trade cycle and a steadily rising level of demand'.[31] Not only had Oxford acquired a working class of some political and industrial interest, but its position within the wider national economy was now of some weight. After 1945, however, attention was bound to be focused less closely on particular 'new' industry towns than it had been in the discussion of the later 1930s, precisely because of the enthusiasm of Keynesian policies which, it was hoped, would regulate demand nationally. In the 1930s the rather imbalanced economies of particular towns had given rise to some anxiety; the solution advanced involved the location of other industries in those towns to protect them against cyclical patterns of demand for particular products. After 1945 greater faith was placed in the management of aggregate demand, rather than in the manipulation of essentially unregulated industrial performance by policies for the location of industry.

Although during the Second World War the position of

[31] Fogarty, *Prospects of the Industrial Areas of Great Britain*, p. 468.

shop stewards and of labour generally was strengthened by government intervention, the wartime interlude period does not constitute a clear dividing line between the inter-war years and the modern period, which has shaped customary impressions of a militant labour force in the industry. The war did create special circumstances in that some of its salient conditions were not expected to persist. Women did not see themselves as permanent members of the labour force, and after the war, at Pressed Steel in particular, there was a fierce period of pay bargaining to establish new piece-work rates.[32] The same was true of union membership. Despite the improved status of unions after the war, the spread of membership was slow. While the position at Pressed Steel was consolidated, the density of membership at Morris's was probably never higher than 50 per cent up to the mid-1950s.[33] It is only since then that the modern characteristics of the industry and its labour relations have appeared clearly and been defined as a national problem.

The failure of the car industry to remain competitive with European and world producers has been seen as a particular and telling example of the decline of the economy as a whole. This is a complete reversal of the inter-war position. At that time the performance of the car industry offered relief in a desolate landscape. Labour productivity roughly doubled between 1924 and 1935, whereas in manufacturing as a whole it increased by only one quarter.[34] By the end of the 1970s it had emerged that Britain was particularly bad at producing cars; that industry did worse than other ones in comparison with other countries.[35] Further, the fact that the motor industry became one of the most strike-prone[36] provided a political incentive to do something about British industrial relations in general. While these two conditions have been associated with one another, their connection

[32] Interview with Jack Thomas.   [33] Ibid.

[34] R. A. Church and M. Miller, 'Motor Manufacturing', in D. H. Aldcroft and N. Buxton (eds.), *British Industry Between the Wars: Instability and Industrial Development, 1918–1939* (London, 1979), p. 218.

[35] D. S. Jones and S. J. Prais, 'Plant Size and Productivity in the Motor Industry; Some International Comparisons', *Oxford Bulletin of Economics and Statistics,* 40 (1978), 44.

[36] For the strike-proneness of the industry see J. Cronin, *Industrial Conflict in Modern Britain* (London, 1979), table 7.3, p. 165.

does not provide the whole answer to the decline of the British motor industry. Analysis of the strikes which affected the industry from the mid-1950s to the later 1960s has suggested that their impact on economic performance can be overstated, even though car producers elsewhere were not so affected.[37] Lost production often occurred at times of slack demand, for example. Although in the 1970s overmanning and strikes seemed to explain the divergence with foreign companies,[38] these factors by themselves were not unambiguously the key problem. Lack of size was paramount: British car factories, whether native or foreign owned, were simply not big enough to compete with major firms elsewhere.[39] Better labour relations and work practices would by themselves not have been enough to overcome this difficulty. Yet the solution of labour problems, whether as strikes or as restrictions on productivity, has been high on the agendas of governments and car producers, and it is into this context that Cowley has to be fitted.

There were basic differences between the inter-war period and post-war conditions. Before 1939 the industry concentrated its main efforts on supplying the home market, which meant selling small cars to the increasingly better-off middle classes.[40] Export performance was less significant, and was restricted in the main to the Empire. Despite some indications of weakening competitiveness—the growing share of trade taken by the German industry being one—the position of the British industry was not noticeably weaker than that of European ones. Although inevitably the Americans were ahead on productivity because of the size of their market, the major divergence between Britain and Europe was to emerge after the mid-1950s. When the industry was keyed in more closely to foreign trade after 1945 such aspects of deteriorating comparison became more important. Cowley was right at the centre of these post-war changes, in terms of both the organization of the industry and the efforts to improve labour relations.

[37] Turner, Clack, and Roberts, p. 24.
[38] Jones and Prais, 'Plant Size', p. 146.
[39] As British Leyland's managing director put it in 1975: 'We do not have the volume to compete with the real giants in the cheap end of the market.' Quoted in G. Maxcy, *The Multinational Motor Industry* (London, 1981), p. 220.
[40] Church and Miller, 'Motor Manufacturing', p. 192.

Although Morris Motors at Cowley was already part of a wider organization in the 1930s, in the sense that supply firms had been bought up along with two other car firms, Wolseley in 1927 and Riley in 1938, mergers since the 1950s have produced integration on a far greater scale. This has not meant any loss of status, since within B.M.C. (formed by Austin and Morris in 1952), British Motor Holdings (when they were joined by Jaguar in 1965), and British Leyland (formed in 1968 with Leyland which itself had absorbed the Rover company) Cowley has remained, with Longbridge, the main centre of volume production. This was confirmed when Pressed Steel merged with B.M.C. in 1966. It is likely to remain so, with the application of automated machinery to produce a medium-sized car promised for the near future, and the transfer there from Birmingham of Rover production. Even though this post-war integration has still not produced a plant of sufficient size to compete abroad, it has provided an element of security. Successive governments have been committed to maintaining a British car industry, and even in extreme conditions the high cost of closure in the short term has made that course of action unpalatable.[41] While such commitment has given the labour force some security against the threats of management in the mid-1970s about the dire consequences of not meeting production targets, in the longer run the failure of governments and management to provide a sound footing for the industry has been to labour's disadvantage. The cycle of events since the mid-1950s has been similar to that at Pressed Steel in the 1930s writ large: initial growth of shop steward strength, incorporation into the industrial relations 'system' of the firm in the mid-1970s, followed by erosion and weakness towards the end of the decade.

The problems for labour in the motor industry in the 1950s and 1960s were rather similar to those in the interwar period—fluctuations in pay and insecurity of employment—but the context was different. The growth in numbers of shop stewards and the greater power of the shop-floor through the secular trend to 'full' employment produced 'aggressive militancy on wage connected issues

[41] *The Economist*, 31 Jan. 1981, p. 48.

during good years to compensate for insecurity and short time working during bad'.[42] Piece-work bargaining enabled the car workers to emerge as the highest paid group of industrial workers in the 1960s, and the more frequent the negotiations the sharper the rise in earnings, which often outstripped productivity.[43] Whereas between the wars insecurity of employment heightened the sense of dependence on the employer and reinforced an awareness of wider depression in the labour market, in the context of 'full' employment and expectations of rising living standards these same factors proved far more productive of unrest.

Since the 1970s the position of the car workers has become more defensive. The deflation in demand during the oil crisis and the competition from foreign producers because of lower tariffs placed British Leyland in a serious position.[44] In 1971 the firm succeeded in containing wage drift by switching from piece-rates to measured day work which involved flat-rate payments for a certain level of output. Although high levels of strikes persisted, shop stewards were in a difficult position. The introduction of measured day work was a serious defeat, and subsequently defensive action against management has posed tactical problems.[45] The rank and file could not be continually led into battle, and by the later 1970s shop stewards were finding it difficult to keep their following when critical issues which appeared to affect the company's survival were at stake. Thus in September 1979 the stewards' opposition to company plans involving significant redundancies was weakened by overwhelming support for such strategies expressed in a ballot of the labour force.[46] In the spring of 1980 the company held firm to a pay award linked with changes in working practices, and a strike called by the stewards was only partially supported. The labour force was not completely subdued: when working practices were modified at plant level small stoppages did

[42] Turner, Clack, and Roberts, p. 128.   [43] Ibid., p. 157.
[44] For the problems of the 1970s caused by government policies and external conditions see P. S. Dunnett, *The Decline of the British Motor Industry: the Effects of Government Policy 1945–79* (London, 1980), chs. 6 and 7.
[45] R. Taylor, 'The Cowley Way of Work', *New Society*, 2 May 1974, p. 251.
[46] 'Chronicle of Industrial Relations in the United Kingdom, August–November 1979', *British Journal of Industrial Relations*, 18 (1980), 126.

take place. It was simply difficult for the stewards to mobilize the work-force over major issues when the survival of the firm was at stake. But they had lost some ground over pay bargaining too. By 1980 changes in work practice were no longer subject to negotiation with shop stewards.[47]

Industrially Oxford was as representative of labour relations in car production in the years after 1945 as it had been before 1939, but in a manner which showed the reduced importance of local social conditions. As the Morris workers moved slowly to unionization theirs became the more strike-prone of the two factories, a reversal from pre-war experience caused at least in part by the competition between unions trying to win members in that factory. The sources of behaviour had therefore changed: while it makes sense to consider the social background of labour in the inter-war period as a factor shaping industrial relations, local particularities cease to be so relevant after 1945. For one thing, trade union membership required a much less narrowly defined and demanding set of social attitudes than had been the case before 1939, when unions at the centre were much weaker than they were to be after 1945. In the 1950s and 1960s labour relations in the Oxford motor industry were affected far more by specifically industrial matters, such as pay comparisons within the industry and the policies of unions, than they were by the origins of labour. For those investigating the motor industry in the 1960s, 'more refined, though less neat, explanations look first at jobs rather than at communities or places'.[48] It is therefore reasonable to describe Cowley as shedding its local characteristics as a motor industry town after 1945; it ceased to carry with it any of the associations with Oxford which had been apparent before 1939. Changes in the composition of the labour force may well have had the same effect. While labour has continued to leave agriculture since 1951, the increase in employment in the service sector and the relative decline of the working class means that recently the distributive sector has probably sent fewer into the motor industry than was the case in the inter-war

[47] 'Chronicle', *BJIR*, 18 (1980), 388.
[48] Turner, Clack, and Roberts, p. 165.

period.[49] The heterogeneity of labour in the motor industry is probably less marked than it was before 1939, with a stronger degree of recruitment from within the industrial working class. Successive generations have become accustomed to an industrial and urban milieu, and to regarding labour organizations as a means of defending their interests in a way that was not true earlier.[50] When the motor industry was investigated in the 1960s, the proposition that it suffered from inputs of 'green' labour—that is, workers unused to industrial conditions—was found to be false. On the contrary, 'The problem, in fact, may well often be, not that labour is "green", but that it is far from it.'[51] The motor industry, in marked contrast to what it had done in the 1920s and 1930s, was recruiting those who not only had some industrial experience but had also been in trade unions.

These broad changes in patterns of employment in the economy have produced a reassertion of Oxford's traditional functions in health and education as part of a wider growth in the service sector. While in the post-war period the level of employment at Cowley went beyond the 16,000 workers thought desirable, by 1971 the proportion employed in the service sector was again increasing, having declined since 1921.[52] It is the expanding University rather than the motor industry which now poses the chief planning problems in the town.[53] The persistence of this dual identity has been apparent in politics too. Before 1939 two reasons were usually given for Labour's poor showing in parliamentary elections,

[49] The numbers in agriculture declined from 10,345 in 1951 to 6,100 in 1971. C. H. Lee, *British Regional Employment Statistics 1841–1971* (Cambridge, 1979) n.p.

[50] For the general argument to this effect see J. H. Goldthorpe, 'The Current Inflation: Towards a Sociological Account', in F. Hirsch and J. H. Goldthorpe (eds.), *The Political Economy of Inflation* (London, 1979), pp. 204–6.

[51] Turner, Clack, and Roberts, p. 175.

[52] *V.C.H. Oxfordshire*, vol. 4, table XIII, p. 219, lists 31 per cent of the occupied population in the motor industry in 1951, and 61 per cent in services (building, distributive trades, local government, and the professions). By 1971 the proportions were 28 per cent and 65 per cent respectively. R. Bacon and W. A. Eltis, when arguing in 1976 that too many resources were being devoted to the production of 'non-marketable' output in the British economy, remarked that 'The Oxfordshire County Council now employs more workers in Oxfordshire than British Leyland.' *Britain's Economic Problem: Too Few Producers* (London, 1976), p. 13.

[53] Sir Norman Chester, 'The University in the City', in T. Rowley (ed.), *Oxford Region*, pp. 179-82.

one being the exclusion of the greater part of the new industrial area, the second being the absence of union organization amongst the Morris workers.[54] After the war both these conditions were satisfied to a degree, but Labour did not win the seat until 1966. It was not simply that, in terms of numbers, the working-class element was 'diluted' by the 'professional' groups, but that, according to the sociologists, 'defections' to the Conservatives from the working class have been higher where affiliations with white collar groups are in evidence.[55] This factor might well explain Labour's problems post-war and its continued dependence upon middle-class voting patterns.

[54] See comments of Jack Thomas in the *Oxford Mail*, 11 May 1938.
[55] J. H. Goldthorpe, D. Lockwood, F. Bechhofer, and J. Platt, *The Affluent Worker: Political Attitudes and Behaviour* (Cambridge, 1968), ch. 4.

CONCLUSION

It is appropriate now to say something about the place of the inter-war period within the longer-run themes of labour history. Attention has recently focused on the persistence of informal organization by the rank and file at the point of production. Control over the way work is done, or, at the very least, over those aspects of work which determine pay, has been seen as one of the means by which labour has defended its interests and hampered managerial authority. Interest in the growth and activities of trade unions, which have not had a major effect on the distribution of wealth in the long term, has been replaced by analysis of activity on the shop-floor, which is argued to have had a limiting effect on the performance of the economy. As Professor Price has put it: 'the failure of the auto industry to cope success-fully with worker resistance is central not only to the economic decline of that industry but suggestive of the wider story of British capitalism as a whole since the mid-1950's'.[1] The key point is that such worker resistance is seen not merely as a product of full employment and a burgeoning shop stewards' movement in the 1950s, nor simply as the expression of spontaneous or 'instrumental' ambitions which require no deeper explanation, but as part of a historically continuous tradition of informal organization at work going back to the 1890s.[2] Labour, in retaining some residual control over work, has always forced employers to accept some element of compromise in the way their enterprises have been run. Once this point is made, the important question, as Dr Zeitlin has put it, is how 'patterns of craft control were diffused and adopted from the older sectors to the new mass production

---

[1] R. Price, 'Rethinking Labour History: the Importance of Work', in J. E. Cronin and J. Schneer (eds.), *Social Conflict and Political Oder in Modern Britain* (London, 1982), p. 196.

[2] Ibid., p. 190.

industries which emerged during the inter-war years, and
from the minority of skilled workers to the vast number of
unskilled and semi-skilled workers in the new industries'.[3]

The aims of these unofficial or informal activities have
been identified as fourfold: control over negotiations, control
over the regulation or organization of work ('workers'
control'), determination of overtime, and the maintenance
of job security.[4] It has been admitted that they constituted
at best a persistent tendency and have only rarely been
elevated to the status of an articulated theory. But even with
these qualifications, the arguments about work-place regulation have tended to overemphasize its continuity and exag-
gerate its effects.

The relevance of the inter-war period to such longer-run
themes is obvious. Not only were there regional and industrial shifts within the economy away from the export
staples to the newer industries which have been of 'strategic'
importance since 1945, but the technological changes occurring in the motor industry, for example, were quite considerable. Assembly-line methods relying on a high input of semi-
skilled labour had been adopted by the mid-1930s.[5] The
moving assembly line appeared to eliminate labour's discretion of the pace of work, and the subdivision of jobs down to
cycles of no more than 2½ minutes' duration, so permitting
mobility of workers within the factories, reduced any
identification with a particular process. The response of
labour to these changes therefore bears closely upon arguments about the continuities and effectiveness of informal
regulation.

Even though the technology of car production appeared
to reduce to a minimum discretion over work, employers
still believed that forms of incentive payment and provision
for non-monetary factors had a part to play in achieving
efficient production. G. D. H. Cole argued that in mass
production 'what is needed is a high uniform rate of work
which all will observe. In order to get men to do this it is

[3] J. Zeitlin, 'The Emergence of Shop Steward Organisation and Job Control in
the British Car Industry: a Review Essay', *History Workshop Journal*, 10 (1980),
120.
[4] Price, 'Rethinking Labour History', pp. 191-4.
[5] Turner, Clack, and Roberts, p. 86.

necessary to offer them a special inducement; but the appropriate inducement is a high time rate and not a piecework rate.'[6] But only Ford's went this far; other firms persisted with piece-work systems in the belief that some form of incentive was necessary to achieve high output. Moreover, even where pay was regarded as central to industrial relations, as at Morris's in the 1920s, provision of wider social benefits crept in. There was, then, some agreement that labour had a discretionary role to play in car production.

Moreover, at Pressed Steel at least, there were recognizable precursors in the inter-war period of aspects of work-place industrial relations which were to arouse such anxiety in the 1950s and beyond. The control of negotiations with the company, the 'short-circuiting' of disputes procedures, and the regulation of manning levels were all pursued with vigour, if not complete or lasting success. Shop stewards in that factory also went beyond their rather circumscribed role in the formal agreements governing the engineering industry, and a system of informal bargaining arrangements certainly existed for a short time in the 1930s.

While the shop-floor bargaining of the 1950s is not surprisingly found to have some antecedents in the inter-war period, the linkages with earlier forms of job regulation and craft control are rather harder to establish. In the motor industry divisions of skill tended to diverge sharply so that neither the skilled toolmaker or patternmaker, nor the semi-skilled assembler bore resemblance to the more traditional turner or fitter. Skill was withdrawn from direct productive activities so that skilled and semi-skilled were separated in both outlook and location within the factory. The skilled groups contributed nothing to the patchy unionization of the semi-skilled before 1939, and their own 'job control' had no direct bearing on the productive process.

For the semi-skilled the main ties with the past were not through any industrial linkages but through the transfer of certain 'community' experiences. The role of the migrants from the older-established industrial centres in the development of union organization has been established. A robust collective attitude towards employers (and often the union

[6] G. D. H. Cole, *The Payment of Wages* (London, 1928), p. 41.

too) was transmitted through the mechanisms of long-distance migration which meant that many of those moving to Oxford were drawn from a small number of mining villages in South Wales. A more specifically industrial connection was unlikely given the heterogeneous background of labour recruited to the motor industry in Oxford. But links through community were themselves transient, on two counts. First, the will to organize amongst the migrants (especially the Welsh) was not always associated with particular cultural patterns of that country: if anything the reverse was true. Second, the Oxford suburbs did not see the generation of a rich, communal working-class life which would have supported an 'oppositional' culture. The rank and file activities existed in a barren social context; the limited sociability of the 'affluent worker' makes an early appearance here.[7] The most impressive example of historically persistent job control in Oxford was provided not by the car workers but by the printers. Their 'control' was far stronger too both over time at work and over the machinery employed. The concerns of the car workers were solely about pay.

In a town like Oxford, where large-scale industry began from scratch in the 1920s, the absence of links with earlier patterns of labour organization is not surprising. What is significant is that in towns where such connections did exist they had ceased to count for much by the end of the 1920s. In Coventry by that time unemployment and dilution had taken their toll, so that labour was not a great deal more strongly placed there than in Oxford. This degree of convergence from such dissimilar starting points was emphasized in the 1930s when it appeared that Coventry provided no special advantages for union organizers trying to revive membership. And so even though Coventry was to a far greater degree than Oxford a working-class town, with a network of working men's clubs to prove it, this counted for very little. The inter-war period for this reason forms a very real hiatus or hiccup in labour organization. In the absence of any firm evidence of transmission of notions of job regulation from the skilled to the semi-skilled, to compensate for

[7] J. H. Goldthorpe, D. Lockwood, F. Bechhofer, and J. Platt, *The Affluent Worker in the Class Structure* (Cambridge, 1969), ch. 4.

the lack of continuity between 1914 and 1945, the historically specific nature of shop-floor organization amongst the semi-skilled can be reaffirmed. It would have been surprising to have found to the contrary. Control by labour over work as a persistent theme required some continuity of experience, as well as some resilience to the fluctuations of the economy. It is therefore predictably found amongst the printers. The efforts of the semi-skilled car workers, themselves a heterogeneous grouping, exposed to economic cycles as well as to movement from job to job, were inevitably more sporadic.

In looking at the activities of the rank and file not simply in terms of 'internal' structure but in their effect, two further points arise. First, the use of leverage by the shop-floor to assuage anxieties over pay and employment does not give any precise indications of wider industrial or political attitudes. While groups of car workers were willing to combat aggressive management and exploit favourable aspects of their position in so doing, a general 'anti-capitalist' bias cannot be inferred. Indeed, it is precisely when these informal shop-floor activities have seemed to carry with them power and influence beyond a particular department or factory that their ambivalence has become clear, as the vulnerability of the shop stewards in the major conflicts at British Leyland in the later 1970s has illustrated. The instrumentality of organization on the assembly lines does provide an adequate explanation for its varying strengths and accounts for the absence of any fully articulated theory. Secondly, employers rarely suffered labour resistance as a constraint upon their performance in the inter-war period, the main problem being rather the misjudgements within their own strategies. The over-long commitment to larger horsepower cars by Morris Motors during the early 1930s, and the reliance on price rather than model competition by Ford's were two examples.[8]

These concluding remarks on the 'place' of the inter-war period may seem somewhat negative in their drift, since they suggest that those years cast no longer shadows into later decades. The elements of 'transition' in fact had a purely local bearing and significance, arising from the way in which

[8] Church and Miller, 'The British Motor Industry', pp. 168–73, 175–80.

Oxford acquired an industrial suburb, having been essentially a non-industrial town before 1914. However, the social aspects of the growth of large-scale industry have defied easy categorization. The sociological study of Banbury found it impossible to encapsulate the impact of an aluminium factory on a market town solely in terms of the old and the new,[9] and this historical study has found tradition and change spread unevenly. While the contrasts between the incoming Welsh and the Oxford natives seemed to crystallize the collision between the industrial and traditional aspects of Oxford, this was neither a statistically preponderant nor a dominant trend. Resistance or indifference to unions and the Labour Movement was as evident in the newly-established motor factories as in the more traditional occupations, and the converse was true. The heterogeneity of labour was fully represented on both sides of Magdalen Bridge.

The relationship between Cowley and Oxford has also varied over time. In the 1930s the influence of the periphery upon the centre was probably at its height. Labour relations in many occupations were irreversibly changed as workers became unionized or pursued claims more vigorously; but even here it is not possible to argue that the unionization of Pressed Steel was the decisive influence. Rather, autonomously derived union growth was making its presence felt as much as the wide-ranging activities of energetic shop stewards from the car factory. In addition, the incorporation of local workers into the negotiating procedures of their particular industries tended to override efforts at 'horizontal' unity across occupations. In elections, where the weight of numbers counted for more, the influence of the periphery was even weaker. The pickings for Labour candidates were always much easier in Cowley or Headington than in the South, East, or West wards.

Later trends have tended to underline segregation rather than encourage contiguity. Labour relations in the car factories were increasingly shaped by factors in the industry and the wider economy; the insularity of pay bargaining based upon local comparisons was very much a feature of the inter-war period and did not survive the changes in the

[9] Stacey, *Tradition and Change*, esp. ch. 9.

organization of the firms in the 1950s and 1960s. In Oxford traditional functions have reasserted themselves, and the expansion of the University in particular now provides the main questions for local politics in the way that suburban growth around the motor industry did in the 1930s. But this is not a return full circle to 1914. Then social order came from a cohesive and comprehensible urban society; now there is still social order, but it comes from a variegated and compartmentalized social structure which is hardly cohesive or smoothly contoured.

BIBLIOGRAPHY

I. ARCHIVAL SOURCES

In Oxford

Abe Lazarus Memorial Library, Ruskin College, Oxford

Minutes of the Trades and Labour Council. Minute Books consulted 1898-1940, and some annual reports and correspondence 1930-5.

Minutes of Trades Hall Committee.

Miscellaneous material concerning Abe Lazarus's activities in Oxford is contained in boxes and files in the library and is in the process of being catalogued. These contain two factory newspapers—the *Spark* and the *Conveyor,* and publications of the tenants' associations, *The Cutteslowe Wallpaper* and *The Florence Park Rent Book.* They also contain material prepared by the Communist Party for elections and strikes.

Minute Books of National Union of Vehicle Builders covering the whole of the inter-war period.

Essays by Arthur Exell on Morris's and Spain, written in 1975.

Minute Book of the West ward of the Labour Party, 1923-8.

Bodleian Library

A. J. Carlyle MSS.
H. A. L. Fisher MSS.
Gilbert Murray MSS.
Marriage registers MSS DD Par Cowley 1923-35
                                 Garsington 1929-38
                                 Wheatley 1920-32
                                 Headington 1923-6
                                 St. Ebbe's 1921-9.
Oxford Diocesan Papers. Visitations of 1928 (c. 388) and 1936 (c. 397).
Oxford Methodist Circuit Minute Book of New Headington Chapel (Wesleyan).

Oriel College
Papers of Provost L. R. Phelps.

Oxford City Library
Records of Oxford City Council. Minute Books of the Housing and Town Planning Committee, Unemployment Committee (1922-7). Housing Allocations Subcommittee. City Rate Books.
Minute Book of Independent (later Labour Party) Group of Councillors 1936-9.
Revd M. Bradyll Johnson, 'An Enquiry into Housing Conditions in the Parish of St. Clements' (2 vol. MS, 1924).

At the Offices of Local Organizations
Minutes of Amalgamated Engineering Union, District Committee.
Minutes of Cowley Workers' Social Club Committee.
Minutes of Oxford City Conservative and Unionist Association.
Minutes of Oxford City Labour Party—Executive Committee and General Management Committee form 1935.
Minutes of Headington Labour Party from 1935; and membership lists from 1924.
Reports of the Oxford University Tutorial Classes Committee 1929-36.
Annual reports of Berks., Bucks., and Oxon. district of W.E.A., 1929-34.
There are no local records of the Transport and General Workers' Union; nor (apart from some balance sheets) from British Leyland, into which Morris Motors and Pressed Steel were incorporated in the post-war period.

Temple Cowley United Reformed Church
Log books of Temple Cowley Congregational Church 1926-39.
Marriage registers 1923-39.

In Coventry

Minutes of Coventry and District Engineering Employers' Association, General Management Committee 1921-38.
City Record Office: Marriage registers for Broad Street (Wesleyan) 1927-39, Lockhurst Lane 1900-39, Alderman's Green, Foleshill 1930-5.

In Pangbourne

Minutes of Typographical Association, held by National Graphical Association.

In London

At Engineering Employers' Federation Headquarters
Records of the Engineering and Allied Employers' Federation relating to local and central conferences concerning Pressed Steel.

Headquarters of Amalgamated Engineering Union
Minutes of Central Conference with E.A.E.F., relevant for Messrs. Lucy and Co. and John Allen and Sons.

Congress House
Minutes of T.U.C. Organization Committee, and files on trades councils, areas, and industries.

Labour Party Headquarters
General Correspondence Files on Affiliations.
Organization Subcommittee of N.E.C. for 1921 and 1938, and Elections Subcommittee of October 1938.

Transport House
Records of T. & G.W.U. Minutes of General Executive Council (including general secretary's quarterly reports). Minutes of Metal, Engineering, and Chemical Trade Group; Passenger Transport Trade Group; Building Trade Group.

P.R.O.
Records of Ministry of Labour on Transference (LAB 8) and Disputes (LAB 34). Records of Ministry of Housing and Local Government (HLG 47 and 48). Ministry of Agriculture and Fisheries (MAF 47).

In Birmingham
Minutes of T. & G.W.U. Area Committee (No. 5).

University of Lancaster
Nuffield biography archive—interview notes and other material collected by P. W. S. Andrews and Elizabeth Brunner for their biography of Lord Nuffield.

II. PRINTED DOCUMENTARY SOURCES

Oxford Charity Organization Society, annual reports.
Minutes of Oxford City Council.
Oxford Liberal Association, annual reports to 1913.
Oxford Municipal Labour Representation Committee—Rules, 1902.

III. TRADE UNION JOURNALS

Amalgamated Engineering Union Journal and Monthly Report.
National Union of General and Municipal Workers' Journal.
National Union of Distributive and Allied Workers' Journal, *New Dawn*.
National Union of Vehicle Builders Journal.
Transport and General Workers' Union Journal, *Record*.

IV. NEWSPAPERS AND PERIODICALS

Automobile Engineer
Journal of Production Engineers
Mechanical Handling
Motor Body Building and Vehicle Construction
Works Manager
Communist Review
Daily Worker
Labour Monthly
Oxford Times
Oxford Mail
Oxford Chronicle

V. OFFICIAL PRINTED SOURCES

Barlow Commission on Geographical Distribution of Industrial Population, Report and Evidence 1940, Cmd. 6153.
Ministry of Labour annual reports.
Ministry of Labour Report on Industrial Transference Board, 1928, Cmd. 3156.
Ministry of Labour *Gazette*.
Reports of Chief Inspector of Factories.

VI. INTERVIEWS (affiliations apply to 1930s)

Donovan Brown, Ruskin College, Communist Party; Norman Brown, Pressed Steel shop steward, Communist Party; J. Clarke, Pressed Steel worker; Harry Cook, N.U.V.B., Morris's; George Currill, secretary, Cowley Labour Party, 1929–31; Arthur Exell, Morris's, Communist Party; Rowland Garrett, president, Cowley Labour Party; William Hawley, city councillor (Labour), 1935–8; Harry Jones, Pressed Steel worker, Communist Party 1934–6; Tom Jones, Pressed Steel worker; Mrs Bessie Ledger, secretary, Oxford City Labour Party, 1938; Kathleen and Marcus Lower, Headington Labour Party; William Spencer, foreman, Morris's; Jack Thomas, district secretary, T. & G.W.U.; Emrys Williams, Pressed Steel worker, South Wales; M. Williams, Pressed Steel worker, South Wales; Richard Williams, Pressed Steel worker, South Wales.

VII. THESES

Carr, F., 'Engineering Workers and the Rise of Labour in Coventry' (Warwick Univ. Ph.D. thesis, 1978).
Daniel, G. H., 'A Sample Analysis of Labour Migration into the Oxford District' (Oxford Univ. D.Phil. thesis, 1939).
Eatwell, R., 'The Labour Party and the Popular Front Movement in Britain in the 1930's' (Oxford Univ. D.Phil. thesis, 1975).

Hyman, R., 'The Worker's Union' (Oxford Univ. D.Phil. thesis, 1968).

Pickard, O. G., 'Midland Immigrations' (Birmingham Univ. B.Com. thesis, 1940).

Smithies, E. D., 'The Contrast between North and South in England 1918-39: Economic, Social and Political Problems with Special Reference to Burnley, Halifax, Luton and Ipswich' (Leeds Univ. Ph.D. thesis, 1974).

Wright, R. A., 'Liberal Party Organisation and Politics in Birmingham, Coventry and Wolverhampton, 1886-1914, with particular reference to the development of independent Labour representation' (Birmingham Univ. Ph.D. thesis, 1978).

VIII. SELECTED SECONDARY WORKS
(published in London unless otherwise indicated)

Aldcroft, D. H. and Richardson, H. W., *Building in the British Economy Between the Wars* (1968).

Alford, B. W. E., 'New Industries for Old? British Industry between the Wars', in R. C. Floud and D. McCloskey (eds.), *The Economic History of Britain since 1700. 2: 1860 to the 1970's* (Cambridge, 1981.

Andrews, P. W. S., *The Eagle Ironworks of Oxford* (Oxford, 1965).

— with E. Brunner, *The Life of Lord Nuffield* (Oxford, 1954).

Ashley, M. and Saunders, C. T., *Red Oxford* (1937).

Attlee, M. E., *Mobility and Labour* (Catholic Guild pamphlet, 1944).

Ball, O., *Sidney Ball: Memories and Impressions of 'An Ideal Don'* (Oxford, 1923).

Barnett House, *A Survey of Social Services in the Oxford District*, ed. A. F. C. Bourdillon, 2 vols. (Oxford, 1938-40).

Bentley, M., *The Liberal Mind 1914-1929* (Cambridge, 1977).

Bowley, M., *Housing and the State* (1945).

Butler, C. V., *Social Conditions in Oxford* (1912).

Chester, Sir Norman, 'The University in the City', in T. Rowley (ed.), *The Oxford Region* (Oxford, 1980).

Church, R. A., *Herbert Austin: the British Motor Car Industry to 1941* (1979).

— and Miller, M., 'The Big Three: Competition, Management and Marketing in the British Motor Industry, 1922-39', in B. Supple (ed.), *Essays in British Business History* (Oxford, 1977).

— — 'Motor Manufacturing', in D. H. Aldcroft and N. Buxton (eds.), *British Industry Between the Wars: Instability and Industrial Development, 1918-1939* (1979).

Clegg, H. A., *General Union in a Changing Society* (Oxford, 1954).

—, *Labour Relations in London Transport* (Oxford, 1950).

—, Fox, A., and Thompson, A. F., *A History of British Trade Unions since 1889* (Oxford, 1964).

Cole, G. D. H., *A Century of Co-operation* (Manchester, 1944).

—, *The Payment of Wages* (1928).

Cole, G. D. H., *British Trade Unionism Today* (1945).
— and Cole, Margaret, *The Condition of Britain* (1937).
Collison, P., *The Cutteslowe Walls* (1963).
Cook, C. P., *The Age of Alignment: Electoral Politics in Britain 1922–29* (1975).
—, 'Liberals, Labour and Local Elections', in C. P. Cook and G. Peale (eds.), *The Politics of Re-appraisal 1918–1939* (1975).
Cronin, J., *Industrial Conflict in Modern Britain* (1979).
Daniel, G. H., 'Some Factors Affecting the Movement of Labour', *Oxford Economic Papers*, 3 (1940).
Dunnett, P. S., *The Decline of the British Motor Industry: the Effects of Government Policy 1945–79* (1980).
Elton, G., *Among Others* (1938).
Exell, A., 'Morris Motors in the 1930's' and 'Morris Motors in the 1940's', *History Workshop Journals* 6 (1978), 7 (1979), and 9 (1980).
Fenby, C., *The Other Oxford: the Life and Times of Frank Gray and his Father* (1970).
Fogarty, M. P., *Prospects of the Industrial Areas of Great Britain* (1945).
Fyrth, H. J. and Collins, H., *The Foundry Workers* (Manchester, 1959).
Gilbert, M., *Winston S. Churchill, V. 1922–29, A Companion* (1979).
Goddard, H. A., 'Profit Sharing and the Amenities of the Nuffield Factories', in Catherwood and Gannett (eds.), *Industrial Relations in Great Britain* (New York, 1939).
Gray, F., *Confessions of a Candidate* (1925).
Harrison, B., 'Miss Butler's Oxford Survey', in A. H. Halsey (ed.), *Traditions of Social Policy* (Oxford, 1976).
Hilton, J., *Are Trade Unions Obstructive?* (1935).
Hinton, J., *The First Shop Stewards' Movement* (1973).
— 'Coventry Communism: a Study of Factory Politics in the Second World War', *History Workshop Journal*, 9 (1980).
Hunt, E. H., *Regional Wage Variations in Britain, 1850–1914* (Oxford, 1973).
Hyman, R., *The Workers' Union* (Oxford, 1971).
Kadish, A., 'Oxford Economists and the Young Extension Movement', in T. Rowley (ed.), *The Oxford Region* (Oxford, 1980).
Kinnear, M., *The British Voter* (1968).
Knowles, K. G. J. C., *Strikes: a Study in Industrial Conflict* (Oxford, 1952).
Liepmann, K., *The Journey to Work* (1944).
McKibbin, R., *The Evolution of the Labour Party 1910–1924* (Oxford, 1975).
—, Matthew, H. C. G., and Kay, J., 'The Franchise Factor in the Rise of the Labour Party', in *English Historical Review*, xci (1976).
McKower, H., Marschak, J., and Robinson, M., 'Studies in the Mobility of Labour', *Oxford Economic Papers*, 2 (1939).
McLean, I., 'Oxford and Bridgwater', in C. P. Cook and J. Ramsden (eds.), *By-Elections in British Politics* (1973).

Marriott, J. A. R., *Memories of Four Score Years* (1946).

Marsh, A. I., *Industrial Relations in Engineering* (1963).

Martin, R., *Communism and the British Trade Unions* (Oxford, 1968).

Maxcy, G., *The Multinational Motor Industry* (1981).

— and Silberston, Z. A., *The Motor Industry* (1959).

Overy, R. J., *William Morris, Viscount Nuffield* (1976).

Pakenham, F., *Born to Believe* (1951).

Parker, J., 'Oxford Politics in the 1920's', *Political Quarterly*, XLV (1974).

Peck, J. S. Foreman, 'Tariff Protection and Economies of Scale, the British Motor Industry before 1939', *Oxford Economic Papers*, NS 31 (1979).

Pelling, H., *A History of British Trade Unionism* (Harmondsworth, 2nd edn., 1971).

Powell, J., *Payment by Results* (1924).

Price, R., 'Rethinking Labour History: the Importance of Work', in J. E. Cronin and J. Schneer (eds.), *Social Conflict and Political Order in Modern Britain* (1982).

Robinson, H. W., 'The Response of Labour to Economic Incentives', in P. W. S. Andrews and T. Wilson (eds.), *Oxford Studies in the Price Mechanism* (Oxford, 1951).

Saunders, C. T., *Seasonal Variations in Employment* (1938).

Sharp, T., *Oxford Re-Planned* (1948).

Spicer, G., *British Engineering Wages* (1928).

Turner, H. A., Clack, G., and Roberts, G., *Labour Relations in the Motor Industry* (1967).

V.C.H. Oxfordshire, vol. 4 *Oxford City* and vol. 5 *Bullingdon Hundred* (1979 and 1957).

Williams, P. H., *Hugh Gaitskell: a Political Biography* (1979).

Woollard, F., *Principles of Mass and Flow Production* (1954).

Wright, A. W., *G. D. H. Cole and Socialist Democracy* (Oxford, 1979).

Yates, M. L., *Wages and Labour Conditions in British Engineering* (1938).

Yeo, E. and S., *Popular Culture and Class Conflict 1590–1914: Explorations in the History of Labour and Leisure* (Sussex, 1981).

Zeitlin, J., 'The Emergence of Shop Steward Organisation and Job Control in the British Car Industry: a Review Essay', *History Workshop Journal*, 10 (1980).

— 'Craft Control and the Division of Labour: Engineers and Compositors in Britain 1890–1930', *Cambridge Journal of Economics*, 3 (1979).

INDEX

Abbott, C. F. 155
Agricultural Wages Board 40
agricultural workers 39–41
Amalgamated Engineering Union:
  in Coventry 47, 49, 99, 100, 101 n.,
    104
  in Oxford 36, 42–3, 65, 79–83,
    108, 112, 119–21, 124, 145,
    180, 182, 183
Amalgamated Society of Engineers 13,
  25
Amalgamated Society of Gas, Munici-
  pal and General workers 109
Amalgamated Society of Woodworkers
  124
Amery, L. S. 35 n.
Appleyard, A. 79
Armstrong-Siddeley 98, 100 n.
Associated Society of Locomotive En-
  gineers and Firemen 13, 15

Baldwin, S. 33, 60
Bull, S. 18, 19, 20, 23
Banbury 89, 95, 108 n., 198
Bannington, A. 26
Bellinger, L. 108 n., 125
Bevin, E. 41 n., 62, 63, 80 n., 114,
  115, 178, 180 n.
Birkenhead, Lord 35 n.
Birmingham 3, 11, 14, 69
Board of Guardians 140, 144–5
Boden, O. 85
Bourne, R. C. 35, 132, 143, 170
Bowles, C. 108, 175 n.
brewery workers 21, 110
Briggs Bodies 101, 102–3
British Leyland 188, 189, 197
British Motor Corporation 188
British Motor Holdings 188
British Union of Fascists 172
British Workers' Sports Association 176
Broadhurst, H. 15
building societies 164–5
building workers 12, 15, 88, 129, 144
Bullingdon estate 161
bus workers 110, 111, 112–17

Butler, Miss C. V. 17, 18, 157

car workers:
  contrasts with rural labour 40, 44
  fluctuations in employment 88–9,
    104
  heterogeneity of 7–8, 38–41, 44,
    103, 105, 177, 191, 196
  housing 165–7
  patternmakers 59, 90, 102, 127
  pay 87–8, 189, 194–5
  relations between skilled and semi-
    skilled 7, 25, 27, 58–60, 65,
    68, 82–3, 98–9, 101–2, 195
  religion 90
  residence 9
  social life 91–3, 176
  strikes 96–8, 187–8, 189
  technology 77–8
  trade unionism 51, 101, 105–6
  vehicle builders 25, 31–2, 43,
    50–1, 98
  women 51 n., 99, 183, 186
  see also shop stewards, and under
    individual firms and trade
    unions
Cardiff 103
Carlyle, A. J. 18–19, 20, 22, 137,
  138 n., 157
Carritt, E. F. 94
Carter, Rev. J. 18
casual labour 13–14, 15, 17, 129,
  145, 147
Charity Organisation Society 17, 18,
  19, 144
Chaundy, T. W. 18, 19, 21 n.
Christian Social Union 17
Church Army Press 29
churches 89–90, 136
Churchill, W. S. 33, 34
cinema 91
Citrine, W. 80 n., 123, 147, 179
City of Oxford Motor Services 113
Clark, G. N. 22
Clarkson, G. W. 156 n., 163
clerical workers 140, 145

shop workers 14, 128, 145
Singer 98
Slough 3, 11 n., 42, 103
Smallbone, S. G. K. 36 n., 153
Smewin, E. 163, 174 n.
Smith, A. L. 137 n.
Smith, Mrs. A. L. 16
Smith, F. 152, 155
Smith, S. 152, 155
Snowden, P. 33, 36
Social-Democratic Federation 23, 26
Sorensen, A. 103
Spain 96
sport 38, 176
Stocks, J. L. 138 n.
strikes:
    in Coventry 24, 49 n., 51 n.
    in Dagenham 102-3
    in motor industry 96-8, 186-7
    in Oxford: British Leyland 189-90
        busmen 110, 115-16, 125
        coalmen 119
        engineers 119
        General Strike 43, 111-12, 140
        Morris Motors 84, 190
        Pressed Steel 58, 63-9, 77-9
        railwaymen 136
        tramway workers 14-15, 22-3
Swindon 89
Sunbeam 6

T.U.C. 48, 52, 104, 123-5, 180
tenants' associations 63, 167-8
Thomas, J. 107 n., 175
Toynbee, Mrs. A. 16
trades unionism 13, 22-3, 37, 39-41,

51-2, 74, 82, 84, 104-5,
108-29 *passim*, 195-6
tramway workers 14-15, 22-3
Transport and General Workers'
    Union:
    in Coventry 98-9, 105
    in Oxford 40-1, 62-70, 75-83,
        112-16, 119, 124, 126, 169,
        175, 180-1, 183
Triumph 49 n.
Typographical Association 12, 108,
    111, 124, 127, 134, 145

unemployed workers 144-5
United Front 80, 123, 168-9
United Patternmakers' Association 59,
    65 n.
Uzzell, H. 152
Uzzell, R. 152

Valentia, Viscount 21, 133
Vauxhall 32, 61, 105, 164, 179, 181

W.E.A. 140, 155
Wale, H. 26
Waterhouse, H. 94
Wells, Mrs. J. 16
Welsh 60-2, 65-6, 70-3, 103-5, 198
Welsh, J. 154
West Ward Housing Association 18
Williams, E. 15
Wiltshire, W. J. 156, 174 n.
Witney 93
Wolseley 6, 188
Workers' Union 14, 24-5, 27, 40-1,
    47, 62, 99, 145